Shakespeare and His Rivals

A Casebook on the Authorship Controversy

"There has been much throwing about of brains."

HAMLET, ACT 2, SCENE 2.

Shakespeare and His Rivals

A CASEBOOK ON THE AUTHORSHIP CONTROVERSY

George McMichael
SAN BERNARDINO-RIVERSIDE STATE COLLEGE

Edgar M. Glenn
CHICO STATE COLLEGE

THE ODYSSEY PRESS · INC · *New York*

Printed in the United States

Library of Congress Catalog Card Number: 62-11942

A 098765432

Acknowledgments

The editors wish to thank the following for their permission to reproduce material in this book.

Charles Scribner's Sons for quotation from *The Letters of Henry James,* ed. by Percy Lubbock, 1920. Cambridge University Press for passages from Caroline F. E. Spurgeon, *Shakespeare's Imagery and What It Tells Us,* 1935; and for portions of William F. and Elizebeth Friedman, *The Shakespearean Ciphers Examined,* 1957. The University of North Carolina Press for sections from Paul Kocher, *Christopher Marlowe: A Study of His Thought, Learning and Character,* 1946. Alfred Harbage and *The New York Times* for Alfred Harbage, "Sweet Will and Gentle Marlowe," June 12, 1955. The University of California Press for portions of Frank W. Wadsworth, *The Poacher from Stratford,* 1958. The Modern Language Association of America for passages from Norman N. Holland, "Freud on Shakespeare," *PMLA,* June, 1960.

The Clarendon Press, Oxford, for extracts from E. K. Chambers, *William Shakespeare: A Study of Facts and Problems,* 1930. "Empty Theory" (*TIME,* May 14, 1956) appears through the courtesy of *TIME;* copyright Time, Inc., 1956. Saturday Review, Inc., for use of material in the following, all of which appeared in *The Saturday Review:* G. B. Harrison, "Was Marlowe the Bard?" July 9, 1955; Bergen Evans, "Good Frend for Iesvs Sake Forbeare: Was Shakespeare Really Shakespeare?" May 7, 1949; and letters to the editor by Gelett Burgess, Oct. 2, 1948, and June 4, 1949; Clark Kinnaird, Nov. 6, 1948; William A. Klutts, June 4, 1949; Marcia M. Roof, June 4, 1949; G. F. Freudenberg, June 4, 1949; Clara Longworth de Chambrun, June 25, 1949; Alden Brooks, Sept. 3, 1949; and F. Y. St. Clair, Sept. 3, 1949. W. & R. Holmes (Books) Ltd. for passages from William Ross, *The Story of Anne Whateley and William Shaxpere,* 1939. W. W. Norton & Company, Inc., for an extract from Sigmund Freud, *An Outline of Psychoanalysis,* trans. by James Strachey, 1949. Robert L. Heilbroner for passages from "The Murder of the Man Who Was William Shakespeare." Published in *Esquire,* Dec., 1954. Oscar J. Campbell for his "Shakespeare Himself." Published in *Harper's Magazine,* July, 1940.

The Board of the *American Bar Association Journal* for sections from the following: Richard Bentley, "Elizabethan Whodunit: Who Was 'William Shakespeare'?" Feb., 1959; Charlton Ogburn, "A Mystery Solved: The True Identity of Shakespeare," Mar., 1959; William W. Clary, "The Case for the Defense: De Vere *et al.*, v. Shakespeare," July, 1959; John N. Hauser, "The Shakespearean Controversy: A Stratfordian Rejoinder," July, 1959; Dorothy and Charlton Ogburn, "The True Shakespeare: England's Great and Complete Man," Sept., 1959. *The American Scholar* and William T. Hastings for extracts from Mr. Hastings' "Shakspere Was Shakespeare," Autumn, 1959. Copyright © 1959 by the United Chapters of Phi Beta Kappa. Stanford University Press for quotation from B. Roland Lewis, *The Shakespeare Documents,* 1940-1941. The Hutchinson Group for passages from Percy Allen, *Talks with Elizabethans Revealing the Mystery of "William Shakespeare,"* c. 1945. Harper & Brothers for "Is Shakespeare Dead?" by Mark Twain. Copyright 1909 bv Harper & Brothers. Reprinted by permission. Calvin Hoffman for material from *The Murder of the Man Who Was Shakespeare.* Published 1955 and 1960. The Folger Shakespeare Library for the protographic reproduction of page 136 of the First Folio.

Introduction

This book is about an intellectual controversy which has raged for more than a century. Though it has taken many forms and directions, the debate has always come to one major question: Did William Shakespeare of Stratford-on-Avon write the poems and plays commonly attributed to him? Or was he actually an ignorant actor who merely provided a pen name for someone else?

Most academic scholars accept the idea that Shakespeare wrote the plays and poems bearing his name. But some students of Shakespeare and the Elizabethan Age are firmly convinced of the contrary, and they have taken their views to the presses to attempt to overthrow what they regard as a false tradition. The traditionalists have counterattacked. The result has been the Shakespearean authorship controversy.

The argument is over a century old, and like other aged institutions, it has many sides: historical, logical, semantic, emotional, stylistic, and no doubt others. The student dealing with the controversy can approach it, therefore, from any one of these sides. He can write a history of the controversy or a biography of Shakespeare. He may want to examine the logic of the controversialists. He may wish to investigate the emotional element in the reasoning presented by partisans. Since some of the debaters are somber, some dramatic, some ingenious, some funny, some irascible, he may wish to deal with the stylistic aspects of the debate. Or he can consider the various meanings that written records have for the interpreters.

As well as being confronted with a variety of approaches, attitudes, problems, and materials, the student will be faced with many of the difficulties that beset the professional biographer, historian, logician, and literary scholar. He will also be exposed to bibliographical form, footnoting, and the mechanics of scholarly writing. On these sacred matters, we leave the student to the tender mercies of his instructor and provide only the raw material, being formally inconsistent so that the student shall not have his work done for him.

The materials presented in this book are, first of all, only a selection. They are arranged historically, beginning with a series of documents related to Stratford-on-Avon and the Shakespeares. They are followed by seventeenth and eighteenth century material referring to William Shakespeare. After that come evidence of the beginnings of doubt about the authorship and, in historical order, the discussions of different persons offered as the true author.

Unless otherwise indicated, each selection in the text has been transcribed as it appeared in its source. Where translation, explanation, or digest is offered, the fact is so indicated. Ellipsis (. . . or * * *) has been used to indicate omission of material appearing in the original source.

The page numbering of the original work is given in bold face in square brackets and precedes the relevant material. Thus, if the instructor wishes, papers may be written with footnotes referring to the pagination of the original work. Otherwise, he may permit his students to refer only to this text and its pages.

Finally, although they sincerely tried to be fair in selecting and balancing the material here assembled, the editors are well aware that space limitations have necessitated the exclusion of much that is worth considering and much that is important. A selective bibliography is appended as partial compensation.

Contents

The Shakespeare Documents 1

Contemporary References to Shakespeare 26

Bacon as Shakespeare 63

Marlowe as Shakespeare 102

Anne Whateley as Shakespeare 145

A Group Theory: Bacon, Oxford, and Shakespeare as Shakespeare 154

Oxford as Shakespeare 159

The Shakespeare Documents

Introduction to the Documents Section

The controversy over who was Shakespeare exists because many people have felt that the works themselves indicate one kind of individual—a genius—whereas the facts actually known about William Shakespeare of Stratford-upon-Avon suggest someone entirely different. There are, then, two major bodies of evidence that have been considered in the controversy: the works of art, that is, Shakespeare's poems and plays, and the recorded facts, such things as court records, legal documents, and parish registers.

The Shakespeare works are easily available elsewhere. Here are presented the documents which relate to the life of the Stratfordian William Shakespeare. The section adheres as closely as possible to chronological order, and thus at first glance a reader may find this material a hodgepodge, yet such is the raw material of history and biography from which Shakespeare scholars have had to work. The student should recognize that even this baffling appearance of hodgepodgery is not without significance: it is one of the main causes of the controversy, for different minds have interpreted the mixed facts in various ways.

The meaning of specific facts may be doubtful or confusing. For example, Shakespeare's father signed his name with a cross. Does this fact prove he was illiterate? Again, do the records directly concerning William Shakespeare himself actually indicate that he was not the sort of man who could have written the works?

The documentary materials may also simply appear useless. Why, for example, include summary and quotation of part of the charter of the borough of Stratford-upon-Avon? For one thing, it is related to the possibility that, whether Shakespeare attended or not, there was a grammar school available to all the youth of the town. The borough records also inform the reader of the duties of the high bailiff. The reader should be able to use that information to make some reasonable assumptions about what John Shakespeare was involved in and, therefore, what his son William was likely to have been familiar with.

The "Payments Made by the Stratford Corporation to Groups of Actors, 1569-1592" is simply a record, made by town officials, listing dates, companies of players, sums paid, and payee. These facts may suggest that Shakespeare probably saw plays as a youth and thus may have begun an unconscious apprenticeship for a career. The same "Payments" list also shows that actors had some sort of connection or familiarity with the Queen or some of the great nobles of the kingdom; that a city or town would not consider it unusual to pay actors for performing; that perhaps not all troupes were as good as others, since payments varied; that acting companies went on tour through the country; that actors earned little or much; that actors were not uncommon in Stratford; and that they brought some sort of culture to the town.

Entries from the parish register can be used to establish part of the family genealogy, to reach conclusions about Elizabethan spelling, and to indicate something about the status of the Shakespeares, who anti-Stratfordians (the doubters) say were ignorant and boorish and who Stratfordians (believers) say were a family of importance and power.

The legal documents pertaining to Shakespeare's father, John, suggest something about John Shakespeare's civic career and local importance, his wealth, his law suits, and his exposure to the technicalities of the law, accounts, and real estate. These, in turn, indicate more about the environment in which William Shakespeare grew up. Upon close examination, most of the documentary material loses its surface confusion. It will become even more revealing and helpful if the reader will ask of each recorded fact as he encounters it, what does this bit of information really reveal? Are the facts consistent? Do they cancel each other out? Do sufficient records remain to support even a partial guess about Shakespeare's personality?

There are some marked and lamentable gaps in the Shakespeare documents. No autograph manuscript of any of Shakespeare's works has been discovered. The author did not care to write his autobiography and explain the genesis and evolution of his mind, as well as claim, in passing, the plays and poems as his own, nor did any of his contemporaries write his biography for him. At any rate, if these things were done, no remnants have been discovered. As a result, the records concerning Shakespeare include only dedications followed by his printed name on books containing his works, contemporary references, epitaphs, and a variety of public records and legal documents. This last group presents two thorny problems in reading, since the records and legal writings are in Latin or in Elizabethan legal English, which is a very specialized thing. Because of these difficulties and the limitations of space, the editors have made a chronological digest of the documents, based on scholarly transcripts, translations, and condensations. Little interpretive or background material has been provided. A few documents have been transcribed in a manner retaining something of the nature and flavor of the Elizabethan originals. But, in general, the entries in the following section should be regarded largely as a series of notes compiled for the reader by the editors. The notes are as complete and accurate as the editors could make them; hence, if there seems to be a lack of important data—for example, facts about Shakespeare's education—it is because the records are not known.

In order to simplify the problem of identifying the sources of the documents in this section, the editors have concocted the following key:

(A) J. O. Halliwell-Phillipps, *Outlines of the Life of Shakespeare,* 2 vols., 10th ed. (Longmans, Green, and Co., 1898, London).

(B) D. H. Lambert, *Cartae Shakespeareanae: Shakespeare Documents.* 1904. George Bell and Sons, London.

(C) Tucker Brooke, *Shakespeare of Stratford: A Handbook for Students.* New Haven: Yale University Press; London: Oxford University Press, 1926.

(D) E. K. Chambers, *William Shakespeare: A Study of Facts and Problems,* 2 vols., The Clarendon Press, Oxford, 1930.

(E) B. Roland Lewis. *The Shakespeare Documents.* 2 vols. Stanford: Stanford University Press; London: Oxford University Press, 1940-1941.

Numbers following the letters indicate volume, where appropriate, and page. Thus (D), I, 6 refers to Chambers, *William Shakespeare . . . ,* volume 1, page 6.

Note also that in the following section, square brackets [ ] are used in two ways: first to enclose source identification material taken from (D) above. These brackets are used by Chambers in his text. Second, they are used to set off page numbers and other editorial inserts from quoted material.

Royal Charter Incorporating Stratford

1553 Royal Charter of Edward VI incorporating Stratford-upon-Avon and thus providing it with a local government: a High Bailiff, fourteen Aldermen and fourteen Burgesses (these three formed the Council), plus other officials such as constables and Sergeants of the Mace. The Bailiff served for a year and was to preside over a Court of Record (limited to matters of dispute, trespass, and debt up to £30); he was also to be a Justice of the Peace, Escheator, Coroner, Almoner, and Clerk of the Market. The Corporation was given the right to certain properties and to the accumulation of a certain amount of income. In turn, one of its responsibilities was to support the Free Grammar School and provide its master with lodgings and £20[1] per annum. Concerning the school, the charter reads in part:

"And furthermore be it known that we, moved by extraordinary love and affection to the end that we bring up the youths of our kingdom in the aforesaid county of Warwick so that the coming generations shall derive from a childhood more cultured and imbued of letters than was accustomed in our times, and that, when they will have come to a more advanced life, they shall go forth more learned, undoubtedly appreciating the English Church of Christ (whose changes in the land we now are carrying out), taught no less in literary affairs than in precedence for the benefit of all our kingdom, we do in reality and to the full create, erect, found, ordain, make, and establish a certain Free Grammar School with one Master to endure forever in the aforesaid village of Stratford-upon-Avon. . . ." (Trans. by B. Roland Lewis.) (E), I, 27-51.

Payments Made by the Stratford Corporation to Groups of Actors, 1569-1592

[The following data derive from the Corporation records.]

1569 9s [shillings] to the Queen's players
12d [pence] to the Earl of Worcester's players
1573 6s8d to the Earl of Leicester's players
1574 17s to "my lord of Warwicks players"

[1] In 1940, Lewis estimated that an Elizabethan pound was worth $40. (E), I, 53.

	5s7d to the Earl of Worcester's players
1577	15s to the Earl of Leicester's players
	3s4d to the Earl of Worcester's players
1579	5s to Lord Strange's men
	14s6d to the Countess of Essex's players
1580?	8s4d to the Earl of Darbey's players
1581	3s4d to the Earl of Worcester's players
	3s2d to the Lord Bartlett's players
1582	5s to the Earl of Worcester's players
1583	5s to Lord Bartlett's players
	3s2d to "Lord Shandowes players"
1584	3s4d to the Earl of Oxford's players
	3s4d to the Earl of Warwick's players
	3s8d to the Earl of Essex's players
1586	5s for the players
1587	20s to the Queen's players
	5s to the Earl of Essex's players
	10s to the Earl of Leicester's players
	4s4d to another company of players
	3s4d to "my lord of Staffords men"
1592	20s for the Queen's players

(E), I, 60, fn. 14.

Entries Selected from the Register of the Church of the Holy Trinity, Stratford-on-Avon

Only relatively major items are given below. *C* stands for christening or baptism, *M* for marriage, and *F* for funeral or burial.

1558, Sept. 15	C	Jone [Joan] Shakspere daughter to John Shakspere
1562, Dec. 2	C	Margareta daughter of John Shakspere*
1563, Apr. 30	F	Margareta daughter of John Shakspere*
1564, Apr. 26	C	Gulielmus filius Johannes Shakspere [William, son of John Shakspere]
1566, Oct. 13	C	Gilbert son of John Shakspere*
1569, Apr. 15	C	Jone the daughter of John Shakspere [apparently the first Jone had died]
1571, Sept. 28	C	Anna daughter of master Shakspere*
1574, Mar. 11	C	Richard sonne to Mr. John Shakspeer

* Items so marked were originally entered in Latin.

1579, Apr. 4	F	Anne daughter to Mr. John Shakspere
1580, May 3	C	Edmund sonne to Mr. John Shakspere
1583, May 26	C	Susanna daughter to William Shakespeare
1585, Feb. 2	C	Hamnet & Judeth sonne and daughter to William Shakspere
1589, Feb. 26	C	Thomas sonne to Richard Queeny
1596, Aug. 11	F	Hamnet son of William Shakspere*
1601, Sept. 8	F	Mr. Johannes Shakspeare
1607, June 5	M	John Hall gentleman [also an Oxford M.A. and a physician] & Susanna Shaxspere
1608, Feb. 21	C	Elizabeth dawghter to John Hall gen.
1608, Sept. 9	F	Mayry Shaxspere wydowe [presumably John Shakespeare's wife, née Mary Arden]
1612, Feb. 3	F	Gilbert Shakspere young man*
1613, Feb. 4	F	Rich:[ard] Shakspeare
1616, Feb. 10	M	Tho. Queeny tow Judith Shakespeare [Quiney was a member of a prominent Stratford family; he failed in business as a vintner.]
1616, Apr. 17	F	Will. Hartt hatter [husband of William Shakespeare's sister Joan]
1616, Apr. 25	F	Will. Shakspere, gent.
1616, Nov. 23	C	Shaksper son of Thomas Quyny gent*
1617, May 8	F	Shakspere son of Tho. Quyny, gent.*
1623, Aug. 8	F	Mrs. Shakspeare [William Shakespeare's wife]
1626, Apr. 22	M	Mr. Thomas Nash to Mrs. Elizabeth Hall
1635, Nov. 26	F	John Hall a most expert physician*
1647, Apr. 5	F	Thomas Nash gent
1649, July 16	F	Mrs. Susanna Hall, widow.
1662, Feb. 9	F	Judith wife of Thomas Quiney gent*

(A), II, 51-52; (D), II, 1-12; (E), I & II, *passim*.[2]

Legal and Official Documents Referring to John Shakespeare, Citizen of Stratford

1552 John Shakespeare Fined by Local Court

Document

Stratford Burgus Visus franci plegii cum cur. illustrissimi principis Domini Edwardi Sexti Dei gratia Angliae ffranciae & Hiberniae regis Fidei defensoris & in terra ecclesiae Anglicanae &

[2] Wherever transcripts disagreed, the editors have arbitrarily followed (E).

Hibernicae supremi capitis ibidem tent. xxix°. die Aprilis anno regni sui sexto

Item [iuratores] present[ant] super sacramentum suum quod Humfrudus Reynoldes (xij.*d.*) Adrianus Quyney (xij.*d.*) & Johannes Shakyspere (xij.*d.*) fecerunt sterquinarium in vico vocato Hendley Strete contra ordinationem curiae Ideo ipsi in misericordia ut patet

Translation[3]

The City of Stratford — View of frank pledge at the court of the most illustrious prince [and] ruler Edward the Sixth by the grace of God King of England, France and Ireland, Defender of the Faith and Supreme Head in the land of the English and Irish Church held on the 29th day of April in the sixth year of his reign

Item: Deponents state under oath that Humphrey Reynolds (12 pence) Adrian Quiney (12 pence) and John Shakespeare (12 pence) have made a muckhill in the street called Hendley Street contrary to the order of the court. Therefore in fine for each as stated.

[According to B. Roland Lewis, the above is the first known reference to John Shakespeare, recording his being fined, with others, about $2.00 for having an illegal refuse dump. Like Reynolds, Quiney, and John Shakespeare, who were or became prominent Stratfordians, many fellow citizens, including the Bailiff and the local clergyman, were fined more than once for minor infractions of the law. Such fines, which were frequent, indicate official alertness. Lewis adds, "While it is not to be denied that Stratford-upon-Avon, from a modern point of view, was rather unsanitary, it is obvious too that the regulations very definitely aimed at good sanitation."] (E), I, 52.

Abstracts of Legal and Official Documents Referring to John Shakespeare

[Items listed under a year are not necessarily in chronological order, nor are they necessarily all the data for a year, although the editors have tried to make the list reasonably complete. The sources used are the five already listed. Where these disagree as to date, the editors have arbitrarily relied on (A).]

[3] Editors' translation.

1556 Complaint brought by Thomas Siche against "John Shakyspere,"[4] glover, to recover £8 debt.

Served twice on Court of Record jury.

Purchased two houses, with gardens, etc., in Stratford.

Appointed aletaster [an official who supervised the quality and sale of foodstuffs, especially bread and ale] for the city of Stratford.

Made complaint in court against Henry Field for the return of eighteen quarters [measures] of barley.

1557 Fined for not performing duty as aletaster.

Complaint against Richard Wagstaff to recover a debt of 10s.

Complaint against Walter Malpes.

Complaint against William Richardson.

Elected Burgess of the Corporation of Stratford-upon-Avon, a civic post held until 1565.

Complaint against John Asshell for a debt of 42s.

1558 Did jury duty twice.

Sued Matthew Bramley.

With Mr. Adrian Quiney, Mr. Hall, Mr. Clopton, and the Bailiff, fined for not keeping his gutter clean.

Action against by Adrian Quiney and Thomas Knight to recover a debt of £6 [apparently John Shakespeare paid].

Complaint by William Malpas [or *Malpes*] to recover a debt of 8s; John Shakespeare opposed the suit, and Malpas was fined 2d by the court for not prosecuting further.

Elected constable.

Complaint against by Francis Herbage to recover 10s.

1559 Summoned for jury duty.

Two complaints against Matthew Bramley for debt.

Action against John Shakespeare by Adrian Quiney and Thomas Knight to recover a debt of £5.

Complaint against Richard Court for a debt of 6s8d.

Complaint against Alice Nevell for a debt, no further action.

Again elected constable.

Elected affeeror [one who determined penalties in cases where the law did not state them].

1560 Summoned to jury duty, but apparently did not serve.

1561 Identified in a bond as administrator of the estate of his father, Richard, of Snitterfield.[5]

Complaint against by Robert Locke to recover a debt.

[4] The spelling of the last name is not consistent in the documents (e.g., *Shaxbere, Shakspeyr, Shakysper*).

[5] Chambers, II, 11, says that the identification is reasonable.

Elected one of the Chamberlains of the Stratford Corporation. Re-elected affeeror.

1562 Re-elected Chamberlain.

1563 Paid 3s by the Corporation for a piece of timber.

As Chamberlain, signed various leases [with a cross].[6]

Complaint against Richard Court regarding debt [settled out of court].

With John Taylor, the other Chamberlain, submitted the annual account of Corporation receipts and disbursals; [signed this document with a cross].[7]

Action against Richard Careles for debt.

1564 Made his report as one of the Chamberlains.

Owed 25s8d by the Stratford Council [the governing body of the Corporation].

Action against Humphrey Gadcliffe for debt.

On four different occasions contributed the following sums to the relief of the poor: 12d, 6d, 6d, 8d.

Was repaid £3·2s7½d, an "old det," owed him by the Corporation. [Halliwell-Phillipps regards this as a sign that John Shakespeare was affluent.]

1565 Appointed alderman [and so remained until 1586].

Record of presence at six Council meetings and absence from one.

Complaint versus John Mille regarding debt.

Member of a Court of Record jury.

1566 Apparent from the Chamberlains' Report that John Shakespeare had superintended the Chamberlains' accounts for 1564 and 1565.

Corporation paid John Shakespeare an indebtedness of 7s3d.

Called into court for debt by John Pagge.

Legal entanglement because of standing bail and perhaps security for Richard Hathaway, Anne Hathaway's father.

1567 Assessed for goods and paid levies of 3s4d and 2s6d.

Nominated for bailiff.

Attended four Council meetings.

1568 Paid 7s3d owed him by the Corporation.

Again nominated for bailiff; elected High Bailiff.

"As High Bailiff, John Shakespeare was Justice of the Peace, the Queen's Chief Officer, and Judge of the Court of Record. As such, moreover, by very [p. 60] quality and

[6] As far as is known, we have no signature of John Shakespeare; only his marks or crosses exist.

[7] Note how controversialists interpret this fact.

rank of the office, he was eligible for a coat of arms—for the gentryhood." (E), I, 59-60.

[As High Bailiff] presided at two sessions of the Court of Record and one meeting of the Council.

1569 Paid an allowance of 14s by the Corporation.

Witnessed a contingent lease on some property formerly belonging to Robert Arden.

Arbitrator in a suit between Henry Bragge and John Ball.

As High Bailiff, presided over three Council meetings and nine of the Court of Record.

1570 Present at four Council meetings.

During 1569-1570, received £6 from the Corporation chamberlains.

1571 Elected Chief Alderman for the year; this office made him also a justice of the peace.

Present at eight Council meetings.

Action against Richard Quiney for £50.

1572 Complaint against John Luther for a debt of £50; secured judgment plus 33s4d damages.

Present at seven Council meetings.

1573 Action by Henry Higford to recover debt of £30.

Attended two Council meetings.

"John Shaxbere" [name so spelled by Walter Roche, former master of the Stratford Grammar School] witnessed a conveyance of a piece of land.

1574 Present at four Council meetings.

1575 Witnessed the sale of two houses in Stratford.

Paid £40 to Edmund and Emma Hall for two houses & land in Henley Street.

Attended three Council meetings.

1576 Present at three Council meetings.

1577 Attended only one out of six Council meetings.

1578 Assessed half the sum for an alderman in a military levy, being taxed 3s4d.

Exempted from a weekly levy of 4d [for aldermen] for poor relief.

Owed Roger Saddeler £5, Edmund Lambert being one of John Shakespeare's securities.

Absent from eight out of the nine Council meetings at which attendance was recorded.

1579 John and Mary, his wife, conveyed an estate in Aston Cantlow to Edmund Lambert for £40.

John and Mary leased property to Thomas Webbe and Humphrey Hooper.

Listed as not having paid his assessment of 3s4d in a citizens' levy.

Sold an interest in an estate at Snitterfield to Robert Webbe for £4.

Listed as absent at seven out of ten Council meetings, no record of attendance being kept for three of the ten.

1580 Fined £40 for failure to appear before the Court of the Queen's Bench and for acting as surety for another who failed to appear there.

John and Mary sold part of a Snitterfield estate to Robert Webbe for £40.

Absent from all eight recorded Council meetings.

1581 Absent from all six Council meetings.

1582 Witness in a suit concerning the Arden-Snitterfield estates.

Present at one out of ten Council meetings.

1583 Absent from all fourteen Council meetings.

1584 Known to be absent from eight out of nine Council meetings.

1585 Sued by John Browne for debt.

Not present at nine Council meetings; at the tenth attendance was not recorded.

1586 On two Court of Record juries.

Went bail for Michael Price, indicted for felony.

Absent from five Council meetings prior to release.

Released as alderman for non-attendance.

1587 Action by Nicholas Lane to recover £10 of a debt contracted by Henry Shakespeare, John's brother, for whom John had acted as surety.

1588 Complaint against John Tompson for debt.

Complaint against John Lambert concerning the property conveyed to his father, Edmund Lambert, in 1579, and agreements made concerning it and, in addition, suit for £30 damages.

1589 Complaint against William Greene for debt; settlement reached.

Suits against John Tompson and Richard Sutton for debts.

1590 Served on Court of Record jury.

Survey of the Earl of Warwick's possessions showing that John Shakespeare still owned properties in Henley Street.

1591 Sued by Adrian Quiney, Humphrey Plumley, and Richard Hill for debt.

Complaint against Robert Jones for a debt of 9s1d.

Recovered a piece of movable property from Thomas West [apparently a cauldron].

Complaint against Robert Young.

Served on Court of Record jury.

1592 Served on committees evaluating the goods of the late Ralph Shawe and the late Henry Field.

Named on the county list of those who were or were suspected of being "Jhesuites, seminarye preestes, fugitives, or recusants" under the subheading: "It is sayd that these laste nine coom not to churche for fear of processe for debtts."

Action by John Burbage to end a lease.

1593 Complaint by Richard Tyler regarding debt.

1595 With Philip Green and Henry Rogers, sued by Adrian Quyney and Thomas Barber for a debt of £5.

1596 Probably witnessed a marriage settlement between Robert Fulwood and Elizabeth Hill.

Applied for and was granted a coat of arms; the draft of the grant notes that John "hathe Land[es] & tene[men]t[es] of good wealth & Substance $500^{li.}$."

1597 Sold a strip of land to George Badger for £2·10s.

A second suit against John Lambert regarding the property conveyed to his father and indicating that John and Mary Shakespeare wished to recover the property. Apparently the suit failed.

1599 Suit against John Walford of Marlborough to recover £21 for wool sold to Walford, plus £10 damages.

1601 Member of a committee of five that drew up suggestions to aid the Corporation in an action brought against it by Sir Edward Greville, Lord of the Manor of Stratford.

Records Relating to William Shakespeare

[Unless a code number following an entry indicates another source, the following material is largely a duplication of pertinent items, with modification or expansion, given in the "List of Documents" in each volume of (E).]

1582 Nov. 27. Entry in the Register of the Diocese of Worcester of a marriage license issued to "w^{m} Shaxpere et Annā whateley de Temple grafton." [There were Whateleys in and around Stratford.]

Nov. 28. Entry in above register of the marriage bond for "willm Shagspere . . . and Anne hathwey of Stratford in the Dioces of worcester maiden." The bond indicates that "the said will[ia]m and Anne" had been issued a license allowing for a single publication of the banns, instead of the usual three.

1593 Stationers' Register entry of *Venus and Adonis.* Approximately ten editions before 1616.

1594 Stationers' Register entry of *Lucrece;* at least five editions printed between 1594 and 1616.

Stationers' Register entry of *Titus Andronicus;* editions published in 1594, 1600, and 1611; none of the title pages gives the author's name.

1595 Entry in Public Record Office MS: "To William Kempe, William Shakespeare & Richard Burbage, servants to the Lord Chamberlain, upon the council's warrant dated at Whitehall, 15th March 1594, for two several comedies or interludes showed by them before her Majesty in Christmas time last past, viz. upon St. Stephen's day and Innocents' day £13·6s8d and by way of her Majesty's reward £6·13s4d; in all, £20." [Spelling, punctuation, etc., have been modernized by the editors.]

1596 Writ of attachment [court order for arrest] issued against William Shakespeare, Francis Langley, Dorothy Soer, and Anna Lee at the complaint of William Wayte, who wanted them placed under bond to keep the peace.

Documentary evidence that Shakespeare lived "in Southwark near the Bear-Garden, in 1596" and "that he continued to reside in Southwark to the year 1608." (D), II, 88.

1597 Record of purchase of New Place in Stratford from William Underhill for £60.

Stationers' Register entry of *Richard II.* First edition this year without author's name, which does appear, however, on title pages of the four editions between 1598 and 1615. Stationers' Register entry of *Richard III,* published this year without author's name. Shakespeare given as author in four editions between 1598 and 1612.

First edition of *Romeo and Juliet;* perhaps three others printed in Shakespeare's lifetime, only one bearing his name.

London record listing "Shackspere," of St. Helen's parish, in default of taxes [5s] on goods valued at £5 and among those who have died, moved or skipped.

1598 Jan. 24. Letter from Abraham Sturley to Richard Quiney advising that Shakespeare has money and may buy land. Oct. 25. Letter from Richard Quiney to Shakespeare seeking a loan of £30 from Shakespeare.

Oct.-Nov. Letter from Adrian Quiney to Richard Quiney, his son, mentioning bargaining with "Wm. Sha. . . ."

Nov. 4. Letter from Abraham Sturley to Richard Quiney again mentioning that Shakespeare might obtain money for them.

London record naming Shakespeare [same parish as above, 1597] among tax defaulters.

Folio [pub. 1616] of Ben Jonson's works: Shakespeare named as one of the "principall Comoedians" having acted in *Every Man in His Humor* in 1598 and also as one of the leading actors in *Sejanus,* 1603.

Stationers' Register entry of *1 Henry IV,* published this year without the author's name. Four other editions in Shakespeare's lifetime, only one [1599] bearing his name.

Stratford list citing Shakespeare as one of numerous citizens hoarding grain in time of scarcity.

Love's Labour's Lost published, author's name given on title page as "W. Shakespere."

Stationers' Register entry of *The Merchant of Venice,* published 1600 as "Written by William Shakespeare."

Stratford *Chamber Account* records: "pd to mr Shaxpere for on lod of ston xd." (D), II, 96.

1599 Property inventory of Sir Thomas Brend showing Shakespeare [only person named] and others to be occupying the Globe theater.

Tax roll list: Shakespeare cited as tax defaulter [same parish as above, 1597]; again so listed in 1600.

The Passionate Pilgrime, by "W. Shakespeare," published: a miscellany in which only a few of the poems were by Shakespeare; at least one other edition attributed to him before 1616.

1600 Stationers' Register entry of *2 Henry IV,* published in 1600, Shakespeare being named as author. The first SR entry to name William Shakespeare as author of a play.

Stationers' Register entry of *Henry V,* no author given. No author named in first three editions [1600, 1602, 1619].

Stationers' Register entry of *Much Ado About Nothing;* play published same year with Shakespeare given as author.

Court record of suit brought against John Clayton by a

"Willelmus Shackspere" for a £7 debt, which had been acknowledged in 1592 in Cheapside. [Not all scholars agree that this "Shackspere" was from Stratford.]

Stationers' Register entry of *A Midsummer-Night's Dream,* published the same year with Shakespeare named as author on title page.

1601 Extract from will of Thomas Whittington, shepherd of Richard Hathaway, Anne's father: "Item I geve and bequeth unto the poore people of Stratford 40s that is in the hand of Anne Shaxspere, wyf unto Mr. Wyllyam Shaxspere, and is due debt unto me. . . ."

1602 Stationers' Register entry of *The Merry Wives of Windsor,* published this year with Shakespeare as author on title page.

Recording of Shakespeare's purchase of 107 acres of land with appurtenances from William and John Combe for £320; the land was near Stratford.

Documents challenging and justifying Shakespeare's eligibility for a coat of arms [a heralds' dispute involving the arms of a number of persons].

Walter Getley's transfer of cottage with garden, Walker's Street, Stratford, to Shakespeare.

Stationers' Register entry of *Hamlet,* printed in 1603 as "By William Shake-speare"; republished perhaps thrice in Shakespeare's lifetime and attributed to him.

1603 King James's Royal Warrant ordering a patent to be issued to the Lord Chamberlain's Men; Shakespeare and others are named and authorized "freely to vse and exercise the Arte and facultie of playing Comedies Tragedies," etc.

Stationers' Register entry of *Troilus and Cressida.*

Letters Patent making the Lord Chamberlain's Men the King's Men: Shakespeare and others named in the document and authorized to give plays at the Globe or any other suitable place in the realm.

1604 List of the Master of the Wardrobe naming William Shakespeare as one of the King's Men and recording gifts to him and others of the players' company of four yards of scarlet cloth each. The gifts were connected with James's royal entry into London.

Record of suit against Philip Rogers to recover a debt of 35s10d.

Payment of £21·12s to the King's Men for eighteen days' attendance on the Spanish ambassador.

1605 Record of Shakespeare's payment of £440 for a thirty-one-year lease of part of the Stratford tithes.

Extract from the will of Augustine Phillips: "Item I geve and bequeathe to my Fellowe William Shakespeare a thirty shillings peece in gould, To my Fellowe Henry Condell one other thirty shillinge peece in gould, To my Servaunte Christopher Beeston thirty shillings in gould, To my Fellowe Lawrence Fletcher twenty shillings in gould. . . ." (D), II, 73.

1607 Stationers' Register entry of "Master William Shakespeare *his 'historye of Kinge Lear' . . . played before the kinges maiestie at Whitehall vppon Sainct Stephens night at Christmas Last by his maiesties servantes playinge vsually at the 'Globe'. . . .*" Play first published in 1608, Shakespeare given as author; apparently not reprinted in Shakespear's lifetime.

1608 Suit against John Addenbrooke for debt of £6.

Stationers' Register entry of *Pericles,* published in 1609 with Shakespeare as author; two other editions in Shakespeare's lifetime. Entry also made for *Antony and Cleopatra,* which was not published at this time.

1609 Second Stationers' Register entry for *Troilus and Cressida,* which, when published this year, bore on its title page *"Written by William Shakespeare."*

Stationers' Register entry of *Shake-speares Sonnets,* so entitled when published this year, the only edition in Shakespeare's lifetime.

1611 Stratford record listing Shakespeare as contributing to a fund for the repair of highways.

Bill of complaint in the Court of Chancery concerning Shakespeare's holding of Stratford tithes.

1612 Summons for Shakespeare and others to testify in the Belott-Mountjoy case, involving a marriage settlement of 1604. Legal documents reveal that Shakespeare had resided with Mountjoy and had known him and his son-in-law, Belott, for about ten years. [Mountjoy, a prosperous tiremaker living in St. Olave's parish, and Belott were French.]

Deposition of "Will[ia]m Shakespeare of Stratford vpon Aven in the Countye of Warwicke gen[tleman]" in the Mountjoy-Belott case.

1613 Record in the King's Chamber Account of payment of £153·6s8d for twenty plays performed by the King's Men, including *Much Ado about Nothing, The Tempest, The*

Winter's Tale, Othello, 1 & 2 Henry IV, and *Julius Caesar.*

Deed by which Shakespeare, William Johnson, John Jackson, and John Heminges purchased a property in Blackfriars, London, for £140.

Record that Shakespeare was paid 44s for work on an impresa [symbolic design on a shield] for the Earl of Rutland.

Court entry of suit for slander brought against John Lane by Susanna Hall.

Will of John Combe: bequest of £5 to "Mr William Shackspere."

Deed by which Shakespeare, *et al.,* mortgaged the Blackfriars property to Henry Walker.

1614 Agreement with William Replingham safeguarding Shakespeare's tithes.

Shakespeare listed as freeholder of four yards of land[8] in Welcombe.

1615 Bill of complaint entered in the Court of Chancery by Shakespeare and others to obtain possession of documents relating to the Blackfriars property.

1615 Court plea of Thomasina Ostler listing Shakespeare as shareholder in the Globe and Blackfriars theaters.

1616 Last will and testament of William Shakespeare, March 25.

Stratford Parish Register entry of the burial of William Shakespeare, April 25.

1604-1605 *The* Revels Account[9]

The Plaiers.		The poets which mayd the plaies.
By the Kings Maiesties plaiers.	Hallamas Day being the first of Nouembar A Play in the Banketinge house att Whit-Hall Called The Moor of Venis.	
By his Maiesties plaiers.	The Sunday ffollowinge A play of the Merry wiues of winsor.	

[8] A yard-land is an English land measure varying from place to place; it may include as few as 15 or as many as 40 acres. Lewis says that the reference here is to the 107 acres that Shakespeare purchased from the Combes in 1602. (E), II, 457.

[9] An official list of plays performed at court. For a fuller list of performances at court and elsewhere see (D), II, 303-353.

By his Maiesties plaiers.	On St Stiuens night in the Hall A play Caled Mesur for Mesur.	Shaxberd.
By his Maiesties plaiers.	On Inosents night The plaie of Errors.	Shaxberd.
By his Maiesties plaiers.	Betwin Newers Day and Twelfe day A play of Loues Labours Lost.	
By his Maiesties plaiers.	On the 7 of January was played the play of Henry the fift.	
By his Maiesties plaiers.	The 8 of January A play Cauled Euery on out of his Vmor.	[p. 332]
By his Maiesties plaiers.	On Candlemas night A playe Euery one In his Vmor. The Sunday ffolowing A playe provided And discharged.	
By his Maiesties plaiers.	On Shrousunday A play of the Marthant of Venis.	Shaxberd.
By his Maiesties plaiers.	On Shroumonday A Tragidye of The Spanishe Maz.	
By his Maiesties plaiers.	On Shroutusday A play Cauled the Martchant of Venis Againe Commanded By the Kings Maiestie.	Shaxberd.

(D), II, 331-332.

1593 *The Dedication of* Venus and Adonis *to the Earl of Southampton*

To the Right Honorable Henry Wriothesley, Earl of Southampton, and Baron of Titchfield. [p. 12]

Right Honorable: I know not how I shall offend in dedicating my unpolished lines to your Lordship, nor how the world will censure me for choosing so strong a prop to support so weak a burthen; only if your Honor seem but pleased, I account myself highly praised, and vow to take advantage of all idle hours till I have honored you with some graver labor. But if the first heir of my invention prove deformed, I shall be sorry it had so noble a godfather, and never after ear [plough] so barren a land for fear it yield me still so bad a harvest. I leave it to your honorable survey, and your Honor to your heart's content, which I wish may always answer your own wish and the world's hopeful expectation.

Your Honor's in all duty,

WILLIAM SHAKESPEARE.[10]

(C), 11-12.

1594 *The Dedication of* Lucrece

To the Right Honourable Henry Wriothesley, Earl of Southampton, and Baron of Titchfield.

The love I dedicate to your Lordship is without end; whereof this Pamphlet, without beginning is but a superfluous Moity. The warrant I have of your Honourable disposition, not the worth of my untutored lines, makes it assured of acceptance. What I have done is yours, what I have to doe is yours, being part in all I have, devoted yours. Were my worth [p. 13] greater, my duety would shew greater, meantime, as it is, it is bound to your Lordship, to whom I wish long life, still lengthened with all happiness.

Your Lordships in all duety,

William Shakespeare.

(B), 12-13.

1616 *Shakespeare's Will*

In the name of God, Amen! I William Shackspeare, of Stratford upon Avon in the countie of Warr., gent., in perfect health and memorie, God be praysed, doe make and ordayne this my last will and testament in manner and forme followeing, that ys to saye, ffirst, I comend my soule into the hands of God my Creator, hoping and assuredlie beleeving, through thonelie merites, of Jesus Christe my Saviour, to be made partaker of lyfe everlastinge, and my bodye to the earth whereof yt ys made. Item, I gyve and bequeath unto my [sonne and][11] daughter Judyth one hundred and fyftie poundes of lawfull English money, to be paied unto her in the manner and forme foloweng, that ys to saye, one hundred poundes *in discharge*

[10] Bracketed word and modernization of spelling and punctuation were supplied by the editor of (C).

[11] The words which were *erased* in the original will but which are still legible, have been put in brackets by the editors. Words which were *added* to the original will have been italicized.

of her marriage porcion within one yeare after my deceas, with consideracion after the rate of twoe shillings in the pound for soe long tyme as the same shalbe unpaied unto her after my deceas, and the fyftie poundes residwe thereof upon her surrendring *of,* or gyving of such sufficient securitie as the overseers of this my will shall like of, to surrender or graunte all her estate and right that shall discend or come unto her after my deceas, [p. 84] or *that shee* nowe hath, of, in, or to, one copiehold tenemente, with thappurtenaunces, lyeing and being in Stratford upon Avon aforesaied in the saied countye of Warr., being parcell or holden of the mannour of Rowington, unto my daughter Susanna Hall and her heires for ever. Item, I gyve and bequeath unto my saied daughter Judith one hundred and fyftie poundes more, if shee or anie issue of her bodie be lyvinge att thend of three yeares next ensueing the daie of the date of this my will, during which tyme my executours are to paie her consideracion from my deceas according to the rate aforesaied; and if she dye within the saied tearme without issue of her bodye, then my will ys, and I doe gyve and bequeath one hundred poundes thereof to my neece Elizabeth Hall, and the fiftie poundes to be sett fourth by my executours during the lief of my sister Johane Harte, and the use and proffitt thereof cominge shalbe payed to my saied sister Jone, and after her deceas the saied l.*li.*[12] shall remaine amongst the children of my saied sister, equallie to be divided amongst them; but if my saied daughter Judith be lyving att thend of the saied three yeares, or anie yssue of her bodye, then my will ys, and soe I devise and bequeath the saied hundred and fyftie poundes to be sett out *by my executours and overseers* for the best benefitt of her and her issue, and *the stock* not *to be* paied unto her soe long as she shalbe marryed and covert baron [by my executours and overseers]; but my will ys, that she shall have the consideracion yearelie paied unto her during her lief, and, after her deceas, the saied stocke and consideracion to bee paied to her children, if she have anie, and if not, to her executours or assignes, she lyving the saied terme after my deceas. [p. 85] Provided that yf suche husbond as she shall att thend of the saied three years be marryed unto, or att anie after, doe sufficientlie assure unto her and thissue of her bodie landes awnswereable to the porcion by this my will gyven unto her, and to be adjudged soe by my executours and overseers, then my will ys, that the said cl.*li.*[13] shalbe paied to such husbond as shall make such assurance, to his owne use. Item, I gyve and bequeath unto my saied sister Jone xx.*li.* and

[12] That is, £50.

[13] £150.

all my wearing apparrell, to be paied and delivered within one yeare after my deceas; and I doe will and devise unto her *the house* with thappurtenaunces in Stratford, wherein she dwelleth, for her naturall lief, under the yearlie rent of xij.[d.] Item, I gyve and bequeath unto her three sonnes, William Harte, ——— Hart, and Michaell Harte, fyve pounds a peece, to be paied within one yeare after my deceas [to be sett out for her within one yeare after my deceas by my executours, with thadvise and direccions of my overseers, for her best profitt, untill her mariage, and then the same with the increase thereof to be paied unto her]. Item, I gyve and bequeath unto [her] *the saied Elizabeth Hall,* all my plate, *except my brod silver and gilt bole,* that I now have att the date of this my will. Item, I gyve and bequeath unto the poore of Stratford aforesaied tenn poundes; to Mr. Thomas Combe[14] my sword; to Thomas Russell esquier fyve poundes; and to Frauncis Collins, of the borough of Warr. in the countie of Warr. gentleman, thirteene poundes, sixe shillinges, and eight pence, to be paied within one yeare after my deceas. Item, I gyve and bequeath to [Mr. Richard Tyler thelder] *Hamlett Sadler* xxvj.[s.] viij.[d.] to buy him a ringe; to *William Raynoldes gent., xxvj.*[s.] *viij.*[d.] *to buy him a ringe;* to [p. 86] my godson William Walker xx[s.] in gold; to Anthonye Nashe gent. xxvj.[s.] viij.[d.]; and to Mr. John Nashe xxvj.[s.] viij.[d.] [in gold]; *and to my fellowes John Hemynges, Richard Burbage, and Henry Cundell, xxvj.*[s.] *viij.*[d.] *a peece to buy them ringes.* Item, I gyve, will, bequeath, and devise, unto my daughter Susanna Hall, *for better enabling of her to performe this my will, and towards the performans thereof,* all that capitall messuage or tenemente with thappurtenaunces, *in Stratford aforesaid,* called the New Place, wherein I nowe dwell, and two messuages or tenementes with thappurtenaunces, scituat, lyeing, and being in Henley streete, within the borough of Stratford aforesaied; and all my barnes, stables, orchardes, gardens, landes, tenementes, and hereditamentes, whatsoever, scituat, lyeing, and being, or to be had, receyved, perceyved, or taken, within the townes, hamletes, villages, fieldes, and groundes, of Stratford upon Avon, Oldstratford, Bushopton, and Welcombe, or in anie of them in the saied countie of Warr. And alsoe all that messuage or tenemente with thappurtenaunces, wherein one John Robinson dwelleth, scituat, lyeing and being, in the Blackfriers in London, nere the Wardrobe; and all my other landes, tenementes, and hereditamentes whatsoever, To have and to hold all and singuler the saied premisses, with theire appurtenaunces, unto the saied Susanna Hall, for and during the terme of her naturall lief, and

[14] Nephew of John Combe, subject of the epitaphs from (D), II, 246.

after her deceas, to the first sonne of her bodie lawfullie yssueing, and to the heires males of the bodie of the saied first sonne lawfullie yssueinge; and for defalt of such issue, to the second sonne of her bodie, lawfullie issueinge, and to the heires males of [p. 87] the bodie of the saied second sonne lawfullie yssueinge; and for defalt of such heires, to the third sonne of the bodie of the saied Susanna lawfullie yssueing, and of the heires males of the bodie of the saied third sonne lawfullie yssueing; and for defalt of such issue, the same soe to be and remaine to the ffourth [sonne], ffyfth, sixte, and seaventh sonnes of her bodie lawfullie issueing, one after another, and to the heires males of the bodies of the saied fourth, fifth, sixte, and seaventh sonnes lawfullie yssueing, in such manner as yt ys before lymitted to be and remaine to the first, second, and third sonns of her bodie, and to theire heires males; and for defalt of such issue, the said premisses to be and remaine to my sayed neece Hall, and the heires males of her bodie lawfullie yssueinge; and for defalt of such issue, to my daughter Judith, and the heires males of her bodie lawfullie issueinge; and for defalt of such issue, to the right heires of me the saied William Shackspeare for ever. *Item, I gyve unto my wief my second best bed with the furniture.* Item, I gyve and bequeath to my saied daughter Judith my broad silver gilt bole. All the rest of my goodes, chattel, leases, plate, jewels, and household stuffe whatsoever, after my dettes and legasies paied, and my funerall expenses dischardged, I give, devise, and bequeath to my sonne in lawe, John Hall gent., and my daughter Susanna, his wief, whom I ordaine and make executours of this my last will and testament. And I doe intreat and appoint *the saied* Thomass Russell esquier and Frauncis Collins gent. to be overseers hereof, and doe revoke all former wills, and publishe this to be my last will and testament. In witness whereof I have [p. 88] hereunto put my [seale] *hand,* the daie and yeare first abovewritten.

By me William Shakspeare

Witnes to the publyshing hereof,

Fra: Collyns,
Julyus Shawe,
John Robinson,
Hamnet Sadler,
Robert Whattcott.[15]

(B), 83-88.

[15] The editors have omitted the heading of the will, which dates it March 25; the note at its end, indicating that it was probated June 22, 1616; and two of what B. R. Lewis calls the "three autograph signatures of the dramatist"; these appear at the bottoms of the first two sheets of the will.

Shakespeare's Epitaphs at Stratford

From the gravestone:

Good frend for Iesvs sake forbeare,
To digg the dvst encloased heare!
Bleste be ye man yt spares thes stones,
And cvrst be he yt moves my bones.

From the monument:

Ivdicio Pylivm, genio Socratem, arte Maronem:
Terra tegit, popvlvs maeret, Olympvs habet.[16]

Stay Passenger, why goest thov by so fast?
Read if thov canst, whom enviovs Death hath plast,
With in this monvment Shakspeare: with whome,
Qvick natvre dide: whose name doth deck ys Tombe,
Far more then cost: sieh all, yt He hath writt,
Leaves living art, bvt page, to serve his witt.
obiit año do[i] 1616
Ætatis · 53 die 23 Ap[r].[17]

1635 The Lord Chamberlain's Books (V, 133, p. 44), c. August 1, 1635: Extracts from legal reply of Cuthbert Burbage, *et al.*, to a petition made by Robert Benfield and Heliard Swanton.

Wee your humble suppliantes, Cutbert Burbage and Winifrid his brothers wife, and William his sonne, doe tender to your honorable consideration for what respectes and good reasons wee ought not in all charity to bee disabled of our livelyhoodes by men soe soone shott up. . . . The father of us, Cutbert and Richard Burbage, was the first builder of playhowses, and was himselfe in his younger yeeres a player. The Theater hee built with many hundred poundes

[16] Editors' literal translation: In judgment a Nestor, in wit a Socrates, in art a Virgil: earth covers, the nation mourns, heaven has.

[17] (D), II, 181-182. The above text follows Chambers as closely as possible. Chambers notes that the verses appear in Dugdale, *Antiquities of Warwickshire* (1656), where the transcription is accurate as to substance, if not to orthography. It is Chambers' opinion that the monument was erected between 1616 and 1623 and, except for refurbishing, has remained substantially the same ever since. For the monument, see inside of back cover.

taken up at interest. The players that lived in those first times had onely the profitts arising from the dores, but now the players receave all the commings in at the dores to themselves and halfe the galleries from the houskepers. Hee built this house upon leased ground, by which meanes the landlord and hee had a great suite in law, and, by his death, the like troubles fell on us, his sonnes; wee then bethought us of altering from thence, and at like expence built the Globe, with more summes of money taken up at interest, which lay heavy on us many yeeres; and to ourselves wee joyned those deserveing men, Shakspere, Hemings, Condall, Philips and others, partners in the profittes of that they call the House. . . . [p. 520] Now for the Blackfriers, that is our inheritance; our father purchased it at extreame rates, and made it into a playhouse with great charge and troble; which after was leased out to one Evans that first sett up the boyes commonly called the Queenes Majesties Children of the Chappell. In processe of time, the boyes growing up to bee men . . . and were taken to strengthen the Kings service; and the more to strengthen the service, the boyes dayly wearing out, it was considered that house would bee as fitt for ourselves, and soe purchased the lease remaining from Evans with our money, and placed men players, which were Hemings, Condall, Shakspeare, &c. . . . Then, to shew your Honor against these sayinges, that wee eat the fruit of their labours, wee referre it to your Honors judgement to consider their profittes . . . , for it appeareth by their owne accomptes for one whole yeere last past . . . each of these complainantes gained severally, as hee was a player and noe howskeeper, 180 *li.* Besides Mr. Swanston hath receaved from the Blackfriers this yeere, as hee is there a houskeeper, above 30 *li.* . . . (E), II, 519-520.

1635 *The Will of John Hall, Shakespeare's Son-in-Law*[18]

The last Will and Testament nuncupative of John Hall of Stratford-upon-Avon in the county of Warwick, gentleman, made and declared the five and twentith of November, 1635. Imprimis, I geve unto my wife my house in London. Item, I geve unto my daughter Nash [née Elizabeth Hall] my house in Acton. Item, I geve unto my daughter Nash my meadowe. Item, I geve my goodes

[18] From recorded copy, Registry of the Prerogative Court of Canterbury.

and money unto my wife and my daughter Nash, to be equally devided betwixt them. Item, concerning my study of bookes, I leave them, sayd he, to you, my sonn Nash, to dispose of them as yow see good. As for my manuscriptes, I would have given them to Mr. Boles, if hee had been here; but forasmuch as hee is not heere present, yow may, son Nash, burne them, or doe with them what yow please. Wittnesses hereunto,—*Thomas Nash. Simon Trapp.* (A), II, 61.

Contemporary References to Shakespeare 1592-1641

1930 *William Shakespeare: A Study of Facts and Problems.* By E. K. Chambers. Published by the Clarendon Press at Oxford, England. Two volumes.

[In volume 2, Chambers lists 58 contemporaries who refer to Shakespeare, some more than once. The following selections, which come from "Appendix B. Contemporary Allusions," are typical only of those that refer clearly and directly to Shakespeare. The only exception is the passage from Greene.]

[p. 188] *Robert Greene, 1592*[1]

[From *Greenes Groats-worth of Wit* . . . .][2]

To those Gentlemen his Quondam acquaintance, that spend their wits in making plaies, R. G. wisheth a better exercise, and wisdome to preuent his extremities. . . .

Base minded men all three of you, if by my miserie you be not warnd: for vnto none of you (like mee) sought those burres to cleaue: those Puppets (I meane) that spake from our mouths, those Anticks garnisht in our colours. Is it not strange, that I, to whom they all haue beene beholding: is it not like that you, to whome they all haue beene beholding, shall (were yee in that case as I am now) bee both at once of them forsaken? Yes trust them not: for

[1] Dates after authors' names in this section are those of the works whose names or titles are indicated in the bracketed material.

[2] The material identifying the source of a passage is quoted from Chambers. For the sake of convenience, the quotation marks have been omitted.

there is an vpstart Crow, beautified with our feathers, that with his *Tygers hart wrapt in a Players hyde,* supposes he is as well able to bombast out a blanke verse as the best of you: and beeing an absolute *Iohannes fac totum,* is in his owne conceit the onely Shake-scene in a countrey. O that I might intreat your rare wits to be imploied in more profitable courses: & let those Apes imitate your past excellence, and neuer more acquaint them with your admired inuentions. I knowe the best husband of you all will neuer proue an Usurer, and the kindest of them all will neuer proue a kind nurse: yet, whilest you may, seeke you better Maisters; for it is pittie men of such rare wits, should be subiect to the pleasure of such rude groomes.

In this I might insert two more, that both haue writ against these buckram Gentlemen: but lette their owne [p. 189] workes serue to witnesse against their owne wickednesse, if they perseuere to maintaine any more such peasants. For other new-commers, I leaue them to the mercie of these painted monsters, who (I doubt not) will driue the best minded to despise them: for the rest, it skils not though they make a ieast at them.[3]

[p. 192] *Anonymous, 1594*

[From commendatory verses to *Willobie his Avisa . . . .*]

Though Collatine *haue deerely bought,*
To high renowne, a lasting life,
And found, that most in vaine haue sought,
To haue a Faire, *and* Constant *wife,*
  Yet Tarquyne *pluckt his glistering grape,*
  And Shake-speare, *paints poore Lucrece rape.*

[3] Greene, educated at Cambridge, was a prominent but spendthrift writer and playwright who was impoverished and dying at the time he wrote the above passage. Scholars regard the passage as containing one of the earliest allusions to Shakespeare.

[p. 193] *Francis Meres, 1598*

[From *Palladis Tamia: Wits Treasury* . . . .] [p. 194]

A comparatiue discourse of our English Poets
with the *Greeke, Latine, and Italian Poets.*

. . . The English tongue is mightily enriched, and gorgeouslie inuested in rare ornaments and resplendent abiliments by sir *Philip Sidney, Spencer, Daniel, Drayton, Warner, Shakespeare, Marlow* and *Chapman*. . . .

As the soule of *Euphorbus* was thought to liue in *Pythagoras:* so the sweete wittie soule of *Ouid* liues in mellifluous & hony-tongued *Shakespeare,* witnes his *Venus* and *Adonis,* his *Lucrece,* his sugred Sonnets among his priuate friends, &c.

As *Plautus* and *Seneca* are accounted the best for Comedy and Tragedy among the Latines: so *Shakespeare* among the English is the most excellent in both kinds for the stage; for Comedy, witnes his *Gentlemen of Verona,* his *Errors,* his *Loue labors lost,* his *Loue labours wonne,* his *Midsummers night dreame,* & his *Merchant of Venice:* for Tragedy his *Richard the* 2. *Richard* the 3. *Henry the* 4. *King Iohn, Titus Andronicus* and his *Romeo* and *Iuliet.*

As *Epius Stolo* said, that the Muses would speake with *Plautus* tongue, if they would speak Latin: so I say that the Muses would speak with *Shakespeares* fine filed phrase, if they would speake English. . . .

As *Ouid* saith of his worke . . . as *Horace* saith of his . . . so say I seuerally of sir *Philip Sidneys, Spencers, Daniels, Draytons, Shakespeares,* and *Warners workes;*

Non Iouis ira, imbres, Mars, ferrum, flamma, senectus,
Hoc opus vnda, lues, turbo, venena ruent. . . .

As *Pindarus, Anacreon* and *Callimachus* among the Greekes; and *Horace* and *Catullus* among the Latines are the best Lyrick Poets: so in this faculty the best among our Poets are *Spencer* (who excelleth in all kinds) *Daniel, Drayton, Shakespeare, Bretton*. . . .

These are our best for Tragedie, the Lorde *Buckhurst,* Doctor *Leg* of Cambridge, Doctor *Edes* of Oxforde, maister *Edward Ferris,* the Author of the *Mirrour for Magistrates, Marlow, Peele, Watson, Kid, Shakespeare, Drayton, Chapman, Decker,* and *Beniamin Johnson*. . . .

The best for Comedy amongst us bee, *Edward* Earle of [p. 195]

Oxforde, Doctor *Gager* of Oxforde, Maister *Rowley* once a rare Scholler of learned Pembrooke Hall in Cambridge, Maister *Edwardes* one of her Maiesties Chappell, eloquent and wittie *John Lilly, Lodge, Gascoyne, Greene, Shakespeare, Thomas Nash, Thomas Heywood, Anthony Mundye* our best plotter, *Chapman, Porter, Wilson, Hathway,* and *Henry Chettle. . . .*

These are the most passionate among us to bewaile and bemoane the perplexities of Loue, *Henrie Howard* Earle of Surrey, sir *Thomas Wyat* the elder, sir *Francis Brian,* sir *Philip Sidney,* sir *Walter Rawley,* sir *Edward Dyer, Spencer, Daniel, Drayton, Shakespeare, Whetstone, Gascoyne, Samuell Page* sometimes fellowe of *Corpus Christi* Colledge in Oxford, *Churchyard, Bretton.*

[p. 196] *Gabriel Harvey, c. 1598-1601*

[From MS. note in copy of Speght's *Chaucer* (1598) . . . .][4]

[p. 197] The younger sort takes much delight in Shakespeares Venus, & Adonis: but his Lucrece, & his tragedie of Hamlet, Prince of Denmarke, haue it in them, to please the wiser sort. . . . [p. 198] His [Sir Edward Dyer's] Amaryllis, & Sir Walter Raleighs Cynthia, how fine & sweet inuentions? Excellent matter of emulation for Spencer, Constable, France, Watson, Daniel, Warner, Chapman, Siluester, Shakespeare, & the rest of our florishing metricians. . . .

[p. 199] *Anonymous, 1599?, 1601?*

[From *Parnassus,* ed. W. D. Macray (1886), a series of plays: (1) *The Pilgrimage to Parnassus,* (2) *The Returne from Parnassus,* Part I, (3) *The Returne from Parnassus,* Part II, performed at St. John's, Cambridge, probably at the Christmases of 1598-9, 1599-1600, and 1601-2; . . .][5] [p. 200]

(a) [From *2 Parnassus* (1599?).]

[iii. I. 1006-55.] *Gull(io).* Pardon, faire lady, thoughe sicke-thoughted Gullio maks amaine unto thee, and like a bould-faced sutore 'gins to woo thee.

[4] The note was written by Harvey in a copy of Chaucer edited by Speght.
[5] Author(s) unknown.

Ingen(ioso). (We shall have nothinge but pure Shakspeare and shreds of poetrie that he hath gathered at the theators!)

Gull. Pardon mee, moy mittressa, ast am a gentleman, the moone in comparison of thy bright hue a meere slutt, Anthonio's Cleopatra a blacke browde milkmaide, Hellen a dowdie.

Ingen. (Marke, Romeo and Juliet! O monstrous theft! I thinke he will runn throughe a whole booke of Samuell Daniell's!)

Gull. Thrise fairer than myselfe (—thus I began—)
The gods faire riches, sweete above compare,
Staine to all nimphes, (m)ore lovely the(n) a man.
More white and red than doves and roses are!
Nature that made thee with herselfe had (at) strife,
Saith that the worlde hath ending with thy life.

Ingen. Sweete Mr. Shakspeare! . . .

Ingen. My pen is youre bounden vassall to commande. But what vayne woulde it please you to have them in?

Gull. Not in a vaine veine (prettie, i'faith!): make mee them in two or three divers vayns, in Chaucer's, Gower's and Spencer's and Mr. Shakspeare's. Marry, I thinke I shall entertaine those verses which run like these;

Even as the sunn with purple coloured face
Had tane his laste leave on the weeping morne, &c.

O sweet Mr. Shakspeare! I'le have his picture in my study at the courte.

[iv. I. 1211-27.] *Gull.*—Let mee heare Mr. Shakspear's veyne.

Ingen. Faire Venus, queene of beutie an dof love,
Thy red doth stayne the blushinge of the morne,
Thy snowie necke shameth the milkwhite dove,
Thy presence doth this naked worlde adorne;
Gazinge on thee all other nymphes I scorne.
When ere thou dyest slowe shine that Satterday,
Beutie and grace muste sleepe with thee for aye! [**p. 201**]

Gull. Noe more! I am one that can judge accordinge to the proverbe, *bovem ex unguibus.* Ey marry, Sir, these have some life in them! Let this duncified worlde esteeme of Spencer and Chaucer, I'le worshipp sweet Mr. Shakspeare, and to honoure him will lay his Venus and Adonis under my pillowe, as wee reade of one (I doe not well remember his name, but I am sure he was a kinge) slept with Homer under his bed's heade.

(b) [From *3 Parnassus* (1601?)]

[i. 2. 304.] *Ingenioso .... William Shakespeare.*

Iudicio. Who loues not *Adons* loue, or *Lucrece* rape?
His sweeter verse contaynes hart trobbing line,
Could but a graver subiect him content,
Without loues foolish lazy languishment.

[iv. 3. 1806-79.] *Kempe.*[6] Few of the vniuersity men pen plaies well, they smell too much of that writer *Ouid,* and that writer *Metamorphosis,* and talke too much of *Proserpina* & *Iuppiter.* Why heres our fellow *Shakespeare* puts them all downe, I and *Ben Ionson* too. O that *Ben Ionson* is a pestilent fellow, he brought vp *Horace* giuing the Poets a pill, but our fellow *Shakespeare* hath giuen him a purge that made him beray his credit:

Burbage.[7] Its a shrewd fellow indeed: I wonder these schollers stay so long, they appointed to be here presently that we might try them: oh, here they come....

Bur. I like your face, and the proportion of your body for *Richard* the *3.* I pray, M. *Phil.* let me see you act a little of it.

Philomusus. 'Now is the winter of our discontent, Made glorious summer by the sonne of Yorke.'

[p. 212] *John Manningham, 1602*

[From *Diary* in *Harl*[eian] *MS.* 5353, f. 29v....]

13 March 1601 (1602) . . . Vpon a tyme when Burbidge played Rich. 3. there was a citizen greue soe farr in liking with him, that before shee went from the play shee appointed him to come that night vnto hir by the name of Ri: the 3. Shakespeare overhearing their conclusion went before, was intertained, and at his game ere Burbidge came. Then message being brought that Rich. the 3.[d] was at the dore, Shakespeare caused returne to be made that William the Conquerour was before Rich. the 3. Shakespeare's name William. *(Mr. Curle.)* [Manningham's informant.]

[6] Kempe was a very famous actor of the Elizabethan era.

[7] Burbage was an Elizabethan actor and theater owner. Both Kempe and Burbage were associated with Shakespeare.

[p. 215] *William Camden, 1605*

[From *Remaines of a greater Worke concerning Britaine,* Poems 8.]

These may suffice for some Poeticall descriptions of our auncient Poets, if I would come to our time, what a world could I present to you out of Sir *Philipp Sidney, Ed. Spencer, Samuel Daniel, Hugh Holland, Ben: Johnson, Th. Campion, Mich. Drayton, George Chapman, Iohn Marston, William Shakespeare,* & other most pregnant witts of these our times, whom succeeding ages may iustly admire.

[p. 218] *John Webster, 1612*

[From *Epistle* to *The White Devil* . . . .]

Detraction is the sworne friend to ignorance: For mine owne part I haue euer truly cherisht my good opinion of other mens worthy Labours, especially of that full and haightned stile of Maister *Chapman:* The labor'd and vnderstanding workes of Maister *Johnson;* The no lesse worthy composures of the both worthily excellent Maister *Beamont* & Maister *Fletcher:* And lastly (without wrong last to be named), the right happy and copious industry of M. *Shake-speare,* M. *Decker,* & M. *Heywood,* wishing what I write may be read by their light: Protesting, that, in the strength of mine owne iudgement, I know them so worthy, that though I rest silent in my owne worke, yet to most of theirs I dare (without flattery) fix that of *Martiall.*

—non norunt, Haec monumenta mori.

[p. 222] *Francis Beaumont, c. 1615*

[I give the poem . . . from two copies, both in 17th-century manuscript anthologies and not autograph. . . .][8]

[p. 224] . . . heere I would let slippe
(If I had any in mee) schollershippe,
And from all Learninge keepe these lines as (cl)eere
as Shakespeares best are, which our heires shall heare . . . .

[8] The poem is addressed to Ben Jonson. The editors have given only the lines mentioning Shakespeare.

[p. 228] *John Heminges and Henry Condell, 1623*

(a) [*Epistle* to the Earls of Pembroke and Montgomery, on third preliminary leaf to Fl (i.e., Folio 1). . . .][9]

Right Honourable,

Whilst we studie to be thankful in our particular, for the many fauors we have receiued from your L. L we are falne vpon the ill fortune, to mingle two the most diuerse things that can bee, feare, and rashnesse; rashnesse in the enterprize, and feare of the successe. For, when we valew the places your H. H. sustaine, we cannot but know their dignity greater, then to descend to the reading of these trifles: and, while we name them trifles, we haue depriu'd our selues of the defence of our Dedication. But since your L. L. haue beene pleas'd to thinke these trifles something, heeretofore; and haue prosequuted both them, and their Author liuing, with so much fauour: we hope, that (they out-liuing him, and he not hauing the fate, common with some, to be exequutor to his owne writings) you will vse the like indulgence toward them, you haue done vnto their parent. There is a great difference, whether any Booke choose his Patrones, or finde them: This hath done both. For, so much were your L L. likings of the seuerall parts, when they were acted, as before they were published, the Volume ask'd to be yours. We haue but collected them, and done an office to the dead, to procure his Orphanes, Guardians; without ambition either of selfe-profit, or fame: onely to keepe the memory of so worthy a Friend, & Fellow aliue, as was our SHAKESPEARE, by humble offer [p. 229] of his playes, to your most noble patronage. . . . therefore, we most humbly consecrate to your H. H. these remaines of your seruant *Shakespeare;* that what delight is in them, may be euer your L. L. the reputation his, & the faults ours, if any be committed, by a payre so carefull to shew their gratitude both to the liuing, and the dead, as is

Your Lordshippes most bounden,
John Heminge.
Henry Condell.

(b) [*To the great Variety of Readers,* on fourth preliminary leaf of Fl.]

. . . And though you be a Magistrate of wit, and sit on the Stage at *Black-Friers,* or the *Cock-pit,* to arraigne Playes [p. 230] dailie,

[9] The source here is the First Folio, the first collection purporting to contain all of Shakespeare's dramatic works. It was published in 1623.

know, these Playes haue had their triall alreadie, and stood out all Appeales; and do now come forth quitted rather by a Decree of Court, then any purchas'd Letters of commendation.

It had bene a thing, we confesse, worthie to haue bene wished, that the Author himselfe had liu'd to haue set forth, and ouerseen his owne writings; But since it hath bin ordain'd otherwise, and he by death departed from that right, we pray you do not envie his Friends, the office of their care, and paine, to haue collected & publish'd them; and so to haue publish'd them, as where (before) you were abus'd with diuerse stolne, and surreptitious copies, maimed, and deformed by the frauds and stealthes of iniurious impostors, that expos'd them: euen those, are now offer'd to your view cur'd, and perfect of their limbes; and all the rest, absolute in their numbers, as he conceiued them. Who, as he was a happie imitator of Nature, was a most gentle expresser of it. His mind and hand went together: And what he thought, he vttered with that easinesse, that wee haue scarce receiued from him a blot in his papers. But it is not our prouince, who onely gather his works, and giue them you, to praise him. It is yours that reade him. . . .

John Heminge.
Henrie Condell.

[p. 231] *Leonard Digges, 1623*

[For Digges' commendatory verses, printed on the eighth preliminary leaf of the Folio, see Hastings' "Shakespeare Was Shakespeare," page 246 of this text. Digges was an Oxford man and a translator.]

[p. 234] *I. M., 1623*

[From the eighth preliminary leaf to Fl . . . .]

To the memorie of M. W. Shake-speare.

Wee wondred *(Shake-speare)* that thou went'st so soone
From the Worlds-Stage, to the Graues-Tyring-roome.
Wee thought thee dead, but this thy printed worth,
Tels thy Spectators, that thou went'st but forth
To enter with applause. An Actors Art,

Can dye, and liue, to acte a second part.
That's but an *Exit* of Mortalitie;
This, a Re-entrance to a Plaudite.

I.M.

Further References to Shakespeare by His Contemporaries—from a Variety of Sources

---

1623 "To the memory of my beloued, The AVTHOR Mr. William Shakespeare: And what he hath left vs." By Ben Jonson. *The Poems: The Prose Works,* Volume 8, of *Ben Jonson,* edited by C. H. Herford and Percy and Evelyn Simpson. 11 volumes. Published at Oxford, the Clarendon Press, 1925-1952. Volume 8 appeared in 1947.

[p. 390]

To draw no enuy *(Shakespeare)* on thy name,
Am I thus ample to thy Booke, and Fame:
While I confesse thy writings to be such,
As neither *Man,* nor *Muse,* can praise too much.
'Tis true, and all mens suffrage. But these wayes
Were not the paths I meant vnto thy praise:
For seeliest Ignorance on these may light,
Which, when it sounds at best, but eccho's right; [p. 391]
Or blinde Affection, which doth ne're aduance
The truth, but gropes, and vrgeth all by chance;
Or crafty Malice, might pretend this praise,
And thinke to ruine, where it seem'd to raise.
These are, as some infamous Baud, or Whore,
Should praise a Matron. What could hurt her more?
But thou art proofe against them, and indeed
Aboue th'ill fortune of them, or the need.
I, therefore will begin. Soule of the Age!
The applause! delight! the wonder of our Stage!
My *Shakespeare,* rise; I will not lodge thee by
Chaucer, or *Spenser,* or bid *Beaumont* lye

A little further, to make thee a roome:
  Thou art a Moniment, without a tombe,
And art aliue still, while thy Booke doth liue,
  And we haue wits to read, and praise to giue.
That I not mixe thee so, my braine excuses;
  I meane with great, but disproportion'd *Muses:*
For, if I thought my iudgement were of yeeres,
  I should commit thee surely with thy peeres,
And tell, how farre thou didst our *Lily* out-shine,
  Or sporting *Kid,* or *Marlowes* mighty line.
And though thou hadst small *Latine,* and lesse *Greeke,*
  From thence to honour thee, I would not seeke
For names; but call forth thund'ring *Æschilus,*
  Euripides, and *Sophocles* to vs,
Paccuuius, Accius, him of *Cordoua* dead,
  To life againe, to heare thy Buskin tread,
And shake a Stage: Or, when thy Sockes were on,
  Leaue thee alone, for the comparison
Of all, that insolent *Greece,* or haughtie *Rome*
  Sent forth, or since did from their ashes come.
Triúmph, my *Britaine,* thou hast one to showe,
  To whom all Scenes of *Europe* homage owe.
He was not of an age, but for all time!
  And all the *Muses* still were in their prime, **[p. 392]**
When like *Apollo* he came forth to warme
  Our eares, or like a *Mercury* to charme!
Nature her selfe was proud of his designes,
  And ioy'd to weare the dressing of his lines!
Which were so richly spun, and wouen so fit,
  As, since, she will vouchsafe no other Wit.
The merry *Greeke,* tart *Aristophanes,*
  Neat *Terence,* witty *Plautus,* now not please;
But antiquated, and deserted lye
  As they were not of Natures family.
Yet must I not giue Nature all: Thy Art,
  My gentle *Shakespeare,* must enioy a part.
For though the *Poets* matter, Nature be,
  His Art doth giue the fashion. And, that he,
Who casts to write a liuing line, must sweat,
  (Such as thine are) and strike the second heat
Vpon the *Muses* anuile: turne the same,
  (And himselfe with it) that he thinkes to frame;
Or for the lawrell, he may gaine a scorne,

For a good *Poet's* made, as well as borne.
And such wert thou. Looke how the fathers face
Liues in his issue, euen so, the race
Of *Shakespeares* minde, and manners brightly shines
In his well torned, and true-filed lines:
In each of which, he seemes to shake a Lance,
As brandish't at the eyes of Ignorance.
Sweet Swan of *Auon!* what a sight it were
To see thee in our waters yet appeare,
And make those flights vpon the bankes of *Thames,*
That so did take *Eliza,* and our *Iames!*
But stay, I see thee in the *Hemisphere*
Aduanc'd, and made a Constellation there!
Shine forth, thou Starre of *Poets,* and with rage,
Or influence, chide, or cheere the drooping Stage;
Which, since thy flight from hence, hath mourn'd like night,
And despaires day, but for thy Volumes light.

Ben: Ionson.[10]

1623 Folio of Shakespeare's Works, title page: Mr. WILLIAM/SHAKESPEARES/COMEDIES,/HISTORIES, &/TRAGEDIES./Published according to the True Originall Copies./[Portrait[11] signed by] *Martin Droeshout: sculpsit London*/LONDON/Printed by Isaac Iaggard, and Ed. Blount. 1623. (E), II, 553 & 554.

From the ninth preliminary leaf to the Folio:

"The Names of the Principall Actors in all these Playes.

William Shakespeare.	Samuel Gilburne.
Richard Burbadge.	Robert Armin.
John Hemmings.	William Ostler.
Augustine Phillips.	Nathan Field.
William Kempt.	John Vnderwood.
Thomas Poope.	Nicholas Tooley.
George Bryan.	William Ecclestone.
Henry Condell.	Joseph Taylor.
William Slye.	Robert Benfield.
Richard Cowly.	Robert Goughe.

[10] This poem was first published in the 1623 Folio edition of Shakespeare's plays.
[11] See inside front cover—the editors.

John Lowine.
Samuell Crosse.
Alexander Cooke.
Richard Robinson.
Iohn Shancke.
Iohn Rice." (D), II, 77.

List of dramas in the First Folio (1623):

Comedies. The Tempest, folio 1; The Two Gentlemen of Verona, 20; The Merry Wives of Windsor, 38; Measure for Measure, 61; The Comedy of Errours, 85; Much adoo about Nothing, 101; Loves Labour lost, 122; Midsommer Nights Dreame, 145; The Merchant of Venice, 163; As you Like it, 185; The Taming of the Shrew, 208; All is well that Ends well, 230; Twelfe-Night, or what you will, 255; The Winters Tale, 304.—*Histories.* The Life and Death of King John, fol. 1; the Life and Death of Richard the Second, 23; the First Part of King Henry the Fourth, 46; The Second Part of K. Henry the fourth, 74; The Life of King Henry the Fift, 69; The First part of King Henry the Sixt, 96; The Second part of King Hen. the Sixt, 120; The Third part of King Henry the Sixt, 147; The Life and Death of Richard the Third, 173; The Life of King Henry the Eight, 205.—*Tragedies.* The Tragedy of Coriolanus, fol. 1; Titus Andronicus, 31; Romeo and Juliet, 53; Timon of Athens, 80; The Life and death of Julius Caesar, 109; The Tragedy of Macbeth, 131; The Tragedy of Hamlet, 152; King Lear, 283; Othello, the Moore of Venice, 310; Anthony and Cleopater, 346; Cymbeline King of Britaine, 369. (B), 101-102.

1641 From Ben Jonson's *Timber: or, Discoveries; Made Vpon Men and Matter* as reprinted on pp. 583-584 in volume 8, *The Poems: The Prose Works* (1947) of *Ben Jonson,* edited by C. H. Herford and Percy and Evelyn Simpson. 11 volumes. Published at Oxford, the Clarendon Press, 1925-1952.

[p. 583]

I remember, the Players have often mentioned it as an honour to *Shakespeare,* that in his writing, (whatsoever he penn'd) hee never blotted out line. My answer hath beene, Would he had blotted a thousand. Which they thought a malevolent speech. I had not told posterity this, but for their ignorance, who choose that circumstance to commend their friend by, wherein he most faulted. And to justifie mine owne candor, (for I lov'd the man, and doe honour his [p. 584] memory (on this side Idolatry) as much as any.) Hee was (indeed) honest, and of an open, and free nature: had an excellent *Phantsie;* brave notions, and gentle expressions: wherein hee flow'd with that facility, that sometime it was necessary he should be stop'd: *Sufflaminandus erat;*[12] as *Augustus* said of *Haterius.* His wit was in his owne power; would the rule of it had beene so too. Many times hee fell into those things, could not escape laughter: As when hee said in the person of *Caesar,* one speaking to him; *Caesar, thou dost me wrong.* Hee replyed: *Caesar did never wrong, but with just cause:*[13] and such like; which were ridiculous. But hee redeemed his vices, with his vertues. There was ever more in him to be praysed, then to be pardoned.[14]

[12] The brakes ought to have been applied.

[13] *Julius Caesar,* III, i, 31-47.

[14] Published in 1640-41, after Jonson's death, *Timber: or, Discoveries* is a collection of the author's miscellaneous papers. It consists of notes, reflections, translations and extracts of various sorts.

Early Shakespeare Biography and Tradition 1662-1780

[The following excerpts are from E. K. Chambers, *William Shakespeare: A Study of Facts and Problems,* II, Appendix C, which is entitled: "The Shakespeare-Mythos."]

[p. 238] [. . . We may share the regrets of Malone . . . that . . . so many persons of Shakespeare's generation or the next, who lived to the end of the 17th century or the beginning of the 18th, yet died with unconsulted memories, before Nicholas Rowe . . . made the first attempt at a considered *Life* in 1709. . . . Many[1] which emerged in the 18th and even the 19th centuries are, of course, of doubtful origin and still more doubtful validity. . . . I have brought together as many as possible in this Appendix. . . . It is, I think, possible to underestimate the value of biographical tradition, where it is not inconsistent with other evidence. Provincial memories are long-lived, and so are those of professions which, like that of the stage, are largely recruited as hereditary castes. There is, of course, a tact to be exercised in taking the gist of a statement, without laying too much stress on its details. And it must be admitted that after all there is much here which throws less light upon Shakespeare than upon the mental processes which lead to the development of myths. There are three streams of tradition, deriving respectively from London, from Oxford, and from Stratford. The London tradition is mainly theatrical. Its main channel of transmission seems to have been through Sir William Davenant (1606-68) and his associate Thomas Betterton (*c.* 1635-1710), who also

[1] *I.e.,* notices of Shakespeare.

visited Stratford on behalf of Rowe. . . . [p. 239] The Oxford tradition only concerns itself with the relations between Shakespeare and the Davenants. . . . The Stratford contribution is of a very miscellaneous kind. The nearest approach to a personal reminiscence is Plume's story. . . . But Stratford was not unaware of the reputation of its distinguished inhabitant, and became a place of pilgrimage at an early date. . . .][2]

[p. 242] *Lieutenant Hammond, 1634*

[1634, Sept. 9. From *A Relation of a Short Survey of 26 Counties . . . By a Captaine, a Lieutennant and an Ancient, All three of the Military Company of Norwich* (*Lansd. MS.* 213, f. 315). . . . The narrator was evidently the lieutenant, who says that the town-clerk of Maldon (one Hammond in 1635) was his namesake. . . .]

In that dayes trauell we came by Stratford vpon Auon, where in the Church in that Towne there are some Monuments which Church was built by Archbishop Stratford; Those worth obseruing and of which wee [p. 243] tooke notice of were these. . . . A neat Monument[3] of that famous English Poet, Mr. William Shakespeere; who was borne heere.

And one of an old Gentleman a Batchelor, Mr Combe, vpon whose name, the sayd Poet, did merrily fann vp some witty, and facetious verses, which time would nott giue vs leaue to sacke vp.

[p. 243] *Sir Nicholas L'Estrange, 1629-55*

[From *Merry Passages and Jeasts* (*Harl. MS.* 6395, f. 2). . . .]

Shake-speare was Godfather to one of *Ben: Johnsons* children, and after the christning being in a deepe study, Johnson came to cheere him vp, and askt him why he was so Melancholy? no faith *Ben:* (sayes he) not I, but I haue beene considering a great while what should be the fittest gift for me to bestow vpon my God-child, and I haue resolu'd at last; I pry'the what, sayes he? I faith *Ben:* I'le e'en

[2] The editors once again put Chambers' introductory comment or source identification within brackets.

[3] See inside of back cover—the editors.

giue him a douzen good Lattin Spoones, and thou shalt translate them.

[p. 244] *Thomas Fuller, 1662*

[From *Worthies, Warwickshire,* 126.][4]

William Shakespeare was born at *Stratford* on *Avon* in this County, in whom three eminent Poets may seem in some sort to be compounded. [p. 245]

1. *Martial* in the *Warlike* sound of his Sur-name (whence some may conjecture him of a *Military extraction,*) *Hasti-vibrans,* or *Shake-speare.*

2. *Ovid,* the most *naturall* and *witty* of all Poets, and hence it was that Queen *Elizabeth,* coming into a Grammar-School, made this extemporary verse,

'*Persius* a Crab-staffe, Bawdy *Martial,*
Ovid a fine Wag.'

3. *Plautus,* who was an exact Comædian, yet never any Scholar, as our *Shake-speare* (if alive) would confess himself. Adde to all these, that though his Genius generally was *jocular,* and inclining him to *festivity,* yet he could (when so disposed) be *solemn* and *serious,* as appears by his Tragedies, so that *Heraclitus* himself (I mean if secret and unseen) might afford to smile at his Comedies, they were so *merry,* and *Democritus* scarce forbear to sigh at his Tragedies they were so *mournfull.*

He was an eminent instance of the truth of that Rule, *Poeta not* [sic] *fit, sed nascitur,* one is not *made,* but *born* a Poet. Indeed his Learning was very little, so that as *Cornish diamonds* are not polished by any Lapidary, but are pointed and smoothed even as they are taken out of the Earth, so *nature* it self was all the *art* which was used upon him.

Many were the *wit-combates* betwixt him and *Ben Johnson,* which two I behold like a *Spanish great Gallion* and an *English man of War;* Master *Johnson* (like the former) was built far higher in Learning; *Solid,* but *Slow* in his performances. *Shake-spear,* with the *English-man of War,* lesser in *bulk,* but lighter in *sailing,* could turn

[4] The more complete title is *The History of the Worthies of England;* the work is arranged in alphabetical order by counties, of which Warwickshire is one. Date(s) following an author's name indicate date of publication or of the writing of a manuscript or letter; for handwritten materials, sometimes only an approximate date or span of time can be indicated.

with all tides, tack about and take advantage of all winds, by the quickness of his Wit and Invention. He died *Anno Domini* 16 . . , and was buried at *Stratford* upon *Avon,* the Town of his Nativity.

[p. 246] *Anonymous, c. 1650*

[From *Bodl. Ashm. MS.* 38, a collection of verses. . . .]

(a)

On John Combe A Coueteous rich man mr Wm. Shakspear wright this att his request while hee was yett Liueing for his Epitaphe

Who Lies In this Tombe
Hough; Quoth the Deuill, Tis my Sonn John A Combe.

finis

but being dead, and making the poore his heiers hee after wrightes this for his Epitaph

How ere he liued Judge not
John Combe shall neuer be forgott
While poor, hath Memmorye, for hee did gather
To make the poore his Issue; hee their father
As record of his tilth and seede
Did Crowne him In his Latter deede.

Finis W: Shak.

(b)

mr Ben: Johnson and mr. Wm: Shake-speare Being Merrye att a Tauern, mr Jonson haueing begune this for his Epitaph

Here lies Ben Johnson that was once one

he gives ytt to mr Shakspear to make vpp who presently wrightes

Who while hee liu'de was a sloe things
and now being dead is Nothinge.

finis

[p. 249] *John Ward, 1661-3*

[From C. Severn, *Diary of John Ward* (1839), 183. The note-books of Ward (1629-81), who was vicar of Stratford (1662-81) came into the possession of the Medical Society of London towards the end of the 18th century. . . .]

Shakespear had but 2 daughters, one whereof M. Hall, y[e] physitian, married, and by her had one daughter, to wit, y[e] Lady Bernard of Abbingdon. . . .

I have heard y[t] M[r]. Shakespeare was a natural wit, without any art at all; hee frequented y[e] plays all his younger time, but in his elder days lived at Stratford: and supplied y[e] stage with 2 plays every year, and for y[t] had an allowance so large, y[t] hee spent att y[e] Rate of a 1,000*l.* a year, as I have heard.

[p. 250] Rememb*er* to peruse Shakespears plays, and bee versd in *them,* y[t] I may not bee ignorant in y[t] matter. . . .

Shakespear, Drayton, and Ben Jhonson [sic], had a merry meeting, and itt seems drank too hard, for Shakespear died of a feavour there contracted. . . .

[p. 250] *Robert Dobyns, 1673*

[Printed by B. Dobell in *Athenaeum* (19 Jan. 1901) from . . . a MS. in his possession. . . .]

In 1673 I Robert Dobyns being at Stratford upon Avon & visiting the church there transcribed these two Epitaphs, the first is on William Shakespeare's monument:[5] the other is upon ye monument of a noted usurer.

1. Good friend for Jesu sake forbeare
To dig the Dust that lyeth incloased here
Blessed is the man that spareth these stones
Cursed be he yt moveth these bones. [p. 251]

2. Tenn in the hundred here lyeth engraved
A hundred to tenn his soule is now saved
If anny one aske who lyeth in this Tombe
Oh ho quoth the Divell tis my John a Combe.

[5] See inside of back cover—the editors.

Since my being at Stratford the heires of Mr Combe have caused these verses to be razed, so yt now they are not legible.

[p. 252] *John Aubrey, 1681*

[Aubrey (1626-97) collected his *Brief Lives* as material for the *Athenae Oxonienses* of Anthony Wood. . . .]

(a) [from *Bodl*[*eian Library*] *Aubrey MS*. 8. . . .]

the more to be admired q(uia) he was not a company keeper
lived in Shoreditch, wouldnt be debauched, & if invited to writ; he was in paine.

W. Shakespeare.

q(uaere) Mr Beeston[6] who knows most of him . . . .

(b) [From *Bodl*[*eian Library*] *Aubrey MS*. 6. . . .]

M^r. William Shakespear. . . . was borne at Stratford vpon Avon, in the County of Warwick; his father was a Butcher, & I have been told heretofore by some of the neighbours, that when he was a boy he exer-[p. 253]cised his father's Trade, but when he kill'd a Calfe, he would doe it in a *high style*, & make a Speech. There was at that time another Butcher's son in this Towne, that was held not at all inferior to him for a naturall witt, his acquaintance & coetanean, but dyed young. This Wm. being inclined naturally to Poetry and acting, came to London I guesse about 18. and was an Actor at one of the Play-houses and did act exceedingly well: now B. Johnson was never a good Actor, but an excellent Instructor. He began early to make essayes at Dramatique Poetry, which at that time was very lowe; and his Playes tooke well: He was a handsome well shap't man: very good company, and of a very readie and pleasant smooth Witt. The Humour of . . . the Constable in a Midsomersnight's Dreame, he [i.e., Shakespeare] happened to take at Grendon . . . in Bucks which is the roade from London to Stratford, and there was living that Constable about 1642 when I first came to Oxon. M^r. Jos. Howe is of that parish and knew him. Ben Johnson and he did gather Humours of men dayly where ever they came. One time as he was at the Tavern at Stratford super Avon, one Combes an old

[6] Chambers' introductory note explains that William Beeston was "a Caroline and Restoration actor, and the son of Christopher Beeston, a Chamberlain's man in 1598."

rich Usurer was to be buryed, he makes there this extemporary Epitaph

Ten in the Hundred the Devill allowes
But *Combes* will have twelve, he sweares & vowes:
If any one askes who lies in this Tombe:
Hoh! quoth the Devill, 'Tis my John o' Combe.

He was wont to goe to his native Country once a yeare. I thinke I have been told that he left 2 or 300[li] per annum there and therabout: to a sister. . . . I have heard S[r] Wm. Davenant and M[r]. Thomas Shadwell (who is counted the best Comoedian we have now) say, that he had a most prodigious Witt, and did admire his naturall parts beyond all other Dramaticall writers. He was wont to say, That he never blotted out a line in his life: sayd Ben: Johnson, I wish he had blotted out a thousand. [p. 254] [*In margin,* 'B. Johnsons Underwoods'.] His Comoedies will remaine witt, as long as the English tongue is understood; for that he handles mores hominum; now our present writers reflect so much upon particular persons, and coxcombeities, that 20 yeares hence, they will not be understood. Though as Ben: Johnson sayes of him, that he had but little Latine and lesse Greek, He understood Latine pretty well: for he had been in his younger yeares a Schoolmaster in the Countrey. [*In margin,* 'from M[r] —— Beeston'.]

(c) [From *Bodl*[*eian Library*] *Aubrey MS.* 6. . . .] [Passages in the orginal manuscript which were lined out have been reinserted within brackets. Editors' note.]

S[r] William Davenant Knight Poet Laureate was borne in —— street in the City of Oxford, at the Crowne Taverne. . . . His father was John Davenant a Vintner there, a very grave and discreet Citizen: his mother was a very beautifull woman, & of a very good witt and of conversation extremely agreable. . . . M[r] William Shakespeare was wont to goe into Warwickshire once a yeare, and did commonly in his journey lye at this house in Oxon: where he was exceedingly respected. [I have heard parson Robert D(avenant) say that M[r] W. Shakespeare here gave him a hundred kisses.] Now Sr. W[m] would sometimes when he was pleasant over a glasse of wine with his most intimate friends e.g. Sam: Butler (author of Hudibras) &c. say, that it seemed to him that he writt with the very spirit that Shakespeare, and was *seemed* contentended [sic] enough to be thought his Son: he would tell them the story as above. [in which way his mother had a very light report, whereby she was called a whore.]

[p. 255] *Richard Davies, 1688-1708*

[From *Fulman MS.* xv . . . (in the library of Christ Church College) Oxford. . . .][7]

[p. 257] William Shakespeare,

William Shakespeare was born at Stratford upon Avon in Warwickshire about 1563·4.

much given to all unluckinesse in stealing venison & Rabbits particularly from Sr *Lucy who had him oft whipt & sometimes Imprisoned & at last made Him fly his Native Country to his great Advancem*^{t}. *but His reveng was so great that he is his Justice Clodpate and calls him a great man & y*^{t} *in allusion to his name bore three lowses rampant for his Arms*

From an Actor of Playes, he became a Composer
Ætat. 53.

He dyed Apr. 23. 1616. probably at Stratford, for there he is buryed, and hath a Monument[8] *on w*^{c} *He lays a Heavy curse vpon any one who shal remoove his bones He dyed a papist.*

[p. 259] *Mr. Dowdall, 1693*

[1693, Apr. 10. From *Letter* written to a Mr. Southwell from John Dowdall at Butler's Marston, Warwickshire. . . .]

The 1st Remarkable place in this County y^{t} I visitted was Stratford super avon, where I saw the Effigies[9] of our English tragedian, m^{r} Shakspeare. . . .

the clarke that shew'd me this Church is aboue 80 y^{rs} old; he says that this *Shakespear* was formerly in this Towne bound apprentice to a butcher; but that he Run from his master to London, and there was Rec^{d} Into the playhouse as a serviture, and by this meanes had an oppertunity to be w^{t} he afterwards prov'd. he was the best of his family but the male Line is extinguished; not one for feare of the

[7] The portions italicized by the editors were written by Davies on William Fulman's manuscript. Davies was a clergyman and became Archdeacon of Coventry; he died in 1708.

[8] See inside of back cover—the editors.

[9] See inside of back cover—the editors.

Curse aboues[d] Dare Touch his Grave Stone, tho his wife and Daughters Did Earnestly Desire to be Layd in the same Graue wth him.

[p. 260] *William Hall, 1694*

[From *Letter* of W. Hall to Edward Thwaites. . . .]

Dear Neddy,

I very greedily embraced this occasion of acquainting you with something which I found at Stratford upon Avon. That place I came unto on Thursday night, and y[e] next day went to visit y[e] ashes of the Great Shakespear which lye interr'd in that Church. . . . There is in this Church a place which they call the bone-house, a repository for all bones they dig up; which are so many that they would load a great number of waggons. The Poet being willing to preserve his bones unmoved, lays a curse [i.e., in his tombstone epitaph] upon him that moves them; and haveing to do with Clarks and Sextons, for y[e] most part a very (i)gnorant sort of people, he descends to y[e] meanest of their capacitys; and disrobes himself of that art, which none of his Co-temporaryes wore in greater perfection. Nor has the design mist of its effect; for lest they should not onely draw this curse upon themselvs, but also entail [p. 261] it upon their posterity, they have laid him full seventeen foot deep, deep enough to secure him. And so much for Stratford. . . .

Your friend and Servant
W[m]. Hall.

Direct your letter for
W[m]. Hall Jun[r]. at y[e]
White-hart in Lichfield.

[p. 264] *Nicholas Rowe, 1709*

[Extracts from *Life* in *Works of Shakespeare* (1709), i. I. . . .]

. . . He was the Son of M[r]. *John Shakespear,* and was Born at *Stratford* upon *Avon,* in *Warwickshire,* in *April* 1564. His Family, as appears by the Register and Publick Writings relating to that Town, were of good Figure and Fashion there, and are mention'd as Gentlemen. His Father, who was a considerable Dealer in Wool, had so large a Family, ten Children in all, that tho' he was his eldest Son, he could give him no better Education than his own Employment. He had bred him, 'tis true, for some time at a Free-School, where 'tis probable he acquir'd that little *Latin* he was Master of: But the narrowness of his Circumstances, and the want of his assistance at Home, forc'd his Father to withdraw him from thence, and unhappily prevented his further Proficiency in that Language. . . . Upon his leaving School, he seems to have given intirely into that way of Living which his [**p. 265**] Father propos'd to him; and in order to settle in the World after a Family manner, he thought fit to marry while he was yet very Young. His Wife was the Daughter of one *Hathaway,* said to have been a substantial Yeoman in the Neighbourhood of *Stratford.* In this kind of Settlement he continu'd for some time, 'till an Extravagance that he was guilty of, forc'd him both out of his Country and that way of Living which he had taken up; and tho' it seem'd at first to be a Blemish upon his good Manners, and a Misfortune to him, yet it afterwards happily prov'd the occasion of exerting one of the greatest *Genius*'s that ever was known in Dramatick Poetry. He had, by a Misfortune common enough to young Fellows, fallen into ill Company; and amongst them, some that made a frequent practice of Deer-stealing, engag'd him with them more than once in robbing a Park that belong'd to Sir *Thomas Lucy* of *Cherlecot,* near *Stratford.* For this he was Prosecuted by that Gentleman, as he thought, somewhat too severely; and in order to revenge that ill Usage, he made a Ballad upon him. And tho' this, probably the first Essay of his Poetry, be lost, yet it is said to have been so very bitter, that it redoubled the Prosecution against him to that degree, that he was oblig'd to leave his Business and Family in *Warwickshire,* for some time, and shelter himself in *London.*

It is at this Time, and upon this Accident, that he is said to have made his first Acquaintance in the Play-house. He was receiv'd into the Company then in being, at first in a very mean Rank; but his admirable Wit, and the natural Turn of it to the Stage, soon distinguish'd him, if not as an extraordinary Actor, yet as an excellent Writer. His Name is Printed, as the Custom was in those Times, amongst those of the other Players, before some old Plays, but without any particular Account of what sort of Parts he us'd to play; and tho' I have inquir'd, I could never meet with any further Account of him this way, than that the top of his Performance was the Ghost in his own *Hamlet.* . . . Mr *Dryden* seems to think that *Pericles* is one of his first Plays; but there is no judgment [**p. 266**] to be form'd on that, since there is good Reason to believe that the greatest part of that Play was not written by him; tho' it is own'd, some part of it certainly was, particularly the last Act. . . . Besides the advantages of his Wit, he was in himself a good-natur'd Man, of great sweetness in his Manners, and a most agreeable Companion; so that it is no wonder if with so many good Qualities he made himself acquainted with the best Conversations of those Times. Queen *Elizabeth* had several of his Plays Acted before her, and without doubt gave him many gracious Marks of her Favour: . . . She was so well pleas'd with that admirable Character of *Falstaff,* in the two Parts of *Henry* the Fourth, that she commanded him to continue it for one Play more, and to shew him in Love. This is said to be the Occasion of his Writing *The Merry Wives* of Windsor. How well she was obey'd, the Play it self is an admirable Proof. . . . What Grace soever the Queen confer'd upon him, it was not to her only he ow'd the Fortune which the Reputation of his Wit made. He had the Honour to meet with many great and uncommon Marks of Favour and Friendship from the Earl of *Southampton,* famous in the Histories of that Time for his Friendship to the unfortunate Earl of *Essex*. It was to that Noble Lord that he Dedicated his *Venus* and *Adonis,* the only Piece of his Poetry which he ever publish'd himself, tho' many of his Plays were surrepticiously and lamely Printed in his Life-time. There is one instance so singular in the Magnificence of this Patron of *Shakespear's,* that if I had not been assur'd that the Story was handed down by Sir *William D'Avenant,* who was probably very well acquainted with his Affairs, I should not have ventur'd to have inserted, that my Lord *Southampton,* at one time, gave him a thousand Pounds, to enable him to go through with a Purchase which he [p. 267] heard he had a mind to. A Bounty very great, and very rare at any time, and almost equal to that profuse Generosity the present Age has shewn to *French* Dancers and *Italian* Eunuchs.

What particular Habitude or Friendships he contracted with private Men, I have not been able to learn, more than that every one who had a true Taste of Merit, and could distinguish Men, had generally a just Value and Esteem for him. His exceeding Candor and good Nature must certainly have inclin'd all the gentler Part of the World to love him, as the power of his Wit oblig'd the Men of the most delicate Knowledge and polite Learning to admire him. . . . His Acquaintance with *Ben Johnson* began with a remarkable piece of Humanity and good Nature; M[r] *Johnson,* who was at that Time altogether unknown to the World, had offer'd one of his Plays to the Players, in order to have it Acted; and the Persons into whose Hands it was put, after having turn'd it carelessly and superciliously over, were just upon returning it to him with an ill-natur'd Answer, that it would be of no service to their Company, when *Shakespear* luckily cast his Eye upon it, and found something so well in it as to engage him first to read it through, and afterwards to recommend Mr *Johnson* and his Writings to the Publick. After this they were profess'd Friends; tho' I don't know whether the other ever made him an equal return of Gentleness and Sincerity. . . .

Falstaff is allow'd by everybody to be a Master-piece; . . . Amongst other Extravagances, in *The Merry Wives of* Windsor, he has made him a Dear-stealer, that he might [p. 268] at the same time remember his *Warwickshire* Prosecutor, under the Name of Justice *Shallow;* he has given him very near the same Coat of Arms which *Dugdale,* in his Antiquities of that County, describes for a Family there, and makes the *Welsh* Parson descant very pleasantly upon 'em. . . .

. . . I must own a particular Obligation to him [i.e., the actor Betterton], for the most considerable part of the Passages relating to his Life, which I have here transmitted to the Publick; his Veneration for the Memory of *Shakespear* having engaged him to make a Journey into *Warwickshire,* on purpose to gather up what Remains he could of a Name for which he had so great a Value. . . .

. . . The latter Part of his [Shakespeare's] Life was spent, as all Men of good Sense will wish theirs may be, in Ease, Retirement, and the Conversation of his Friends. He had the good Fortune to gather an Estate equal to his Occasion, and, in that, to his Wish; and is said to have spent some Years before his Death at his native *Stratford.* His pleasurable Wit, and good Nature, engag'd him in the Acquaintance, and entitled him to the Friendship of the Gentlemen of the Neighbourhood. Amongst them, it is a Story almost still remember'd in that Country, that he had a particular Intimacy with Mr *Combe,* an old Gentleman noted thereabouts for his Wealth and Usury: It happen'd, that in a pleasant Conversation amongst their common Friends, Mr *Combe* told *Shakespear* in a laughing manner, that he fancy'd, he intended to write his Epitaph, if he happen'd to out-live him; and since he could not know what might be said of him when he was dead, he desir'd it might be done immediately: Upon which *Shakespear* gave him these four Verses. [p. 269]

Ten in the Hundred lies here ingrav'd,
'Tis a Hundred to Ten, his Soul is not sav'd:
If any Man ask, Who lies in this Tomb?
Oh! ho! quoth the Devil, 'tis my John-a-Combe.

But the Sharpness of the Satyr is said to have stung the Man so severely, that he never forgave it.

He Dy'd in the 53d Year of his Age, and was bury'd on the North side of the Chancel, in the Great Church at *Stratford,* where a Monument[10]. . . . is plac'd in the Wall. . . .

He had three Daughters, of which two liv'd to be marry'd; *Judith,* the Elder, to one Mr *Thomas Quiney,* by whom she had three Sons, who all dy'd without Children; and *Susannah,* who was his Favourite, to Dr *John Hall,* a Physician of good Reputation in that Country. She left one Child only, a Daughter, who was marry'd first to *Thomas Nash,* Esq; and afterwards to Sir John *Bernard* of *Abington,* but dy'd likewise without Issue.

This is what I could learn of any Note, either relating to himself or Family: The Character of the man is best seen in his Writings. . . .

[p. 272] *John Roberts, 1729*

[From *An Answer to Mr. Pope's Preface to Shakespear . . . By a Stroling Player,* 45 . . . ascribed to John Roberts. Sir William Bishop (1626-1700) was of Bridgetown, a hamlet partly in Stratford. There was in fact a disastrous fire at Warwick in 1694, but certainly no descendant of Shakespeare dwelt there, and French (*Shakespeareana Genealogica,* p.) 397 shows no Hart.]

How much it is to be lamented, that *Two* large *Chests* full of this Great Man's *loose Papers* and *Manuscripts,* in the Hands of an ignorant *Baker* of Warwick, (who married one of the Descendants from *Shakespear*) were carelesly scatter'd and thrown about, as Garret Lumber and Litter, to the particuler Knowledge of the late *Sir William Bishop,* till they were all consum'd in the generall Fire and Destruction of that Town? . . .

[p. 273] *Charles Macklin, 1742*

[Macklin (*c.* 1697-1797) was an actor in London and Dublin. In May 1742 . . . he visited Stratford with Garrick, where they were entertained under the New Place mulberry by Sir Hugh Clopton. The

[10] See inside of back cover—the editors.

stories he gathered were probably given orally to Malone. . . .]

[From Malone (. . . Var. ii. 623).][11]

Sir Hugh Clopton, who was born two years after her death, mentioned to Mr Macklin, in the year 1742, an old tradition that she (Lady Bernard) had carried away with her from Stratford many of her grandfather's papers.

[p. 276] *William Oldys*, c. *1743-61*

[From G. Steevens, *Works of Sh.* (1778) i. 202 (after Rowe's *Life*), 223. . . .]

Mr Rowe . . . has told us that he derived the principal anecdotes in his account of Shakspeare, from Betterton the player, whose zeal had induced him to visit Stratford for the sake of procuring all possible intelligence concerning a poet to whose works he might justly think himself under the strongest obligations. Notwithstanding this assertion, in the manuscript papers of the late Mr Oldys it is said, that one Bowman (according to Chetwood, p. 144, 'an actor more than half an age on [p. 277] the London theatres') was unwilling to allow that his associate and contemporary Betterton had ever undertaken such a journey. . . .

[p. 286] *Anonymous, 1762*

[From *Letter from the Place of Shakespear's Nativity* in *British Magazine Or Monthly Repository for Gentlemen and Ladies,* iii. 301.]

I . . . put up at the White Lion. . . My chearful landlord . . . took me to the house where the poet was born and there I saw a mulberry-tree of that great man's planting, a piece of which I brought away with me, to make tobacco-stoppers for our vicar. . . . From thence my landlord was so complaisant as to go with me to visit two young women, lineal descendants of our great dramatic poet: they

[11] "Var." refers to *The Plays and Poems of William Shakespeare. With a Life of the Poet and an Enlarged History of the Stage.* By the late E. Malone. Edited by J. Boswell. 21 vols., 1821.

keep a little ale-house, some small distance from Stratford. [p. 287] On the road thither, at a place called Bidford, he shewed me in the hedge, a crab-tree, called Shakespear's canopy, because under it our poet slept one night; for he, as well as Ben Johnson, loved a glass for the pleasure of society; and he, having heard much of the men of that village as deep drinkers and merry fellows, one day went over to Bidford, to take a cup with them. He enquired of a shepherd for the Bidford drinkers; who replied they were absent; but the Bidford sippers were at home; and, I suppose, continued the sheep-keeper, they will be sufficient for you: and so, indeed, they were. He was forced to take up his lodging under that tree for some hours.

[p. 287] *Samuel Johnson, 1765*

[From *Works* of Shakespeare (1765), i. clii, where it follows a reprint of Rowe's *Life* and copies of the 1599 grant of arms and the will.]

To the foregoing accounts of Shakespear's life, I have only one passage to add, which Mr Pope related, as communicated to him by Mr Rowe.

In the time of *Elizabeth,* coaches being yet uncommon, and hired coaches not at all in use, those who were too proud, too tender, or too idle to walk, went on horse-back to any distant business or diversion. Many came on horse-back to the play, and when *Shakespear* fled to *London* from the terrour of a criminal prosecution, his first ex- [p. 288] pedient was to wait at the door of the play-house, and hold the horses of those that had no servants, that they might be ready again after the performance. In this office he became so conspicuous for his care and readiness, that in a short time every man as he alighted called for *Will. Shakespear,* and scarcely any other waiter was trusted with a horse while *Will. Shakespear* could be had. This was the first dawn of better fortune. *Shakespear* finding more horses put into his hand than he could hold, hired boys to wait under his inspection, who when *Will. Shakespear* was summoned, were immediately to present themselves, *I am* Shakespear's *boy, Sir.* In time *Shakespear* found higher employment, but as long as the practice of riding to the play-house continued, the waiters that held the horses retained the appellation of Shakespear's *Boys.*

[p. 296] *Edmund Malone, 1780*[12]

There is a stage tradition that his first office in the theatre was that of [*Call-boy,* or] prompter's attendant; whose employment it is to give the performers notice to be ready to enter, as often as the business of the play requires their appearance on the stage.

[12] From Malone's *Supplement to the Edition of Shakespeare's Plays Published in 1778 by Samuel Johnson and George Steevens,* 2 vols., 1780. Passage is from volume I, page 67. Bracketed words in the text above were added in 1790.

Signs of Doubt and Their History

1957 "The Great Controversy," *The Shakespearean Ciphers Examined,* William F. and Elizebeth S. Friedman, Cambridge University Press, 1957, pp. 1-4.

[p. 1] It seems that the first man to question Shakespeare's sole authorship of the plays was a certain 'Captain' Goulding. In a small book called *An Essay Against Too Much Reading,* published in 1728, he hinted at one of the anti-Stratfordian arguments. The plays, he said, are so superlative that '*Shakespear* has frighten'd three parts of the World from attempting to write; and he was no Scholar, no Grammarian, no Historian, and in all probability cou'd not write *English.*' Goulding [continues] . . .

> Although his Plays were historical . . . the History Part was given him in concise and short, by one of those Chuckles that could give him nothing else. . . . I will give you a short Account of Mr. *Shakespear's* Proceeding; and that I had from one of his intimate Acquaintance. His being imperfect in some Things, was owing to his not being a Scholar, which obliged him to have one of those chuckle-pated Historians for his particular Associate . . . and he maintain'd him, or he might have starv'd upon his History. And when he wanted anything in his Way . . . he sent to him. . . . Then with his natural flowing Wit, he work'd it into all Shapes and Forms, as his beautiful Thoughts directed. The other put it into Grammar. . . .

One may see here the germ of much future ingenuity. . . .

In 1769—some forty years later—there was published in England a curious little allegory with a historical framework, called *The Life and Adventures of Common Sense.* It is anonymous, [and] [p. 2] contains what has been considered to be one of the first references to Bacon as Shakespeare.

In the allegory, *Common Sense*, his father *Wisdom*, and his companions *Genius* and *Humour* arrive in London together; they meet on their arrival a *Stranger*,

> a Person belonging to the Playhouse; this Man was a profligate in his Youth, and, as some say, had been a Deer-stealer. . . . This Man . . . took the first opportunity . . . to rob them of every Thing he could lay his Hands on. . . . Amongst my Father's Baggage, he presently cast his Eye upon a common place Book, in which was contained, an Infinite Variety of Modes and Forms, to express all the different Sentiments of the human Mind, together with Rules for their Combinations and Connections upon every Subject or Occasion that might Occur in Dramatic Writing. . . . With these Materials, and with good Parts of his own, he commenced Play-Writer, how he succeeded is needless to say, when I tell the Reader that his name was *Shakespear*.

Bacon kept a commonplace book, which has survived. Some Baconians have therefore inferred that Bacon is represented by *Wisdom*, 'my Father', in the allegory.

The first writer to come out firmly for Bacon was the Rev. James Wilmot, D.D. He made the attribution in about 1785, but it seems not to have attracted attention at the time; his priority was recorded and authenticated in 1805 and 1813.

Another allegorical work referred to the authorship of the plays in 1786; this was *The Story of the Learned Pig*, by 'An Officer of the Royal Navy'. It is a small step from the notion of a learned pig to that of the learned Bacon; some readers have been eager to make it. The Pig as he describes himself is a Protean figure—the cliché is justified, for he was successively greyhound, deer and bear. By p. 35 he can state:

> I am now come to a period in which, to my great joy, I once more got possession of a human body. . . . I was early in life initiated in the [p. 3] profession of horseholder to those who came to visit the playhouse, where I was well known by the name of 'Pimping Billy'. . . . I soon after contracted a friendship with that great man and first of geniuses, the 'Immortal Shakespeare', and am happy in now having it in my power to refute the prevailing opinion of his having run his country for deer-stealing, which is as false as it is disgracing. . . . With equal falsehood has he been father'd with many spurious dramatic pieces. 'Hamlet, Othello, As you like it, the Tempest, and Midsummer's Night Dream', for five; of all which I confess myself to be the author.

The tempo now begins to quicken. In 1848 the New York publishers Harper and Brothers issued *The Romance of Yachting* by Joseph C. Hart, a former American consul at Santa Cruz, who had often given it as his opinion that 'the money-lending actor could not have been the author of the plays'. His book has little to say about yachting; . . . but it displays a good deal of anti-Stratfordian scepticism. While it proposes no one specific author, by implication it favours Jonson. Soon afterwards, in 1852, the August issue of Chambers' *Edinburgh Journal* carried an anonymous article called 'Who Wrote Shakespeare?' Again no specific author is named; it is merely suggested that Shakespeare 'kept a poet'.

Bacon was really launched as Shakespeare in 1856. *Putnam's Monthly* published in January an article on 'Shakespeare and His Plays: An Inquiry Concerning Them'. The author, 'D. Bacon', was an American woman, and, as she said, no relation. Delia Bacon wrote more articles; and in 1857 she published a 543-page volume called *The Philosophy of the Plays of Shakespeare Unfolded*. She believed in several authors, but this contention tended to be overlooked as Baconians grew more numerous and more convinced. It is worth noting that both Mark Twain and Nathaniel Hawthorne gave countenance if not support to anti-Stratfordianism. Hawthorne, then consul in Liverpool, was sought out by Miss Bacon and asked to help find a publisher. Instead he wrote a Preface; recording in his *English Notebooks* that she was 'a remarkable woman', and in the Preface the equally judicious remark 'it is for the public to judge whether or not my country woman has proved her theory'.

[p. 4] James Russell Lowell is reputed to have said that Delia Bacon had opened a question that would never be closed. It seemed also as if she had opened a giant valve: the books, the articles, the journals now appeared in a gathering spate: some 'for', but most 'against' Shakespeare.

1910 *Bacon is Shake-speare*. By Sir Edwin Durning-Lawrence, Bart., B.A., LL.B., etc. The John McBride Co. New York, 1910.

[After presenting various arguments to establish his thesis that Bacon was Shakespeare, Durning-Lawrence presents the following authorities as expressing doubts about Shakespeare's authorship.—Editors' note.]

[p. 178] It may however not be without advantage to those who are becoming convinced against their will, if we place before them a few of the utterances of men of the greatest distinction who, without being furnished with the information which we have been able to afford to our readers, were possessed of sufficient intelligence and common sense to perceive the truth respecting the real authorship of the Plays.

Lord Palmerston, b. 1784, d. 1865.

Viscount Palmerston, the great British statesman, used to say that he rejoiced to have lived to see three things—the re-integration of Italy, the unveiling of the mystery of China and Japan, and the explosion of the Shakespearian illusions.—*From the Diary of the Right Hon. Mount-Stewart E. Grant.*

Lord Houghton, b. 1809, d. 1885.

Lord Houghton (better known as a statesman under the name of Richard Monckton Milnes) reported the words of Lord Palmerston, and he also told Dr. Appleton Morgan that he himself no longer considered Shakespeare, the actor, as the author of the Plays.

Samuel Taylor Coleridge, b. 1772, d. 1834.

Samuel Taylor Coleridge, the eminent British critic and poet, although he assumed that Shakespeare was the author of the Plays, rejected the facts of his life and character, and says: "Ask your own hearts, ask your own common sense, to conceive the possibility of the author of the Plays being the anomalous, the wild, the irregular genius of our daily criticism. [p. 179] What! are we to have miracles in sport? Does God choose idiots by whom to convey divine truths to man?"

John Bright, b. 1811, d. 1889.

John Bright, the eminent British statesman, declared: "Any man that believes that William Shakespeare of Stratford wrote Hamlet or Lear is a fool." In its issue of March 27th 1889, the *Rochdale Observer* reported John Bright as scornfully angry with deluded people who believed that Shakespeare wrote Othello.

Ralph Waldo Emerson, b. 1803, d. 1882.

Ralph Waldo Emerson, the great American philosopher and poet, says: "As long as the question is of talent and mental power, the world of men has not his equal to show. . . . . . The Egyptian verdict of the Shakespeare Societies comes to mind that he [i.e., Shakespeare] was a jovial actor and manager. I cannot marry this fact to his verse."—*Emerson's Works. London, 1883. Vol. 4, p. 420.*

John Greenleaf Whittier, b. 1807, d. 1892.

John Greenleaf Whittier, the American poet, declared: "Whether Bacon wrote the wonderful plays or not, I am quite sure the man Shakspere neither did nor could."

Dr. W. H. Furness, b. 1802, d. 1891.

Dr. W. H. Furness, the eminent American scholar, who was the father of the Editor of the Variorum [p. 180] Edition of Shakespeare's Works, wrote to Nathaniel Holmes in a letter dated Oct. 29th 1866: "I am one of the many who have never been able to bring the life of William Shakespeare and the plays of Shakespeare within planetary space of each other. Are there any two things in the world more incongruous? Had the plays come down to us anonymously, had the labor of discovering the author been imposed upon after generations, I think we could have found no one of that day but F. Bacon to whom to assign the crown. In this case it would have been resting now on his head by almost common consent."

Mark Twain, b. 1835, d. 1910.

Samuel Langhorne Clemens, who wrote under the pseudonym of Mark Twain, was,—it is universally admitted,—one of the wisest of men. Last year (1909) he published a little book with the title, "Is Shakespeare dead?" In this he treats with scathing scorn those who can persuade themselves that the immortal plays were written by the Stratford clown. He writes, pp. 142-3: "You can trace the life histories of the whole of them [the world's celebrities] save one—far and away the most colossal prodigy of the entire accumulation—Shakespeare. About him you can find out *nothing*. Nothing of even the slightest importance. Nothing worth the trouble of stowing away in your memory. Nothing that even remotely indicates that he was ever anything more than a distinctly commonplace person. . . ."

[p. 181] Prince Bismarck, b. 1815, d. 1898.

We are told in Sydney Whitman's "Personal Reminiscences of Prince Bismarck," pp. 135-6, that in 1892, Prince Bismarck said, "He could not understand how it were possible that a man, however gifted with the intuitions of genius, could have written what was attributed to Shakespeare unless he had been in touch with the great affairs of state, behind the scenes of political life, and also intimate with all the social courtesies and refinements of thought which in Shakspeare's time were only to be met with in the highest circles.

[p. 182] "It also seemed to Prince Bismarck incredible that the man who had written the greatest dramas in the world's literature could of his own free will, whilst still in the prime of life, have retired to such a place as Stratford-on-Avon and lived there for years, cut off from intellectual society, and out of touch with the world."

The foregoing list of men of the very greatest ability and intelligence who were able clearly to perceive the absurdity of continuing to accept the commonly received belief that the Mighty Author of the immortal Plays was none other than the mean rustic of Stratford, might be extended indefinitely, but the names that we have mentioned are amply sufficient to prove to the reader that he will be in excellent company when he himself realises the truth that

BACON IS SHAKESPEARE.

1920 *The Letters of Henry James,* ed. Percy Lubbock, Vol. I, Charles Scribner's Sons, New York, 1920.

[p. 424] *To Miss Violet Hunt.*

Dictated.

Lamb House, Rye.
Aug. 26th, 1903.

Dear Violet Hunt,

I am very backward with you, being in receipt of more than one unanswered communication. . . . I have still, all the same, to thank you for the photographs of the admirable little niece. . . . Also came the Shakespeare-book back with your accompanying letter—for which also thanks, but to which I can't now pretend to reply. You rebound lightly, I judge, from any pressure exerted on you by the author—but *I* don't rebound: I am "a sort of" haunted by the conviction that the divine William is the biggest and most successful fraud ever practised on a patient world. The more I turn him round and round the more he so affects me. But that is all—I am not pretending to treat the question or to carry it any further. It bristles with difficulties, and I can only express my general sense by saying that I find it *almost* as impossible to conceive that Bacon wrote the plays as to conceive that the man from Stratford, as we know the man from Stratford, did.

For the rest, I have been trying to sit tight and get on with work that has been much retarded. . . .

Believe me yours always,
Henry James.

A List of Candidates for the Authorship of the Shakespearean Works

Each of the following has been offered, either in a group or singly, as writing the Shakespeare works.

William Alexander, Earl of Stirling
Francis Bacon
Anthony Bacon (Francis Bacon's brother)
Sir John Barnard
Barnabe Barnes
Richard Barnfield
Sir Charles Blount, Lord Mountjoy, Earl of Devonshire
Richard Burbage
Robert Burton
William Butts
Robert Cecil, Earl of Salisbury
Henry Chettle
Samuel Daniel
Thomas Dekker
Edward de Vere, Earl of Oxford
Robert Devereux, 2nd Earl of Essex
Walter Devereux, 1st Earl of Essex
John Donne, Dean of St. Paul's
Michael Drayton
Sir Edward Dyer
Queen Elizabeth
Henry Ferrers
John Fletcher
John Florio
Michele Angelo Florio
Robert Greene
Bartholomew Griffin
Thomas Heywood
The Jesuits
Ben Jonson
Thomas Kyd
Thomas Lodge
John Lyly
Roger Manners, 5th Earl of Rutland
Christopher Marlowe
Thomas Middleton
Anthony Munday
Thomas Nashe
Henry, Lord Paget
George Peele
Henry Porter
Sir Walter Raleigh
The Rosicrucians
Thomas Sackville, Lord Buckhurst, Earl of Dorset
Sir Anthony Shirley
Elizabeth Sidney, Countess of Rutland
Mary Sidney, Countess of Pembroke
Sir Philip Sidney
Wentworth Smythe
Edmund Spenser
William Stanley, 6th Earl of Derby
William Warner
Thomas Watson
John Webster
Anne Whateley
Robert Wilson
Thomas, Cardinal Wolsey
Henry Wriothesley, Earl of Southampton

Bacon as Shakespeare

Introduction

Barely one hundred years after Shakespeare died, the suggestion was being made that Sir Francis Bacon, Lord Verulam, was the real author of the Shakespeare works. More than one hundred years after that, in 1856, the first argument in favor of Bacon appeared in print—William Henry Smith's *Bacon and Shakespeare: An Inquiry Touching Players, Playhouses and Play-Writers in the Days of Elizabeth.* One year later came a book written by an American woman named Delia Bacon. She was not related to Sir Francis Bacon, but she believed he, with Sir Walter Raleigh, Edmund Spenser, Sir Philip Sydney, and others, wrote the plays and poems commonly attributed to Shakespeare. Delia Bacon's book, *The Philosophy of the Plays of Shakespeare Unfolded* (1857), popularized the authorship controversy as nothing before had. It raised doubts among the learned and the ignorant alike and brought her support from all sides. She even obtained permission to open Shakespeare's grave to search for more evidence, but just before the grave was to be opened, she began to question the wisdom of the act, and the project was abandoned.

From the appearance of Delia Bacon's book until well into the twentieth century, Francis Bacon was the most popular contender for the authorship of the plays and poems. His cause was vigorously supported by the Bacon Society, which was formed in England in 1885 and inspired further investigation of the case for Bacon, including such cryptological research as Ignatius Donnelly presented in *The Great Cryptogram* (1888).

In 1909, Mark Twain joined the controversy with *Is Shakespeare Dead?* which was primarily an attack on the conventional belief in Shakespeare rather than a claim for Bacon as author. In 1910, Sir Edwin Durning-Lawrence gathered many of the previous arguments into one of the most spectacular anti-Shakespeare books, *Bacon is*

Shakespeare, which used codes, cyphers, anagrams, and cryptic pictures to support the Baconian theory.

Since the first of the twentieth century, interest in the Baconian theory has diminished in the face of numerous arguments for other contenders, though as recently as 1956 an American newspaper printed a series of articles arguing that Bacon wrote the Shakespeare works as well as all of Milton, Spenser, and Marlowe and that he edited the King James Bible and composed a poem which had long been attributed to Edgar Allan Poe: "The Raven."

The Baconian theory has even achieved one distinction which no other theory can claim: An American court of law, considering a law suit which arose out of the controversy, has made the decision that "Francis Bacon is the author."

1909 *Is Shakespeare Dead?* by Mark Twain, Harper and Brothers, New York.

[p. 4] A friend has sent me a new book, from England—*The Shakespeare Problem Restated*—well restated and closely reasoned; and my fifty years' interest in that matter—asleep for the last three years—is excited once more. It is an interest which was born of Delia Bacon's book—away back in that ancient day—1857, or maybe 1856. About a year later my pilot-master, Bixby, transferred me from his own steamboat to the *Pennsylvania,* and placed me under the orders and instructions of George Ealer—dead now, these many, many years. . . . [p. 5] He was a prime chess player and an idolater of Shakespeare. He would play chess with anybody; even with me, and it cost his official dignity something to do that. Also—quite uninvited—he would read Shakespeare to me; not just casually, but by the hour, when it was his watch, and I was steering. . . . [p. 7] He did not use the book, and did not need to; he knew his Shakespeare as well as Euclid ever knew his multiplication table.

Did he have something to say—this Shakespeare-adoring Mississippi pilot—[p. 8] anent Delia Bacon's book? Yes. And he said it; said it all the time, for months—in the morning watch, the middle watch, the dog watch; and probably kept it going in his sleep. . . . He was fiercely loyal to Shakespeare and cor-[p. 9]dially scornful of Bacon and of all the pretensions of the Baconians. So was I—at first. . . .

[p. 10] Then the thing happened which has happened to more persons than to me [p. 11] when principle and personal interest found themselves in opposition to each other and a choice had to be made: I let principle go, and went over to the other side. Not the entire way, but far enough to answer the requirements of the case. That is to say, I took this attitude, to wit: I only *believed* Bacon wrote Shakespeare, whereas I *knew* Shakespeare didn't. . . . Study, practice, experience in handling my end of the matter presently enabled me to take my new position almost seriously; a little bit later, utterly seriously; a little later still, lovingly, gratefully, devotedly; finally: fiercely, rabidly, uncompromisingly. After that, I was welded to my faith, I was theoretically ready to die for it, and I looked down with compassion not unmixed with scorn, upon everybody else's faith that didn't [p. 12] tally with mine. That faith, imposed upon me by self-interest in that ancient day, remains my faith today, and in it I find comfort, solace, peace, and never-failing joy. You see how curiously theological it is. The "rice Christian" of the Orient goes through the very same steps, when he is after rice and the missionary is after *him;* he goes for rice, and remains to worship.

* * *

[p. 15] I answered as my readings of the champions of my side of the great controversy had taught me to answer: that a man can't handle glibly and easily and comfortably and successfully the *argot* of a trade at which he has not personally served. He will make mistakes; he will not, and cannot, get the trade-phrasings precisely and exactly right; and the moment he departs, by even a shade, from a common trade-form, the reader who has served that trade will know the [p. 16] writer *hasn't.*

* * *

[p. 27] For the instruction of the ignorant I will make a list, now, of those details of [p. 28] Shakespeare's history which are *facts*—verified facts, established facts, undisputed facts.

Facts

He was born on the 23d of April, 1564.

Of good farmer-class parents who could not read, could not write, could not sign their names.

At Stratford, a small back settlement which in that day was shabby and unclean, and densely illiterate. Of the nineteen important men charged with the government of the town, thirteen had to "make their mark" in attesting important documents, because they could not write their names.

Of the first eighteen years of his life *nothing* is known. They are a blank.

On the 27th of November (1582) William Shakespeare took out a license to marry Anne Whateley.

[p. 29] Next day William Shakespeare took out a license to marry Anne Hathaway. . . . In a hurry. By grace of a reluctantly-granted dispensation there was but one publication of the banns.

Within six months the first child was born.

About two (blank) years followed, during which period *nothing at all happened to Shakespeare,* so far as anybody knows.

Then came twins—1585. February.

Two blank years follow.

Then—1587—he makes a ten-year visit to London, leaving the family behind.

Five blank years follow. During this period *nothing happened to him,* as far as anybody actually knows.

Then—1592—there is mention of him as an actor.

[p. 30] Next year—1593—his name appears in the official list of players.

Next year—1594—he played before the queen. A detail of no consequence: other obscurities did it every year of the forty-five of her reign. And remained obscure.

Three pretty full years follow. Full of play-acting. Then

In 1597 he bought New Place, Stratford.

Thirteen or fourteen busy years follow; years in which he accumulated money, and also reputation as actor and manager.

Meantime his name, liberally and variously spelt, had become associated with a number of great plays and poems, as (ostensibly) author of the same.

Some of these, in these years and later, were pirated, but he made no protest.

Then—1610-11—he returned to Stratford and settled down for good and all, [p. 31] and busied himself in lending money, trading in tithes, trading in land and houses; shirking a debt of forty-one shillings, borrowed by his wife during his long desertion of his family; suing debtors for shillings and coppers; being sued himself for shillings and coppers; and acting as confederate to a neighbor who tried to rob the town of its rights in a certain common, and did not succeed.

He lived five or six years—till 1616—in the joy of these elevated pursuits. Then he made a will, and signed each of its three pages with his name.

A thoroughgoing business man's will. It named in minute detail every item of property he owned in the world—houses, lands, sword, silver-gilt bowl, and so on—all the way down to his "second-best bed" and its furniture.

It carefully and calculatingly distributed his riches among the members of [p. 32] his family, overlooking no individual of it. Not even his wife: the wife he had been enabled to marry in a hurry by urgent grace of a special dispensation before he was nineteen; the wife whom he had left husbandless so many years; the wife who had had to borrow forty-one shillings in her need, and which the lender was never able to collect of the prosperous husband, but died at last with the money still lacking. No, even this wife was remembered in Shakespeare's will.

He left her that "second-best bed."

And *not another thing;* not even a penny to bless her lucky widowhood with.

It was eminently and conspicuously a business man's will, not a poet's.

It mentioned *not a single book.*

Books were much more precious than swords and silver-gilt bowls and second-[p. 33]best beds in those days, and when a departing person owned one he gave it a high place in his will.

The will mentioned *not a play, not a poem, not an unfinished literary work, not a scrap of manuscript of any kind.*

Many poets have died poor, but this is the only one in history that has died *this* poor; the others all left literary remains behind. Also a book. Maybe two.

If Shakespeare had owned a dog—but we need not go into that: we know he would have mentioned it in his will. If a good dog, Susanna would have got it; if an inferior one his wife would have got a dower interest in it. I wish he had had a dog, just so we could see how painstakingly he would have divided that dog among the family, in his careful business way.

He signed the will in three places.

[p. 34] In earlier years he signed two other official documents.

These five signatures still exist.[1]

There are *no other specimens of his penmanship in existence.* Not a line.

* * *

When Shakespeare died in Stratford *it was not an event.* It made no more stir in England than the death of any other forgotten theatre-actor would have made. Nobody came down from London;

[1] See p. 80—the editors.

there were no lamenting poems, no eulogies, no national tears—there was merely silence, and nothing more. A striking [p. 35] contrast with what happened when Ben Jonson, and Francis Bacon, and Spenser, and Raleigh and the other distinguished literary folk of Shakespeare's time passed from life! No praiseful voice was lifted for the lost Bard of Avon; even Ben Jonson waited seven years before he lifted his.

So far as anybody actually knows and can prove, Shakespeare of Stratford-on-Avon never wrote a play in his life.

So far as anybody knows and can prove, he never wrote a letter to anybody in his life.

So far as any one knows, he received only one letter during his life.

So far as any one *knows and can prove,* Shakespeare of Stratford wrote only one poem during his life. This one is authentic. He did write that one—a fact which stands undisputed; he wrote the whole of it; he wrote the whole of it out [p. 36] of his own head. He commanded that this work of art be engraved upon his tomb, and he was obeyed. There it abides to this day. This is it:

Good friend for Iesus sake forebeare
To digg the dust encloased heare:
Blest be ye man yt spares thes stones
And curst be he yt moves my bones.

In, the list as above set down, will be found *every positively known* fact of Shakespeare's life, lean and meagre as the invoice is. Beyond these details we know *not a thing* about him. All the rest of his vast history, as furnished by the biographers, is built up, course upon course, of guesses, inferences, theories, conjectures—an Eiffel Tower of artificialities rising sky-high from a very flat and very thin foundation of inconsequential facts.

[p. 37] The historians "suppose" that Shakespeare attended the Free School in Stratford from the time he was seven years old till he was thirteen. There is no *evidence* in existence that he ever went to school at all.

The historians "infer" that he got his Latin in that school—the school which they "suppose" he attended.

They "suppose" his father's declining fortunes made it necessary for him to leave the school they supposed he attended, and get to work and help support his parents and their ten children. But there is no evidence that he ever [p. 38] entered or retired from the school they suppose he attended.

* * *

[p. 49] Shall I set down the rest of the Conjectures which constitute the giant Biography of William Shakespeare? It would strain the Unabridged Dictionary to hold them. He is a Brontosaur: nine bones and six hundred barrels of plaster of paris.[2]

[p. 50] In the Assuming trade three separate and independent cults are transacting business. Two of these cults are known as the Shakespearites and the Baconians, and I am the other one—the Brontosaurian.

The Shakespearite knows that Shakespeare wrote Shakespeare's Works; the Baconian knows that Francis Bacon wrote them; the Brontosaurian doesn't really know which of them did it, but is quite composedly and contentedly sure that Shakespeare *didn't,* and strongly suspects that Bacon *did.* We all have to do a good deal of assuming, but I am [p. 51] fairly certain that in every case I can call to mind the Baconian assumers have come out ahead of the Shakespearites. Both parties handle the same materials, but the Baconians seem to me to get much more reasonable and rational and persuasive results out of them than is the case with the Shakespearites. The Shakespearite conducts his assuming upon a definite principle, an unchanging and immutable law—which is: 2 and 8 and 7 and 14, added together, make 165. I believe this to be an error. No matter, you cannot get a habit-sodden Shakespearite to cipher-up his materials upon any other basis. With the Baconian it is different. If you place before him the above figures and set him to adding them up, he will never in any case get more than 45 out of them, and in nine cases out of ten he will get just the proper 31.

* * *

[p. 56] When Shakespeare died, in 1616, great literary productions attributed to him as author had been before the London world and in high favor for twenty-four years. Yet his death was not an event. It made no stir, it attracted no attention. Apparently his eminent literary contemporaries did not realize that a celebrated poet had passed from their midst. Perhaps they knew a play-actor of minor rank had disappeared, but did not regard him as the author of his Works. "We are justified in assuming" this.

* * *

[p. 65] If Shakespeare had really been celebrated, like me, Stratford could have told things about him; and if my experience goes for anything, they'd have done it.

[2] Twain refers to the conjectural reconstruction of prehistoric animals on evidence of a few bones.

[p. 66] If I had under my superintendence a controversy appointed to decide whether Shakespeare wrote Shakespeare or not, I believe I would place before the debaters only the one question, *Was Shakespeare ever a practicing lawyer?* and leave everything else out.

* * *

[p. 67] Experts of unchallengeable authority have testified definitely as to only one of Shakespeare's multifarious craft-equipments, so far as my recollections of Shakespeare-Bacon talk abide with me —his law-equipment. . . .

[p. 68] Other things change, with time, and the student cannot trace back with certainty the changes that various trades and their processes and technicalities have undergone in the long stretch of a century or two and find out what their processes and technicalities were in those [p. 69] early days, but with the law it is different: it is mile-stoned and documented all the way back, and the master of that wonderful trade, that awe-compelling trade, has competent ways of knowing whether Shakespeare-law is good law or not; and whether his law-court procedure is correct or not, and whether his legal shop-talk is the shop-talk of a veteran practitioner or only a machine-made counterfeit of it gathered from books and from occasional loiterings in Westminster.

* * *

[p. 79] The Plays and Poems of Shakespeare supply ample evidence that their author not only had a very extensive and accurate knowledge of law, but that he was well acquainted with the manners and customs of members of the Inns of Court and with legal life generally.

"While novelists and dramatists are constantly making mistakes as to the laws of marriage, of wills, and inheritance, to Shakespeare's law, lavishly as he expounds it, there can neither be demurrer, nor bill of exceptions, nor writ of error." Such was the testimony borne by one of the most distinguished lawyers of the nineteenth cen-[p. 80]tury who was raised to the high office of Lord Chief Justice in 1850, and subsequently became Lord Chancellor. . . .

[p. 81] And what does the same high authority say about Shakespeare? He had "a deep technical knowledge of the law," and an easy familiarity with "some of the most abstruse proceedings in English jurisprudence." And again: "Whenever he indulges this propensity he uniformly lays down good law."

* * *

[p. 102] Did Francis Bacon write Shakespeare's Works?

Nobody knows.

We cannot say we *know* a thing when that thing has not been proved. *Know* is too strong a word to use when the evidence is not final and absolutely conclusive. We can infer, if we want to. . . . [p. 103] Since the Stratford Shakespeare couldn't have written the Works, we infer that somebody did. Who was it, then? This requires some more inferring.

Ordinarily when an unsigned poem sweeps across the continent like a tidal wave, whose roar and boom and thunder [p. 104] are made up of admiration, delight and applause, a dozen obscure people rise up and claim the authorship. Why a dozen, instead of only one or two? One reason is, because there's a dozen that are recognizably competent to do that poem. Do you remember "Beautiful Snow"? Do you remember "Rock Me to Sleep, Mother, Rock Me to Sleep"? Do you remember "Backward, turn backward, O Time, in thy flight! Make me a child again just for to-night"? I remember them very well. Their authorship was claimed by most of the grown-up people who were alive at the time, and every claimant had one plausible argument in his favor, at least: to wit, he could have done the authoring; he was competent.

Have the Works been claimed by a dozen? They haven't. There was good reason. The world knows there was but [p. 105] one man on the planet at the time who was competent—not a dozen, and not two. . . .

There has been only one Shakespeare. There couldn't be two; certainly there couldn't be two at the same time. It takes ages to bring forth a Shakespeare, and some more ages to match him. This one was not matched before his time; nor during his time; and hasn't been [p. 106] matched since. The prospect of matching him in our time is not bright.

The Baconians claim that the Stratford Shakespeare was not qualified to write the Works, and that Francis Bacon was. They claim that Bacon possessed the stupendous equipment—both natural and acquired—for the miracle; and that no other Englishman of his day possessed the like; or, indeed, anything closely approaching it.

Macaulay, in his Essay, has much to say about the splendor and horizonless magnitude of that equipment. Also, he has synopsized Bacon's history: a thing which cannot be done for the Stratford Shakespeare, for he hasn't any history to synopsize. Bacon's history is open to the world, from his boyhood to his death in old age—a history consisting of known facts, displayed in minute and multitudinous details; *facts,* not [p. 107] guesses and conjectures and might-have-beens.

Whereby it appears that he was born of a race of statesmen, and had a Lord Chancellor for his father, and a mother who was "distinguished both as a linguist and a theologian: she corresponded in Greek with Bishop Jewell, and translated his *Apologia* from the Latin so correctly that neither he nor Archbishop Parker could suggest a single alteration." It is the atmosphere we are reared in that determines how our inclinations and aspirations shall tend. The atmosphere furnished by the parents to the son in this present case was an atmosphere saturated with learning; with thinkings and ponderings upon deep subjects; and with polite culture. It had its natural effect. Shakespeare of Stratford was reared in a house which had no use for books, since its owners, his parents, [p. 108] were without education. This may have had an effect upon the son, but we do not know, because we have no history of him of an informing sort.

* * *

[p. 113] When we read the praises bestowed by . . . illustrious experts upon the legal condition and legal aptnesses, brilliances, profundities and felicities so prodigally displayed in the Plays, and try to fit them to the historyless Stratford stage-manager, they sound wild, strange, incredible, ludicrous; but when we put them in the mouth of Bacon they do not sound strange, they seem in their natural and rightful place, they seem at home there. . . . [p. 114] "At every turn and point at which the author required a metaphor, simile or illustration, his mind ever turned *first* to the law; he seems almost to have *thought* in legal phrases; the commonest legal phrases, the commonest of legal expressions were ever at the end of his pen." That could happen to no one but a person whose *trade* was the law; it could not happen to a dabbler in it. Veteran mariners fill their conversation with sailor-phrases and draw all their similes from the ship and the sea and the storm, but no mere *passenger* ever does it, be he of Stratford or elsewhere; or could do it with anything resembling accuracy, if he were hardy enough to try. . . .

* * *

[p. 125] He [Bacon] could have written anything that is in the Plays and Poems. He could have written this:

> The cloud-cap'd towers, the gorgeous palaces,
> The solemn temples, the great globe itself,
> Yea, all which it inherit, shall dissolve,
> And, like an insubstantial pageant faded,
> Leave not a rack behind. We are such stuff

As dreams are made on, and our little life
Is rounded with a sleep.

Also, he could have written this, but he refrained:

Good friend for Iesus sake forbeare
To digg the dust encloased heare:
Blest be ye man yt spares thes stones
And curst be ye yt moves my bones.

When a person reads the noble verses about the cloud-cap'd towers, he ought not to follow it immediately with Good friend for Iesus sake forbeare, because [p. 126] he will find the transition from great poetry to poor prose too violent for comfort. It will give him a shock. You never notice how commonplace and un-poetic gravel is, until you bite into a layer of it in a pie.

[p. 127] Am I trying to convince anybody that Shakespeare did not write Shakespeare's Works? Ah, now, what do you take me for? Would I be so soft as that, after having known the human race familiarly for nearly seventy-four years? It would grieve me to know that any one could think so injuriously of me, so uncomplimentarily, so unadmiringly of me. No-no, I am aware that when even the brightest mind in our world has been trained up from childhood in a superstition of any kind, it will never be possible for that mind, in its maturity, to examine sincerely, dispassionately, and conscientiously any evidence or any circumstance which shall seem to cast a [p. 128] doubt upon the validity of that superstition. I doubt if I could do it myself. We always get at second hand our notions about systems of government; and high-tariff and low-tariff; and prohibition and anti-prohibition; and the holiness of peace and the glories of war; and codes of honor and codes of morals; and approval of the duel and disapproval of it; and our beliefs concerning the nature of cats . . . and our preferences in the matter of religious and political parties; and our acceptance or rejection of the Shakespeares. . . . We get them all at second-hand, we reason none of them out for ourselves. It is the way we are made. It is the way we are all made, and we can't help it, we can't change it. And whenever we have been furnished [p. 129] a fetish, and have been taught to believe in it, and love it and worship it, and refrain from examining it, there is no evidence, howsoever clear and strong, that can persuade us to withdraw from it our loyalty and our devotion. . . .

* * *

[p. 133] One of the most trying defects which I find in these—these—what shall I call them? for I will not apply injurious epithets to them [i.e., Stratfordians], the way they do to us, such violations of courtesy being repugnant to my nature and my dignity. The furthest I can go in that direction is to call them by names of limited reverence—names merely descriptive, never unkind, never offensive, never tainted by harsh feeling. If *they* would do like this, they would feel better in their hearts. Very well, then—to proceed. One of the most trying defects which I find in these Stratfordolaters, these [p. 134] Shakesperoids, these thugs, these bangalores, these troglodytes, these herumfrodites, these blatherskites, these buccaneers, these bandoleers, is their spirit of irreverence. It is detectable in every utterance of theirs when they are talking about us. I am thankful that in me there is nothing of that spirit. When a thing is sacred to me it is impossible for me to be irreverent toward it. I cannot call to mind a single instance where I have ever been irreverent, except toward the things which were sacred to other people. Am I in the right? I think so.

1910 *Bacon is Shake-speare.* By Sir Edwin Durning-Lawrence, Bart., B.A., LL.B., etc. Together with a Reprint of Bacon's *Promus of Formularies and Elegancies.* The John McBride Co. New York.

TO THE READER. [p. v]

The plays known as Shakespeare's are at the present time universally acknowledged to be the "Greatest birth of time," the grandest production of the human mind. Their author also is generally recognised as the greatest genius of all the ages. The more the marvellous plays are studied, the more wonderful they are seen to be.

Classical scholars are amazed at the prodigious amount of knowledge of classical lore which they display. Lawyers declare that their author must take rank among the greatest of lawyers, and must have been learned not only in the theory of law, but also intimately acquainted with its forensic practice. In like manner, travellers feel certain that the author must have visited the foreign cities and countries which he so minutely and graphically describes.

It is true that at a dark period for English literature certain critics denied the possibility of Bohemia being accurately described as by the sea, [p. vi] and pointed out the "manifest absurdity" of speaking of the "port" at Milan; but a wider knowledge of the actual facts have vindicated the author at the expense of his unfortunate critics. It is the same with respect to other matters referred to in the plays. The expert possessing special knowledge of any subject invariably discovers that the plays shew that their author was well acquainted with almost all that was known at the time about that particular subject.

And the knowledge is so extensive and so varied that it is not too much to say that there is not a single living man capable of perceiving half of the learning involved in the production of the plays. One of the greatest students of law publicly declared, while he was editor of the *Law Times,* that although he thought that he knew something of law, yet he was not ashamed to confess that he had not sufficient legal knowledge or mental capacity to enable him to fully comprehend a quarter of the law contained in the plays.

Of course, men of small learning, who know very little of classics and still less of law, do not experience any of these difficulties, because they are not able to perceive how great is the vast store of learning exhibited in the plays.

There is also shewn in the plays the most [p. vii] perfect knowledge of Court etiquette, and of the manners and the methods of the greatest in the land, a knowledge which none but a courtier moving in the highest circles could by any possibility have acquired.

In his diary, Wolfe Tone records that the French soldiers who invaded Ireland behaved exactly like the French soldiers are described as conducting themselves at Agincourt in the play of "Henry V," and he exclaims, "It is marvellous!" (Wolfe Tone also adds that Shakespeare could never have seen a French soldier, but we know that Bacon while in Paris had had considerable experience of them.)

The mighty author of the immortal plays was gifted with the most brilliant genius ever conferred upon man. He possessed an intimate and accurate acquaintance, which could not have been artificially acquired, with all the intricacies and mysteries of Court life. He had by study obtained nearly all the learning that could be gained from books. And he had by travel and experience acquired a knowledge of cities and of men that has never been surpassed.

Who was in existence at that period who could by any possibility be supposed to be this universal genius? In the days of Queen Elizabeth, for the first time in human history, one such man appeared, the man who is described as the marvel and mystery [p. viii] of the age, and this was the man known to us under the name of Francis Bacon.

* * *

[p. 12] But we should remember that . . . the original [Shakespeare] monument was not like the present monument which shews a man with a pen in his hand;[3] but was the very different monument which will be found depicted in Sir William Dugdale's "Antiquities of Warwickshire," published in 1656. . . .[4]

The figure [in the monument as it appears in Dugdale] bears no resemblance to the usually accepted likeness of Shakspeare. It hugs a sack of wool, or a pocket of hops to its belly and does not hold a pen in its hand.

. . . The bust from the monument as it exists at the present time . . . [has a] great pen in the right hand and a sheet of paper under the left hand. . . .

The face [of the present bust] seems copied from the mask of the so-called portrait in the 1623 folio. . . . It is desirable to look at that picture very carefully, because every student ought to know that the portrait in the title-page of the first folio edition of the plays published in 1623, which was drawn by Martin [p. 23] Droeshout, is cunningly composed of two left arms and a mask.[5] Martin Droeshout, its designer, was, as Mr. Sidney Lee tells us, but 15 years of age when Shakspeare died. He is not likely therefore ever to have seen the actor of Stratford, yet this is the "Authentic," that is "Authorised" portrait of Shakespeare, although there *is* no question —there *can be* no possible question—that in fact it is a cunningly drawn cryptographic picture, shewing two left arms and a mask.

The back of the left arm . . . does duty for the right arm. . . . Every tailor will admit that this is not and cannot be the front of the right arm, but is, without possibility of doubt, the back of the left arm.

* * *

Now . . . the mask. Especially note that the ear is a mask ear and stands out curiously; note also how distinct the line shewing the edge of the mask appears. Perhaps the reader will perceive this more clearly if he turns the page upside down.

* * *

[3] See inside back cover—the editors.
[4] See inside back cover—the editors.
[5] See inside front cover—the editors.

[p. 24] While examining this portrait, the reader should study the lines that describe it in the Shakespeare folio of 1623. . . .

To the Reader.

This Figure, that thou here seest put,
It was for gentle Shakespeare cut;
Wherein the Grauer had a strife
with Nature, to out-doo the life:
O, could he but haue dravvne his vvit
As vvell in brasse, as he hath hit
His face; the Print vvould then surpasse
All, that vvas euer vvrit in brasse.
But, since he cannot, Reader, looke
Not on his Picture, but his Booke.
B.I.

[p. 29] "He hath *hit* his face"

It is thought that *hit* means *hid* as in Chaucer's Squiere's Tale, line 512 etc.

"Right as a serpent *hit* him under floures
Til he may seen his tyme for to byte"

If indeed "hit" be intended to be read as "hid" then these ten lines are no longer the cryptic puzzle which they have hitherto been considered to be, but in conjunction with the portrait, they clearly reveal the true facts, that the real author is writing left-handedly, that means secretly, in shadow, with his face hidden behind a mask or pseudonym.

We should also notice "out-doo" is spelled with a hyphen. In the language of to-day and still more in that of the time of Shakespeare all, or nearly all, words beginning with *out* may be read reversed, out-bar is bar out, out-bud is bud out, out-crop is crop out, out-fit is fit out, and so on through the alphabet.

If therefore we may read "out-doo the life" as "doo out the life" meaning "shut out the real face of the living man" we perceive that here also we are told "that the real face is hidden."

The description, with the head line "To the Reader" and the signature "B.I.," forms twelve lines, the words of which can be turned into numerous significant anagrams, etc., to which, however, no allusion is made in the present work. But our readers will find that if all the letters are counted (the two v.v.'s in line nine being counted as four letters) they will amount to the number 287. In subsequent chapters a good deal [p. 30] is said about this number, but here we only desire to say that we are "informed" that the "Great Author" intended to reveal himself 287 years after 1623, the date when the First Folio was published, that is in the present year, 1910, when very numerous tongues will be loosened.

* * *

. . . For about 120 years, this [i.e., the original Shakespeare monument] continued to be the Stratford effigy and shewed nothing that could in any way connect the man portrayed, with literary work. I believe that this was not accidental. I think that everybody in Stratford must have known that William "Sha*c*kspeare" could not write so much as his own name, for I assert that we possess nothing which can by any reasonable possibility be deemed to be his signature.

[p. 35]

CHAPTER III.

The so-called "Signatures."

In Plate 14, . . . are shewn the five so-called signatures.[6] These five being the only pieces of writing in the world that can, even by the most ardent Stratfordians, be supposed to have been written by Shakspeare's pen; let us consider them carefully. The Will commences "In the name of God Amen I Willim Shackspeare."[7] It is written upon three sheets of paper and each sheet bears a supposed signature. . . .

Shakspeare died 23rd April 1616 just four weeks after publishing his will.

I say after "PUBLISHING his Will" advisedly, for such is the attestation, viz., "Witnes to the publyshing hereof,

"Fra: Collyns
Julius Shawe
John Robinson
Hamnet Sadler
Robert Whattcott" [p. 36]

Nothing is said about the witnessing of the signing hereof. The Will might therefore have been, and I myself am perfectly certain that

[6] See p. 80—the editors.
[7] See p. 19—the editors.

it was, marked with the name of William Shakspeare by the Solicitor, Fra (ncis) Collyns, who wrote the body of the Will. He also wrote the names of the other witnesses, which are all in the same hand-writing as the Will; shewing that Shakspeare's witnesses were also unable to write their names.

[p. 37] This fact, that Shakspeare's name is written by the solicitor, is conclusively proved by the recent article of Magdalene Thumm-Kintzel in the Leipzig magazine, *Der Menschenkenner,* which was published in January 1909.

In this publication, photo reproductions of certain letters in the body of the Will, and in the so-called Shakspeare signatures are placed side by side, and the evidence is irresistible that they are written by the same hand. Moreover when we remember that the Will commences "I Willim Sha *c* kspeare" with a "c" between the "a" and "k," the idea that Shakspeare himself wrote his own Will cannot be deemed worthy of serious consideration. The whole Will is in fact in the handwriting of Francis Collyns, the Warwick solicitor, who added the attestation clause.

I myself was sure that the solicitor had added the so-called signatures, when, many years ago, I examined under the strongest magnifying glasses the Will at Somerset House.

Look first at the upper writings and never again call them "signatures." The top one is on the first page of the Will, the second on the second page, the third on the last page of the Will.

The original of the top one has been very much damaged but the "W" remains quite clear. Look first only at the "W's". If the writings were signatures what could induce a man when signing his last Will to make each "W" as different from the others [p. 38] as possible, and why is the second Christian name written Willm?

Compare also the second and third "Shakspeare" and note that every letter is formed in a different manner. Compare the two "S's", next compare the two "h's", the "h" of the second begins at the bottom, the "h" of the third begins at the top, the same applies to the next letter the "a", so also with respect to the "k's"; how widely different these are.

Plate 14 shews at the bottom two other names also.[8] These are taken, the one on the left from a deed of purchase of a dwelling house in Blackfriars dated March 10th 1612-13 (now in the City Library of the Corporation of London); the other on the right is from a mortgage of the same property executed on the following day, viz: March 11th 1612-13, which is now in the British Museum.

[8] See p. 80—the editors.

Neither of these documents states that it was "signed" but only says that it was "sealed," and it was at that date in no way necessary that any signatures should be written over the seals, but the clerks might and evidently did, place upon these deeds an abbreviated name of William Shakspeare over the seal on each document. In the case of the other two parties to the documents, the signatures are most beautifully written and are almost absolutely identical in the two deeds.

Look at these two supposititious signatures. To myself it is difficult to imagine that anyone with eyes to see could suppose them to be signatures by the same hand.

[p. 39] Some years ago by the courtesy of the Corporation of London, the Librarian and the Chairman of the Library Committee carried the Purchase Deed to the British Museum to place it side by side with the Mortgage Deed there.

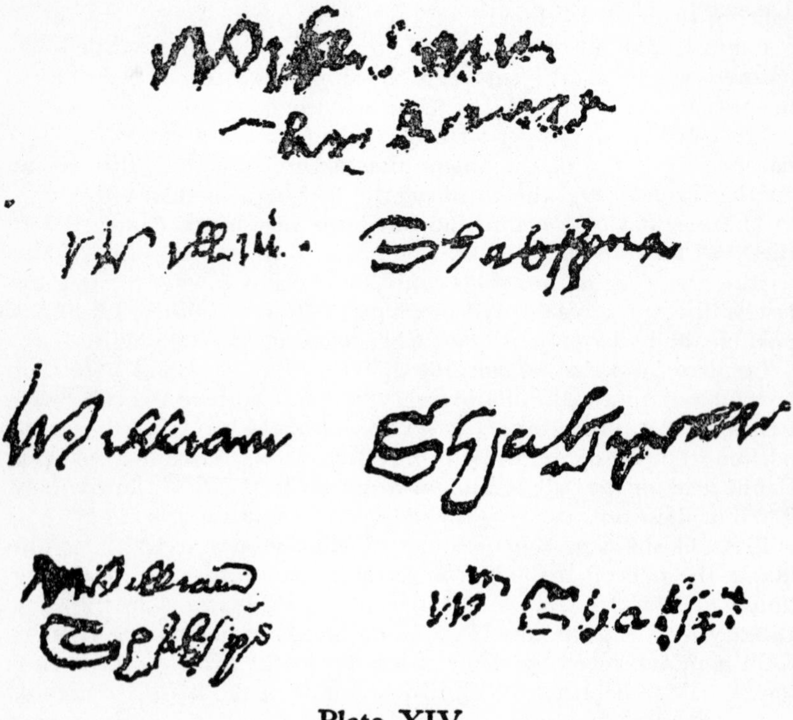

Plate XIV.

THE FIVE SO-CALLED "SHAKESPEARE SIGNATURES."

After they had with myself and the Museum Authorities most carefully examined the two deeds, the Librarian of the City Corporation said to me, there is no reason to suppose that the Corporation deed has upon it the signature of Wm. Shakespeare, and the British Museum Authorities likewise told me that they did not think that the Museum Mortgage Deed had upon it a signature of William Shakespeare.

The more you examine the whole five the more you will be certain, as the writer is, after the most careful study of the Will and of the Deeds, that not one of the five writings is a "signature," or pretends to be a "signature," and that therefore there is a probability, practically amounting to a certainty, that the Stratford Actor could not so much as manage to scrawl his own name.

No! We possess not a scrap of writing, not even an attempt at a signature, that can be reasonably supposed to be written by the Stratford *gentleman.*

He is styled "gentle Shakespeare": this does not refer to anything relating to his character or to his manners but it means that possessing a coat of arms he was legally entitled to call himself a "gentleman."

[p. 40]

CHAPTER IV.

Contemporary Allusions to Shackspere.

Shakspeare the Actor purchased New Place at Stratford-on-Avon in 1597 for £60 and he became a "gentleman" and an esquire when he secured a grant of arms in 1599.

How did the stage "honour" the player who had bought a coat of arms and was able to call himself a "gentleman"?

Three contemporary plays give us scenes illustrating the incident:

1st. Ben Jonson's "Every man out of his humour" which was acted in 1599 the very year of Shakspeare's grant of arms.[9]

2nd. Shakespeare's "As you like it" which was entered at Stationers' Hall in 1600, although no copy is known to exist before the folio of 1623.

3rd. "The Return from Pernassus" which was acted at St. John's College, Cambridge in 1601, though not printed till 1606.

* * *

[9] See pp. 9-10, "1568," and 12, "1596"—the editors.

[p. 41] To commence with Ben Jonson's "Every man out of his humour." The clown who had purchased a coat of arms is said to be the brother of Sordido (a miser), and is described as an "essential" clown (that is an uneducated rustic), and is styled Sogliardo which is the Italian for the filthiest possible name.

[p. 42] The other two characters in the scene (act iii. sc. I) are Puntarvolo who, as his crest is a *Boar,* must be intended to represent Bacon; and Carlo Buffone who is a buffoon or jester.

Enter Sogliardo (the filth), who is evidently the Stratford Clown, who has just purchased a coat of arms:— . . .

Sog. Nay I will haue him, I am resolute for that, by this Parchment Gentlemen, I haue ben so toil'd among the Harrots [meaning *Heralds*] yonder, you will not beleeue; they doe speake i' the straungest language, and giue a man the hardest termes for his money, that euer you knew.

Car. But ha' you armes? ha' your armes?

Sog. Yfaith, I thanke God I can write myselfe Gentleman now, here's my Pattent, it cost me thirtie pound by this breath.

Punt. A very faire Coat, well charg'd and full of Armorie.

Sog. Nay, it has as much varietie of colours in it, as you haue seene a Coat haue, how like you the Crest, Sir?

Punt. I vnderstand it not well, what is 't? [p. 43]

Sog. Marry Sir, it is your Bore without a head Rampant.

Punt. A Bore without a head, that's very rare.

Car. I, . . . and Rampant too: troth I commend the Herald's wit, he has deciphered him well: A Swine without a head, without braine, wit, anything indeed, Ramping to Gentilitie. You can blazon the rest signior? can you not?

. . . .

. . . .

. . . .[10]

[10] The following is the passage omitted by Durning-Lawrence:

Sog. O, I, I haue it in writing here of purpose, it cost me two shillings the tricking.

Car. Let's heare, let's heare.

Punt. It is the most vile, foolish, absurb, palpable, & ridiculous escutcheon, that euer this eye survis'd. Save you, good monsieur FASTIDIVS.

Car. Silence, good knight: on, on.

Sog. GYRONY, of eight *peeces;* AZVRE and GVLES, between three *plates;* a CHEV'RON, *engrailed checkey,* OR, VERT, and ER-

Punt. Let the word be, *Not without mustard,* your Crest is very rare sir.

Shakspeare's "word" that is his "motto" was—non sanz droict—not without right—and I desire the reader also especially to remember Sogliardo's words "Yfaith I thanke God" a phrase which though it appears in the quartos is changed in the 1616 Ben Jonson folio into "I thank *them*" which has no meaning.

Next we turn to Shakespeare's "As you like it." This play, though entered at Stationers' Hall in 1600 and probably played quite as early, is not known in print till it appeared in the folio of 1623. The portion to which I wish to refer is the commencement of Actus Quintus, Scena Prima.

Act 5, Scene I.

Enter Clowne and Awdrie.

Clow. We shall finde a time *Awdrie,* patience gentle Awdrie.
Awd. Faith the priest was good enough, for all the olde gentlemans saying. [p. 44]
Clow. A most wicked Sir *Oliver, Awdrie,* a most vile *Mar-text.* But *Awdrie,* there is a youth heere in the forrest layes claime to you.
Awd. I, I know who 'tis: he hath no interest in mee in the world: here comes the man you meane.

(Enter William)

Clo. It is meat and drinke to me to see a clowne, by my troth, we that haue good wits, haue much to answer for: we shall be flouting: we cannot hold.
Will. Good eu'n *Audrey.*
Awd. God ye good eu'n *William.*
Will. And good eu'n to you sir.
Clo. Good eu'n gentle friend. Couer thy head, couer thy head: Nay prethee bee couer'd.
How olde are you Friend?

MINES; on a *cheefe* ARGENT betweene two ANN'LETS, *sables;* a Bores head, *Proper.*
Car. How's that? on a *cheefe* ARGENT?
Sog. On a *cheefe* ARGENT, a Bores head *Proper,* betweene two ANN'LETS *sables.*
Car. S'lud, it's a hogs-cheeke, and puddings in a pewter field this.
Sog. How like you 'hem, signior?

Will. Fiue and twentie Sir.

Clo. A ripe age: Is thy name *William*?

Will. William, Sir.

Clo. A faire name. Was't borne i' the Forrest heere?

Will. I [Aye][11] Sir, I thanke God.

Clo. Thanke God: A good answer: Art rich?

Will. 'Faith Sir, so, so.

Clo. So, so, is good, very good, very excellent good: and yet it is not, it is but so, so: Art thou wise?

Will. I [Aye][11] sir, I haue a prettie wit.

Clo. Why, thou saist well. I do now remember a saying: The Foole doth thinke he is wise, [p. 45] but the wise man knowes himselfe to be a Foole. . . . . . . You do loue this maid?

Will. I do Sir.

Clo. Giue me your hand: art thou Learned?

Will. No Sir.

Clo. Then learne this of me, To haue is to haue. For it is a figure in Rhetoricke, that drink being powr'd out of a cup into a glasse, by filling the one, doth empty the other. For all your Writers do consent, that *ipse* is hee: now you are not *ipse,* for I am he.

Will. Which he Sir?

Clo. He Sir, that must marrie this woman.

Firstly I want to call your attention to Touchstone the courtier who is playing clown and who we are told "uses his folly like a stalking horse and under the presentation of that he shoots his wit." Notice that Touchstone refuses to be married to Awdrey (who probably represents the plays of Shakespeare) by a *Mar-text,* and she declares that the Clown William "has no interest in mee in the world." William—shall we say Shakspeare of Stratford?—enters and is greeted as "gentle" (*i.e.* he is possessed of a coat of arms). He says "Thank God" he was born in the forest here (Ardennes, very near in sound to Arden).* "Thank God" is repeated by Touchstone and as it is the same phrase that is used by Sogliardo in Ben Jonson's play I expect that it was an ejaculation very characteristic of the real man of Stratford and I [p. 46] am confirmed in this belief because in the folio edition of Ben Jonson's plays the phrase is changed to "I thank *them*" which has no meaning.

The clown of Ardennes is rich but only rich for a Clown (Shakspeare of Stratford was not really rich, New Place cost only £60).

Asked if he is wise, he says "aye," that is "yes," and adds that he

[11] Durning-Lawrence's insertion—the editors.

* There was a forest of Arden in Warwickshire. [Durning-Lawrence's note—the editors.]

has "a pretty wit," a phrase we must remember that is constantly used in reference to the Stratford actor. Touchstone mocks him with a paraphrase of the well-known maxim "If you are wise you are a Foole if you be a Foole you are wise" which is to be found in Bacon's "Advancement of Learning" Antitheta xxxi. Then he asks him *"Art thou learned"* and William replies *"No sir."* This means, *unquestionably,* as every lawyer must know, that William replies that he cannot *read* one line of print. I feel sure the man called Sha*c*kspeare of Stratford was an uneducated rustic, never able to read a single line of print, and that this is the reason why no books were found in his house, this is the reason why his solicitor, Thomas Greene, lived with him in his house at New Place (Halliwell-Phillipps: Outlines, 1889, Vol. I, p. 226);—a well-known fact that very much puzzles those who do not realize the depth of Shakspeare's illiteracy.

[p. 47]

CHAPTER V.

"The Return from Pernassus". . . .

The next play to which attention must be called is "The Return from Pernassus" which was produced at Cambridge in 1601 and was printed in 1606. . . .

The portion to which I wish to direct attention is:—

Actus 5, Scena I.

Studioso. Fayre fell good *Orpheus,* that would rather be [p. 48]
King of a mole hill, then a Keysars slaue:
Better it is mongst fidlers to be chiefe,
Then at plaiers trencher beg reliefe.
But ist not strange this mimick apes should prize
Vnhappy Schollers at a hireling rate.
Vile world, that lifts them vp to hye degree,
And treades vs downe in groueling misery.
England affordes those glorious vagabonds,
That carried earst their fardels on their backes,
Coursers to ride on through the gazing streetes
Sooping it in their glaring Satten sutes,
And Pages to attend their maisterships:
With mouthing words that better wits haue framed,
They purchase lands, and now Esquiers are made.
Philomusus. What ere they seeme being euen at the best
They are but sporting fortunes *scornfull* iests.

Can these last two lines refer to Shakspeare the actor seeming to be the poet? Note that they are spoken by Philomusus that is friend of the poetic muse. Mark also the words "this mimick apes." Notice especially "with mouthing words that *better* wits haue framed, they purchase lands and now Esquiers are made" *i.e.* get grants of arms. Who at [p. 49] this period among mimics excepting W. Shakspeare of Stratford purchased lands and obtained also a grant of arms?

* * *

[p. 65] The immortal plays are the "Greatest Birth of Time," and contain a short summary of the wisdom of the world from ancient times, and they exhibit an extent and depth of knowledge in every branch which has never been equalled at any period of the world's history. In classic lore, as the late Mr. Churton Collins recently pointed out, they evince the ripest scholarship. And this is confirmed by classical scholars all the world over.

None but the profoundest lawyers can realise the extent of the knowledge not only of the theory but of [p. 66] the practice of Law which is displayed. Lord Campbell says that Lord Eldon [supposed to have been the most learned of judges][12] need not have been ashamed of the law of Shakespeare. And as an instance of the way in which the members of the legal profession look up to the mighty author I may mention that some years ago, at a banquet of a Shakespeare Society at which Mr. Sidney Lee and the writer were present, the late Mr. Crump, Q.C., editor of the *Law Times,* who probably possessed as much knowledge of law as any man in this country, declared that to tell him that the plays were not written by the greatest lawyer the world has ever seen, or ever would see, was to tell him what he had sufficient knowledge of law to know to be nonsense. He said also that he was not ashamed to confess that he himself, though he had some reputation for knowledge of law, did not possess sufficient legal knowledge to realise one quarter of the law that was contained in the Shakespeare plays.

It requires a philologist to fully appreciate what the enormous vocabularly employed in the plays implies.

Max Müller in his "Science of Language," Vol. I, 1899, p. 379, says "A well-educated person in England, who has been at a public school and at the University . . . seldom uses more than about 3,000 or 4,000 words. . . . The Hebrew Testament says all that it has to say with 5,642 words, Milton's poetry is built up with 8,000; and Shakespeare, who probably displayed a greater variety of expression

[12] Durning-Lawrence's insertion—the editors.

than any writer in any [p. 67] language . . . produced all his plays with about 15,000 words."

Shakspeare the householder of Stratford could not have known so many as one thousand words.

But Bacon declared that we must make our English language capable of conveying the highest thoughts, and by the plays he has very largely created what we now call the English language. The plays and the sonnets also reveal their author's life.

In the play of "Hamlet" especially, Bacon seems to tell us a good deal concerning himself, for the autobiographical character of that play is clearly apparent to those who have eyes to see. I will, however, refer only to a single instance in that play. In the Quarto of 1603, which is the first known edition of the play of "Hamlet," we are told, in the scene at the grave, that Yorick has been dead a dozen years; but in the 1604 Quarto, which was printed in the following year, Yorick is stated to have been dead twenty-three years. This corrected number, twenty-three, looks therefore like a real date of the death of a real person. The words in the Quarto of 1604 are as follows:—

Hamlet, Act v, Scene i.

"[Grave digger called.] Clow[n] . . . heer's a scull now
"hath lyen you i' th' earth 23 yeeres . . . this same scull,
"sir, was, sir, *Yorick's* skull, the Kings jester. . .
"*Ham*[*let*]. Alas poore *Yoricke,* I knew him *Horatio,*
"a fellow of infinite iest, of most excellent fancie,
"hee hath bore me on his backe a thousand [p. 68] times
". . . Heere hung those lyppes that I haue kist, I know not
"howe oft, where be your gibes now? your gamboles, your
"songs, your flashes of merriment, that were wont to set
"the table on a roare, not one now to mocke your owne
"grinning . . ."

The King's Jester who died about 1580-1, just twenty-three years before 1604 (as stated in the play), was John Heywood, the last of the King's Jesters. The words spoken by Hamlet exactly describe John Heywood, who was wont to set the table in a roar with his jibes, his gambols, his songs, and his flashes of merriment. He was a favourite at the English Court during three if not four reigns, and it is recorded that Queen Elizabeth as a Princess rewarded him. It is an absolutely gratuitous assumption that he was obliged permanently to leave England when she became Queen. Indeed it is believed that he was an intimate friend of the Bacon family, and must have carried little Francis Bacon any number of times upon his back, and the little fellow must have kissed him still more oftentimes. The story in the play of "Hamlet" seems, therefore, to fit in exactly with the facts of Bacon's life; but it is not possible that the most fertile imagination of the most confirmed Stratfordian can suppose that the Stratford actor ever saw John Heywood, who died long before Shakspere came to London.

* * *

CHAPTER X.

[p. 84] Bacon is Shakespeare.

Proved mechanically in a short chapter on the long word Honorificabilitudinitatibus.

The long word found in "Loves Labour's lost" [*sic*] was not created by the author of Shakespeare's plays. . . .

It is believed to have first appeared in the Latin Dictionary by Uguccione, called "Magnae Derivationes," which was written before the invention of printing, in the latter half of the twelfth century. . . . Excerpts from it were . . . included in the "Catholicon" of Giovanni da Genova. . . . [p. 89]

In this "Catholicon," which, though undated, was printed before A.D. 1500, we read

"Ab *honorifico, hic* et *hec honorificabilis,–le* et *hec honororificabilitas,–tis* et *hec honorificabilitudinitas,* et est longissima dictio, que illo versu continetur—
Fulget Honorificabilitudinitatibus iste."

* * *

The long word Honorificabilitudinitatibus occurs in the Quarto edition of "Loues Labor's Lost," which is stated to be "Newly corrected and augmented by W. Shakespere." Imprinted in London by W. W. for Cutbert Burby. 1598.

This is the very first play that bore the name W. Shakespere, but so soon as he had attached the name W. Shakespere to that play, the great author Francis Bacon caused to be issued almost immediately a book attributed to Francis Meres which is called "Palladis Tamia, Wits Treasury" and is stated to be Printed by P. Short for Cuthbert Burbie, 1598.[13] This is the same publisher as the publisher of the

[13] See p. 28—the editors.

Quarto of "Loues Labor's lost" although both the Christian name and the surname are differently spelled.

This little book "Palladis Tamia, Wits Treasury" tells us on page 281, "As Plautus and Seneca are [p. 90] accounted the best for comedy and tragedy among the Latines, so Shakespeare among ye English, is the most excellent in both kinds for the stage; for Comedy, witness his Getleme [*sic*] of Verona, his Errors, his Love Labors lost, his Love Labours wonne, his Midsummers night dreame, and his Merchant of Venice: for Tragedy, his Richard the 2, Richard the 3, Henry the 4, King John, Titus Andronicus, and his Romeo and Juliet."

Here we are distinctly told that eleven other plays are also Shakespeare's work although only Loues Labors lost at that time bore his name.

. . . . For our present purpose it is sufficient to point out that on the very first occasion when the name W. Shakespere was attached to any play, viz., to the play called "Loues Labor's lost," the Author took pains to insert a revelation that would enable him to claim his own when the proper time should arrive. . . .

So far as is known there never was any other edition printed until the play appeared in the Folio of 1623 under the name of "Loues Labour's lost," and we put before the reader a . . . [p. 91] photo reproduction of a portion of the first column of that page. . . .[14]

On comparing the page of the Quarto with that of the Folio, it will be seen that the Folio page commences with the same word as does the Quarto and that each and every word, and each and every italic in the Folio is exactly reproduced from the Quarto excepting that Alms-basket in the Folio is printed with a hyphen to make it into two words. A hyphen is also inserted in the long word as it extends over one line to the next. The only other change is that the lines are a little differently arranged. These slight differences are by no means accidental, because Alms-basket is hyphened to count as two words and thereby cause the long word to be the 151st word. This is exceedingly important and it was only by a misprint in the Quarto that it incorrectly appears there as the 150th word. By the rearrangement of the lines, the long word appears on the 27th line, and the line, "What is A.B. speld backward with the horn on his head" appears as it should do on the 33rd line. At the time the Quarto was issued, when the trouble was to get Shakespere's name attached to the plays, these slight printer's errors in the Quarto—for they are printer's errors—were of small consequence, but when the

[14] See p. 90—the editors.

136 Loues	Number of words in line in ordinary type.
Curat. A most singular and choise Epithat,	6
Draw out his Table-booke.	=
Peda. He draweth out the thred of his verbositie, fi-	9
ner then the staple of his argument. I abhor such pha-	10
naticall phantasims, such insociable and poynt deuise	6
companions, such rackers of ortagriphie, as to speake	8
dout fine, when he should say doubt; det, when he shold	11
pronounce debt; d e b t, not det: he clepeth a Calf, Caufe:	13
halfe, haufe: neighbour *vocatur* nebour; neigh abreuiated	6
ne: this is abhominable, which he would call abhomi-	9
nable: it insinuateth me of infamie: *ne inteligis domine*, to	6
make franticke, lunaticke?	3
Cura. Laus deo, bene intelligo.	=
Peda. Bome boon for boon prescian, a little scratcht, 'twil	4
serue.	1
Enter Bragart, Boy.	=
Curat. Vides ne quis venit?	=
Peda. Video, & gaudio.	=
Brag, Chirra.	1
Peda. Quari Chirra, not Sirra?	3
Brag. Men of peace well incountred.	5
Ped. Most millitarie sir salutation	4
Boy. They haue beene at a great feast of Languages,	9
and stolne the scraps.	4
Clow. O they haue liu'd long on the almes-basket of	10
words. I maruell thy M. hath not eaten thee for a word,	12
for thou art not so long by the head as honorificabilitu-	11
dinitatibus: Thou art easier swallowed then a flapdra-	151
gon.	
Page. Peace, the peale begins.	
Brag. Mounsier, are you not lettred?	
Page. Yes, yes, he teaches boyes the Horne-booke:	
What is Ab speld backward with the horn on his head?	
Peda. Ba, *puericia* with a horne added.	
Pag. Ba most seely Sheepe, with a horne: you heare	
his learning.	

Plate XXI.

PORTION OF PAGE 136, FULL SIZE, AS IN THE SHAKESPEARE FOLIO, 1623.

play was reprinted in the Folio of 1623 all these little blemishes were most carefully corrected.

The long word Honorificabilitudinitatibus is found in "Loues Labour's lost" not far from the commence-[**p. 92**]ment of the Fifth Act, which is called Actus Quartus in the 1623 folio, and on . . . [p. 90 of this text] is given a full size photo facsimile from the folio, of that portion of page 136, in which the word occurs in the 27th line.

* * *

The "revealed" and "all revealing" sentence forms a correct Latin hexameter, and we will proceed to prove that it is without possibility of doubt or question the real solution which the "Author" intended to be known at some future time, when he placed the long word Honorificabilitudinitatibus, which is composed of twenty-seven letters, on the twenty-seventh line of page 136, where it appears as the 151st word printed in ordinary type.

The all-important statement which reveals the [**p. 93**] authorship of the plays in the most clear and direct manner (every one of the twenty-seven letters composing the long word being employed and no others) is in the form of a correct Latin hexameter, which reads as follows—

HI LUDI	F. BACONIS	NATI	TUITI	ORBI
These plays	F. Bacon's	offspring	are preserved	for the world.

* * *

[**p. 97**] This explanation of the real meaning to be derived from the long word honorificabilitudinitatibus seems to be so convincing as scarcely to require further [**p. 98**] proof. But the Author of the plays intended when the time had fully come for him to claim his own that there should not be any possibility of cavil or doubt. He therefore so arranged the plays and the acts of the plays in the folio of 1623 that the long word should appear upon the 136th page, be the 151st word thereon, should fall on the 27th line and that the interpretation should indicate the numbers 136 and 151, thus forming a mechanical proof so positive that it can neither be misconstrued nor explained away, a mechanical proof that provides an evidence which absolutely compels belief.

The writer desires especially to bring home to the reader the manifest fact that the revealed and revealing sentence must have been constructed before the play of "Loues Labor's lost" first appeared in 1598, and that when the plays were printed in their present form in the 1623 folio the scenes and the acts of the preceding plays and the printing of the columns in all those plays as well as in the play of "Loues Labour's lost" required to be arranged with extraordinary skill in order that the revealing page in the 1623 folio should commence with the first word of the revealing page in the original quarto of 1598, and that that page should form the 136th page of the folio, so that the long word "Honorificabilitudinitatibus" should appear on page 136, be the 151st word, and fall upon the 27th line.

Bacon tells us that there are 24 letters in the alphabet (*i* and *j* being deemed to be forms of the same [**p. 99**] letter, as are also *u* and *v*). Bacon was himself accustomed frequently to use the letters of the alphabet as numerals (the Greeks similarly used letters for numerals). Thus A is 1, B is 2 . . . Y is 23, Z is 24. Let us take as an example Bacon's own name–B = 2, a = 1, c = 3, o = 14, n = 13; all these added together make the number 33, a number about which it is possibly [*sic*] to say a good deal. We now put the numerical value to each of the letters that form the long word, and we shall find that their total amounts to the number 287, thus:

H	O	N	O	R	I	F	I	C	A	B	I	L	I	T	U
8	14	13	14	17	9	6	9	3	1	2	9	11	9	19	20

D	I	N	I	T	A	T	I	B	U	S
4	9	13	9	19	1	19	9	2	20	18=287

From a word containing so large a number of letters as twenty-seven it is evident that we can construct very numerous words and phrases; but I think it "surpasses the wit of man" to construct any "sentence" other than the "revealed sentence," which by its construction shall reveal not only the number of the page on which it appears–which is 136–but shall also reveal the fact that the long word shall be the 151st word printed in ordinary type counting from the first word.

On one side of the facsimile reproduction of part of page 136 of the 1623 folio, numbers are placed shewing [**p. 100**] that the long word is on the 27th line, which was a skilfully purposed arrangement, because there are 27 letters in the word. There is also another set of numbers at the other side of the facsimile page which shews that, counting from the first word, the long word is the 151st word. How is it possible that the revealing sentence, "Hi ludi F. Baconis nati tuiti orbi," can tell us that the page is 136 and the position of the long word is the 151st word? The answer is simple. The numerical value of the initial letters and of the terminal letters of the revealed sentence, when added together, give us 136, the number of the page, while the numerical value of all the other letters amount to the number 151, which is the number of words necessary to find the position of the long word "Honorificabilitudinitatibus," which is the 151st word on page 136, counting those printed in ordinary type, the italic words being of course omitted.

The solution is as follows

HI

LUDI

F

BACONIS

NATI

TUITI

ORBI

the initial letters of which are

H L F B N T O [p. 101]

their numerical values being

8 11 6 2 13 19 14 = total 73

and the terminal letters are

I I S I I I

their numerical values being

9 9 18 9 9 9 = total 63

Adding this 63 to 73 we get 136

while the intermediate letters are

U D A C O N I A T U I T R B

their numerical values being

20 4 1 3 14 13 9 1 19 20 9 19 17 2 = 151

Total 287

The reader thus sees that it is a fact that in the "revealed" sentence the sum of the numerical values of the initial letters, when added to the sum of the numerical values of the terminal letters, do, with mathematical certainty produce 136, the number of the page in the first folio, which is 136, and that the sum of the numerical values of the intermediate letters amounts to 151, which gives the position of the long word on that page, which is the 151st word in ordinary type. These two sums of 136 and 151, when added together, give 287, which is the sum of the numerical value of all the letters of the long word "Honorificabilitudinitatibus," which, as we saw . . ., amounted to the same total, 287.

As a further evidence of the marvellous manner in which the Author had arranged the whole plan, the long word of 27 letters is placed on the 27th line. [**p. 102**]

Can anyone be found who will pretend to produce from the 27 letters which form the word "Honorificabilitudinitatibus" another sentence which shall also tell the number of the page, 136, and that the position of the long word on the page is the 151st word?

I repeat that to do this "surpasses the wit of man," and that therefore the true solution of the meaning of the long word "Honorificabilitudinitatibus," about which so much nonsense has been written, is without possibility of doubt or question to be found by arranging the letters to form the Latin hexameter.

HI LUDI F. BACONIS NATI TUITI ORBI

These plays F. Bacon's offspring are preserved for the world.

It is not possible to afford a clearer mechanical proof that

THE SHAKESPEARE PLAYS ARE BACON'S OFFSPRING.

It is not possible to make a clearer and more definite statement that

BACON IS THE AUTHOR OF THE PLAYS.

It is not possible that any doubt can any longer be entertained respecting the manifest fact that

BACON IS SHAKESPEARE.

[p. 103]

CHAPTER XI.

On the revealing page 136 in "Loves Labour's lost."

In the previous chapter it was pointed out that using letters for numbers, Bacon's name is represented by 33.

B	A	C	O	N.
2	1	3	14	13=33

and that the long word possesses the numerical value of 287.

H	O	N	O	R	I	F	I	C	A	B	I	L	I	T	U
8	14	13	14	17	9	6	9	3	1	2	9	11	9	19	20

D	I	N	I	T	A	T	I	B	U	S
4	9	13	9	19	1	19	9	2	20	18=287

In the Shakespeare folio, Page 136, . . . ON LINE 33, we read "What is Ab speld backward with the horn on his head?"

The answer which is given is evidently an incorrect answer, it is "Ba, puericia with a horne added," and the Boy mocks him with "Ba most seely sheepe, with a horne: you heare his learning." [p. 104]

The reply should of course have been in Latin. The Latin for a horn is cornu. The real answer therefore is "Ba corn-u fool."

This is the exact answer you might expect to find on the line 33, since the number 33 indicates Bacon's name. And now, and now only, can be explained the very frequent use of the ornament representing a Horned Sheep, inside and outside "Baconian" books, under whatever name they may be known. An example will be found at the head of the present chapter on page 103. The uninitiated are still "informed" or rather "misinformed" that this ornament alludes to the celebrated Golden Fleece of the Argonauts and they little suspect that they have been purposely fooled, and that the real reference is to Bacon.

It should be noted here that in the Quarto of "Loues Labor's lost," . . . if the heading "Loues Labor's lost" be counted as a line, we read on the 33rd line: "Ba most seely sheepe with a horne: you heare his learning." This would direct you to a reference to Bacon, although not so perfectly as the final arrangement in the folio of 1623.

* * *

[p. 138] The story of the production of the play of "Richard II." is very curious and extremely instructive. It was originally acted with the Parliament scene, where Richard II. is made to surrender, commencing in the Folio of 1623 with the words—

"Fetch hither Richard, that in common view he may surrender," continuing with a description of his deposition extending over 167 lines to the words—

"That rise thus nimbly by a true king's fall."

This account of the deposition of a king reached Queen Elizabeth's ears; she was furiously angry and she exclaimed: "Seest thou not that I am Richard II."

A copy of the play without any author's name was printed in 1597, omitting the story of the deposition of Richard II.; this was followed by a second and probably a third reprint in 1597, with no important alterations, but still without any author's name. Then, after the actor had been sent away to Stratford, Shakespeare's name was put upon a fourth reprint, dated 1598.

The story of Richard II.'s deposition was not printed in the play till 1608, five years after the death of Queen Elizabeth. [**p. 139**]

This history of the trouble arising out of the production of the play of "Richard II." explains why a name had to be found to be attached to the plays. Who would take the risk? An actor was never "hanged," he was often whipped, occasionally one lost his ears, but an actor of repute would probably have refused even a large bribe. There was, however, a grasping money-lending man, of little or no repute, that bore a name called Shaxpur, which might be twisted into Bacon's pen-name Shake-Speare, and that man was secured, but as long as he lived he was continually asking for more and more money. The grant of a coat of arms was probably part of the original bargain. At one time it seems to have been thought easier to grant arms to his father. This, however, was found impossible. But when in 1597 Bacon's friend Essex was Earl Marshall and chief of the Heralds' College, and Bacon's servant Camden (whom Bacon had assisted to prepare the "Annales"—see Spedding's "Bacon's Works," Vol. 6, p. 351, and Letters, Vol. 4, p. 211), was installed as Clarenceux, King-of-Arms, the grant of arms to Shakespeare was recognised, 1599. Shakespeare must have been provisionally secured soon after 1593, when the "Venus and Adonis" was signed with his name, because in the next year, 1594, "The Taming of a Shrew" was printed, in which the opening scene shews a drunken "Warwickshire" rustic [Shakspeare was a drunken Warwickshire rustic],[15] who is dressed up as "My lord," for whom the play had been prepared. (In the writer's possession there is a [**p. 140**] very curious and absolutely unique masonic painting revealing "on the square" that the drunken tinker is Shakspeare and the Hostess, Bacon.)

The early date at which Shakspeare had been secured explains how in 1596 an application for a grant of arms seems to have been made (we say seems) for the date may possibly be a fraud like the rest of the lying document.

[15] Durning-Lawrence's bracketed comment—the editors.

We have referred to Shakspeare as a drunken Warwickshire rustic who lived in the mean and dirty town of Stratford-on-Avon. There is a tradition that Shakespeare as a very young man was one of the Stratfordians selected to drink against "the Bidford topers," and with his defeated friends lay all night senseless under a crab tree, that was long known as Shakespeare's crab tree.

Shakespeare's description of the Stratford man as the drunken tinker in "The Taming of a Shrew" shews that the actor maintained his "drunken" character. . . .

* * *

[p. 143] What then can be the meaning of the statement that the highest point to which the actor, Shakespeare, attained was to play the part of the *Ghost* in "Hamlet"? The rumour is so positive and so persistent that it cannot be disregarded or supposed to be merely a foolish jest or a senselessly false statement put forward for the purpose of deceiving the public. We are compelled, therefore, to conclude that there must be behind this fable some real meaning and some definite purpose, and we ask ourselves; What is the purpose of this puzzle? What can be its real meaning and intention? As usual, the Bacon key at once solves the riddle. The moment we realise that BACON is HAMLET, we perceive that the purpose of the rumour is to reveal to us the fact that the highest point to which the actor, Shakespeare, of Stratford-on-Avon, attained was to play the part of Ghost to Bacon, that is to act as his "Pseudonym," or in other words, the object of the story is to reveal to us the fact that

BACON IS SHAKESPEARE

1916 Frank W. Wadsworth. Berkeley and Los Angeles: University of California Press. *The Poacher from Stratford*. Published 1958.

[p. 74] . . . [A] celebrated courtroom battle . . . took place during . . . the tercentenary of Shakespeare's death. The battle involved, in its legal sense at least, Colonel George Fabyan and William N. Selig. Colonel Fabyan, inspirer of *The Keys for Deciphering the Greatest Work of Sir Francis Bacon* and other similar monographs, was the director of the Riverbank Laboratories of Geneva, Illinois. Strengthened by the presence of Mrs. Elizabeth Wells Gallup, the Laboratories had been conducting an investigation of the Bacon cipher and were preparing publications demonstrating Bacon's authorship of the Shakespearean plays when Selig gained a blocking injunction. Selig, a "motion picture manufacturer," planned to exploit the tercentenary by means of a cinematic tribute to the Bard, and he felt that the publication of the Laboratories' revelations would rather dim the luster of his offer to Shakespeare's memory. The case was heard by Judge Richard S. Tuthill of the Cook County Circuit Court, and his decision made literary, if not legal, history. Here, as reported in the pages of the sedate *Journal of Education* is his verdict.

"That William Shakespeare was born April 23, 1564; that he went to London about 1586 or 1587; that for a time thereafter he made his living working for Burbage; that he later became an actor in Burbage's theatre, and in traveling theatrical companies; that he returned about 1609-1610 to live in Stratford-on-Avon, where he engaged in business to the time of his death, on April 23, 1616, and that Shakespeare was not an educated man, are allegations which the court finds true.

[p. 75] "The court further finds that Francis Bacon was born January 26, 1560 [*sic*]; that he was educated not only in English, but in French, Latin, Italian, German, and had a general education equal or superior to any one of his age; that he was the compiler of a book of 1,560 axioms and phrases selected from the greatest authors and books of all time; that in his youth literary people were frowned upon in England, but in Paris literary people were in the favor of the reigning powers and literature was having a renaissance. Bacon went to Paris in his early youth and spent several years in this atmosphere.

"The court further finds that by the published and accounted works of Francis Bacon there is given a cipher which Bacon devised in his early youth when in Paris, called the Biliteral cipher; that the witness, Elizabeth Wells Gallup, has applied that cipher according to the directions left by Francis Bacon and has found that the name and character of Shakespeare were used as a mask by Francis Bacon to publish facts, stories and statements contributing to the literary renaissance in England which has been the glory of the world.

"The claim of the friends of Francis Bacon that he is the author of said works of Shakespeare, and the facts and circumstances in the real bibliography of the controversy over the question of authority and the proofs submitted herein, convince the court that Francis Bacon is the author."

As concrete evidence of the strength of the court's conviction, Judge Tuthill awarded Colonel Fabyan $5,000 in damages.

1957 *The Shakespearean Ciphers Examined,* by William F. Friedman and Elizebeth S. Friedman, Cambridge University Press, 1957, pp. 106-108, 112.

[**p. 106**] One of the later, but not least impressive, anagrammatists was Sir Edwin Durning-Lawrence. The title he chose for his book (published in 1910) is indicative of his conviction: avoiding the interrogative form, it proclaimed *Bacon is Shakespeare*. Sir Edwin devoted a fair proportion of his space to the long word [honorificabilitudinitatibus], and what he called 'its correct anagrammatic equivalent'. This spondaic hexameter, 'Hi lu-di F Ba-co-nis na-ti tui-ti/ orbi', he translated as 'These plays, F. Bacon's offspring, are preserved for the world'. Sir Edwin was willing to admit that 'from a word containing so large a number of letters as twenty-[**p. 107**]seven, it is evident we can obtain very numerous words and phrases'. But words and phrases were not to the point: he assured his readers that 'it surpasses the wit of man to construct any sentence other than the revealed sentence'.

. . . His conclusion was that the word was skilfully and deliberately contrived to appear where it did in the First Folio; its position was pregnant with significance.

What can be said of these and the many other attempts to find messages in the long word, in order to strengthen the force of the inferences drawn by Baconians . . . ? In the first place, the coincidence in Bacon's, [and] Shakespeare's . . . use of the same word is not so striking as it appears. There is some evidence that it was a popular nonsense-word of the period; it is at any rate clear that it was not invented by Bacon. The first printed occurrence is . . . in a . . . Latin grammar-cum-dictionary, . . . published in Mainz in 1460. . . . It could scarcely be claimed that a writer some hundred years before either Bacon or Shakespeare was born invented the word specifically to conceal messages such as 'These plays, F. Bacon's offspring, are preserved for the world'.

Quite apart from the word's origin, the prolific and diverse labour of the anagrammatists, rather than strengthening their case, is itself a sufficient rebuttal. If the long word had been deliberately planted as a text to conceal a cipher message, it would have to have been chosen to yield one plain, unambiguous message. As it is, as many different 'solutions' emerge as there are different 'solvers'. Anyone can make of the word whatever he manages to make; but whatever he makes of it, someone else is sure to produce an alternative. The effort is damned from [p. 108] the start, for the process is without any fixed rules, without any unique solution, and without any cryptological validity.

* * *

[p. 112] . . . another book, *Is it Shakespeare?* [published in 1903] . . . leaves no doubt of his [the author's] Baconian sympathies. Among the anagrams collected there, he [the author] quotes one from the last two lines of the Epilogue to *The Tempest,* claiming that he does not know who discovered it. The lines are

> As you from crimes would pardon'd be
> Let your indulgence set me free.

and the anagram . . . runs

> Tempest of Francis Bacon, Lord Verulam
> Do ye ne'er divulge me ye words.

The snag, which he fails to notice, is that the anagram has three a's, while the text has only two.

As possible alternatives, we would like to suggest two readings of our own, which contain only the letters which appear in the text. One version suggests a different source of authorship:

> R[eade]r: Believe it or not, my rude
> Play was coded for fun. God save me. CLEMENS

and another upholds Shakespeare's rights in two forthright lines of verse:

> I wrote every line myself. Pursue no code
> E. told me Bacon's a G. D. fraud.

Examples of Baconian anagrammatic 'proofs' could be continued *ad nauseam;* but we have already given some account of the objections that invalidate them. In the absence of a key, any lengthy sequence of letters with the normal proportions of high, medium, and low-frequency vowels and consonants may be anagrammed in a large number of ways. Hence there may be as many 'solutions' as the solver's ingenuity can produce and each will be as valid as any other, but none will carry any objective conviction. . . . There is no place for more than one valid solution in cryptology; a method which allows many bears its own refutation with it. . . .

. . . we have not encountered a single valid or authenticated case in which the writer of a book or play has established his authorship by the anagrammatic method, keyed or unkeyed, within the text of his book or play.

Marlowe as Shakespeare

Introduction

The case for Christopher Marlowe as sole author of the works of Shakespeare is fairly new, though Marlowe has long been offered as one of many who collaborated in the writing of the Shakespeare canon.

As early as 1892, *Our English Homer* suggested that the works of Shakespeare were written by a group composed of Marlowe, Greene, Daniel, Peele, Nashe, Lodge, and Shakespeare himself, with Francis Bacon as editor. Three years later, a novel by Wilbur Ziegler, *It Was Marlowe: A Story of the Secret of Three Centuries,* suggested that Marlowe, Raleigh, and the Earl of Rutland wrote the poems and plays.

The real surge of interest in Marlowe-as-Shakespeare followed the appearance in 1955 of Calvin Hoffman's *The Murder of the Man Who Was 'Shakespeare.'* Hoffman was the first to suggest that Marlowe not only wrote his own plays but also those attributed to William Shakespeare. Like his anti-Shakespearean predecessors, Hoffman believed that Shakespeare lacked the ability and education to write great works of dramatic and poetic art. Marlowe, on the other hand, though he came from the same social class as Shakespeare and was the son of a shoemaker, had been educated at Cambridge University and was well accepted as a great dramatist in his own right—something that other anti-Shakespeareans could not always claim for their candidates.

The major objection made by pro-Shakespeare scholars to the case for Marlowe is the same as that for Oxford, that the claimant died before certain of the plays were written. How Hoffman has met the objection is one of the reasons for the great interest his theory has aroused.

1901 *The Popular Science Monthly,* December 1901, Vol. LX, No. 7, "A Mechanical Solution of a Literary Problem," by Dr. T. C. Mendenhall, pp. 97-105.

[p. 97] Nearly twenty years ago I devised a method for exhibiting graphically such peculiarities of style in composition as seemed to be almost purely mechanical and of which an author would usually be absolutely unconscious. The chief merit of the method consisted in the fact that its application required no exercise of judgment, accurate enumeration being all that was necessary, and by displaying one or more phases of the mere mechanism of composition characteristics might be revealed which the author could make no attempt to conceal, being himself unaware of their existence. It was further assumed that, owing to the well-known persistence of unconscious habit, personal peculiarities in the construction of sentences, in the use of long or short words, in the number of words in a sentence, etc., will *in the long run* manifest themselves with such regularity that their graphic representation may become a means of identification, at least by exclusion. In the present [p. 98] consideration the application of the method has been restricted to a study of the relative frequencies of the use of words of different lengths.

The method of procedure is simple and will be best explained by an example. One thousand words in 'Vanity Fair,' taken in consecutive order of course, were counted and classified as to the number of letters in each with the following result:

Letters—	1	2	3	4	5	6	7	8	9	10	11	12	13	14
Words—	25	169	232	187	109	78	79	48	28	20	10	10	2	3

The graphic exhibition of this result is made by the well-known method of rectangular coordinates. . . . On a sheet of 'squared' paper the numbers showing letters in each word, 1,2,3,4, etc., are placed along the horizontal line and on the vertical above each of these is put a point whose distance from the base shows the number of corresponding words in every thousand, according to the scale shown at the left. These points are then joined by straight lines and the whole broken line may be called the 'word spectrum' or 'characteristic curve' of the author as derived from the group of words considered. The group of 1,000 words from 'Vanity Fair' enumerated above is thus graphically represented by the continuous line in Fig. 1,[1] and the method of constructing the characteristic curve

[1] See p. 104—the editors.

will be readily understood by comparing this with the numbers given. As a thousand is a very small number in a problem of this kind, the curve representing any single group of that number of words is practically certain to differ more or less from that of any other such group. In Fig. 1 the dotted line represents a group of 1,000 words, immediately following that already referred to. Perhaps the most astonishing thing about these two lines is not that they differ, but that they agree as well as they do. It is really remarkable that any marked peculiarity in the use of words is almost sure to be revealed in this way, even in comparatively small groups. In the two diagrams of Fig. 1 it is interesting to note their general sameness, especially as shown in a tendency to equality of words of six and seven letters and also in words of eleven and twelve letters.

When the number of words in each group is increased there is,

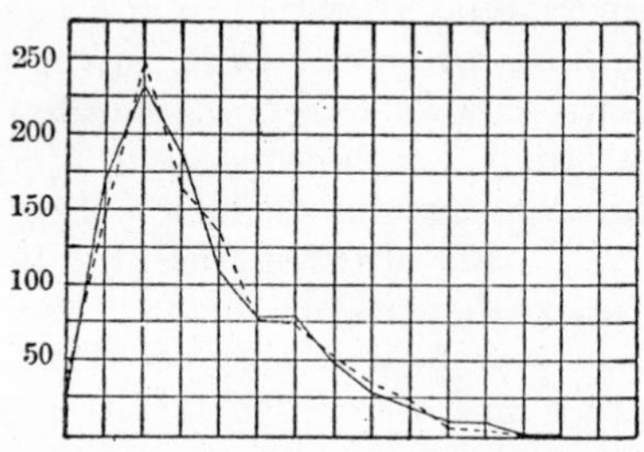

1 2 3 4 5 6 7 8 9 10 11 12 13 14 15 16

FIG. 1. TWO GROUPS—1000 EACH—VANITY FAIR

of **[p. 99]** course, closer agreement of their diagrams, and this became so evident in the earlier stages of the investigation that the conclusion was soon reached that if a diagram be made representing a very large number of words from a given author, it would not differ sensibly from any other diagram representing an equally large number of words from the same author. Such a diagram would then reflect the persistent peculiarities of this author in the use of words of different lengths and might be called the characteristic curve of his composition. Curves similarly formed from anything that he had ever written could not differ materially from this, although curves of other authors might possibly, but would not probably, agree closely with his.

Thus, if this principle were established, the method might be useful as a means of identification of authorship, and it might be relied upon with great confidence to show that a certain author did not write a certain composition.

* * *

[p. 100] The original published description [i.e. of Mendenhall's method, in *Science,* March 11, 1887] . . . concludes as follows:

From the examinations thus far made I am convinced that 100,000 words will be necessary and sufficient to furnish the characteristic curve of a writer—that is to say, if a curve is constructed from 100,000 words of a writer, taken from any one of his productions, then a second curve from another 100,000 words would be practically identical with the first and that this curve would, in general, differ from that formed in the same way from another writer, to such an extent that one could always be distinguished from another. To demonstrate the existence of such a curve would require the enumeration of the letters of several hundred thousand words from each of a number of writers. Should its existence be established the method might then be applied to cases [p. 101] of disputed authorship. If striking differences are found of known and suspected compositions of any writer, the evidence against identity of authorship would be quite conclusive. If the two compositions should produce curves which are practically identical, the proof of a common origin would be less convincing; for it is possible, although not probable, that two writers might show identical characteristic curves.

With this conclusion the matter remained for more than ten years. On innumerable occasions it was suggested that the process ought to be applied to an examination of the writings of Bacon and Shakespeare with a view of forever settling a controversy which will doubtless forever remain unsettled. . . .

That the method has been applied at last to this most curious and yet most interesting question is entirely due to the liberality of Mr. Augustus Heminway, of Boston, who kindly offered to defray the expenses of the work, that is, to employ persons to count and classify nearly two millions of words. . . . [p. 102] After some preliminary work the counting of Shakespeare was seriously begun, and the result from the start with the first group of a thousand words was a decided surprise. Two things appeared from the beginning: Shakespeare's vocabulary consisted of words whose average length was a trifle below four letters, less than that of any writer of English before studied; and his word of greatest frequency was the *four-letter* word, a thing never met with before. His preference for the four-letter word may be said, indeed, to constitute the striking characteristic of his composition. At first it was thought that it might be a general characteristic of the English of his time, but that was found to be not the case. Its appearance in the composition of one or two of his contemporaries will be considered presently. Altogether about 400,000 words of Shakespeare were counted and classified, including, in whole or in part, nearly all of his most famous plays. His 'characteristic curve' is most persistent, that based on the first 50,000 words differing very little from that of the whole count. Two groups have been formed by combining alternate small groups (single plays or parts of plays) in a purely mechanical way, so as to include as nearly as may be the same number of words in each. The curves corresponding to them are plotted in Fig. 4,[2] where, however, the differences have been of necessity somewhat exaggerated in order to make them show at all. The practical identity of these curves must be regarded as convincing evidence of the soundness of the original assumption. . . .

[**p. 103**] The characteristic curve of Bacon was developed along with that of Shakespeare and was based on his 'Henry VII.,' the 'Advancement of Learning' and a large number of his shorter essays, the total number of words being nearly 200,000.

Besides these, extensive counting was done from the writings of Ben Jonson, Addison, Milton, Beaumont and Fletcher, Christopher Marlowe, Goldsmith and Lord Lytton and small groups from a few more modern authors. It is possible, here, to give only general conclusions and to exhibit the diagrams of the more important and interesting results.

One of the first questions likely to be raised is, when an author writes both prose and poetry, will the two styles of composition follow the same general law and show the same characteristic curves? Unfortunately it is not possible to answer this as completely as could be desired, as no one has written enough in two or more different styles, as prose, poetry, history, essay, drama, etc., to produce normal characteristic diagrams. Several of the authors above named were examined with this point in view, and while some of them exhibited somewhat different curves in play writing and in essay or serious prose composition in every case any marked peculiarity found in one style was also found in the other. A good example of this is shown in the two Shakespeare curves of Fig. 5.[3] The continuous line is based on his 'Rape of Lucrece' and 'Venus and Adonis,' while the broken line is his normal curve in play writing.

It will be noted that the Shakespearean peculiarity of an excessive use of four-letter words is shown in the same degree in both and that while there are apparent differences of considerable magnitude the curves are really strikingly alike, every bend in one having a correspond-[**p. 104**]ing flexure in the other. This is typical of all comparisons of different styles of composition by the same author. Undoubtedly there will always be found differences in the graphic

[2] See p. 107—the editors.
[3] See p. 107—the editors.

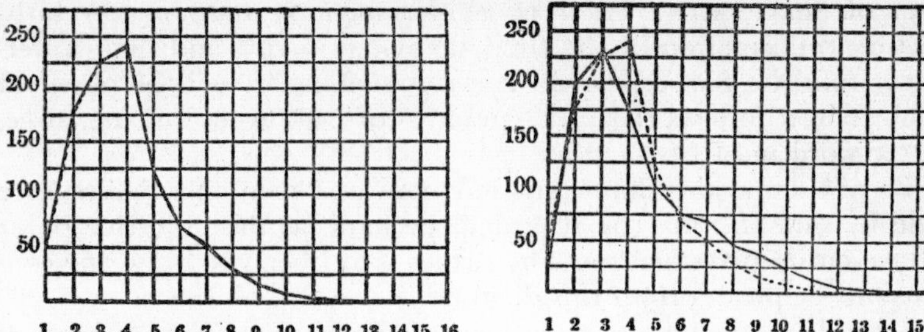

FIG. 4. SHAKESPEARE—TWO GROUPS, ABOUT 200,000 WORDS EACH.

FIG. 7. BACON . . . SHAKESPEARE.

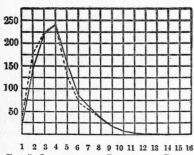

FIG. 5. SHAKESPEARE—POETRY . . . PROSE.

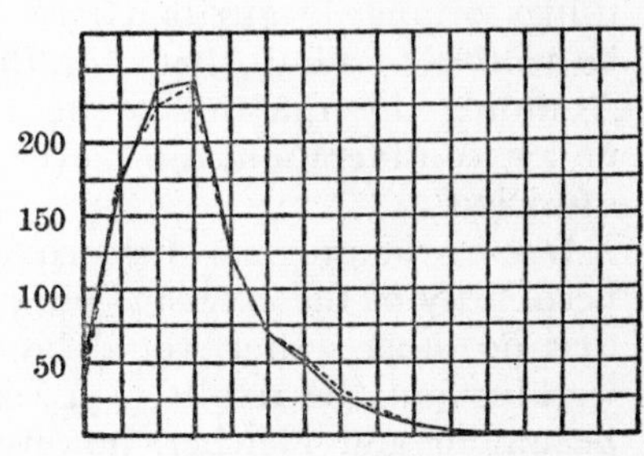

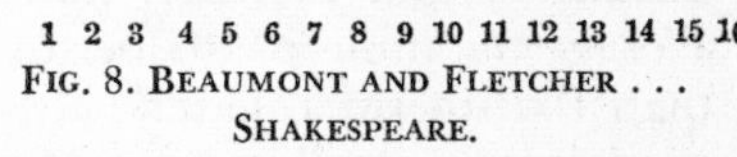

FIG. 8. BEAUMONT AND FLETCHER . . . SHAKESPEARE.

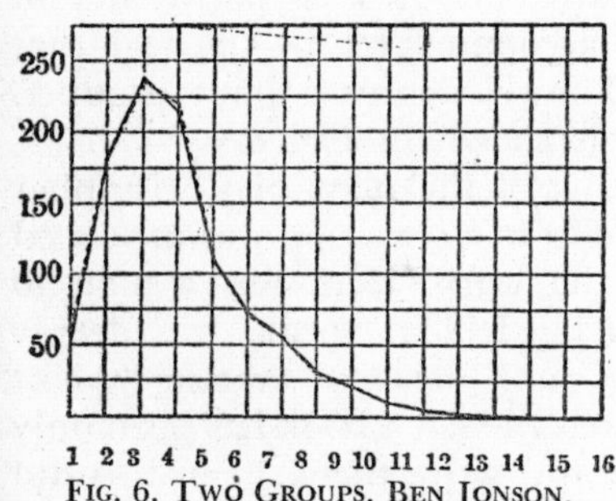

FIG. 6. TWO GROUPS, BEN JONSON.

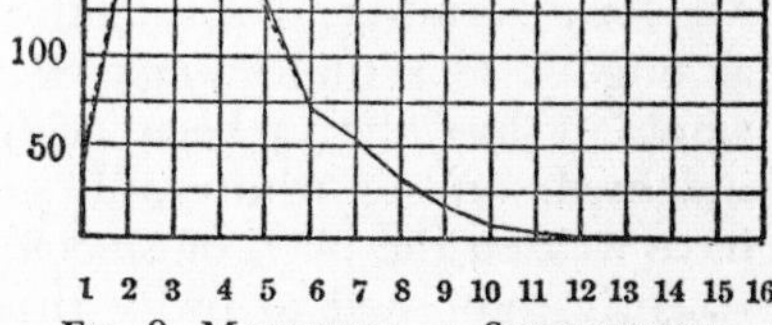

FIG. 9. MARLOWE . . . SHAKESPEARE.

representations of serious prose compositions and those of a higher vein, poetry or play, by the same writer, but the evidence at hand goes to show that the leading personal peculiarities of composition will invariably be found in both.

Fig. 6[4] shows the curves of two groups of about 75,000 words each from the plays of Ben Jonson, the most notable literary contempo-

[4] See above—the editors.

rary of Shakespeare. Their close agreement is another very satisfactory confirmation of the fundamental principle and their difference from the Shakespearean curve is striking. It will be observed that Jonson follows the usual practice of making use of the three-letter word most frequently.

Fig. 7[5] shows the characteristic curves of Bacon and Shakespeare side by side and may be regarded, perhaps, as the objective point of the entire investigation. The reader is at liberty to draw any conclusions he pleases from this diagram.

Should he conclude that, in view of the extraordinary differences in these lines, it is clear that Bacon could not have written the things ordinarily attributed to Shakespeare, he may yet, possibly, be willing to admit that, . . . 'the question still remains, who did?' Assuming this question to be a reasonable one, the method now under consideration can never do more than direct inquiry or suspicion.

During the progress of the count it seemed as if the Shakespearean peculiarity of the excessive use of words of four letters was unique, that no other writer would be found with this characteristic. On working out the results of a very extensive count of the plays of Beaumont and Fletcher, however, it was found that on the final average the num-[**p. 105**]ber of four-letter words was slightly greater than that of three letters, although the excess was by no means so persistent in small groups. The curve of their composition is, on the whole, quite like that of Shakespeare. The lack of persistency of form among small groups may be accounted for by the fact that the work is in a large, though unknown, degree a joint product. The comparison with Shakespeare is shown in Fig. 8.[6]

It was in the counting and plotting of the plays of Christopher Marlowe, however, that something akin to a sensation was produced among those actually engaged in the work. Here was a man to whom it has always been acknowledged, Shakespeare was deeply indebted; one of whom able critics have declared that he 'might have written the plays of Shakespeare.' Indeed a book has been only recently published to prove that he did write them. Even this did not lessen the interest with which it was discovered that in the characteristic curve of his plays Christopher Marlowe agrees with Shakespeare about as well as Shakespeare agrees with himself, as is shown in Fig. 9.[7] Finally, an interesting incident developed in an examination of a bit of dramatic composition by Professor Shaler.

[5] See p. 107—the editors.
[6] *Ibid.*
[7] *Ibid.*

of Harvard University, entitled 'Armada Days.' It was a brochure of only about twenty thousand words, printed for private circulation, in which the author had endeavored to compose in the spirit and style of the Elizabethan Age. Although too small to produce anything like a 'normal curve' it was counted and plotted, and the diagram indicated that Professor Shaler had not only caught the spirit of the literature of the time, but that he had also unconsciously adopted the mechanism which seems to characterize it. In the excess of the four-letter word and in other respects the curve was rather decidedly Shakespearean, although it was written before its author knew anything of such an analysis as this.

1935 *Shakespeare's Imagery and What It Tells Us,* by Caroline F. E. Spurgeon, New York, The Macmillan Company, and Cambridge, England, The University Press.

[p. 12] As I have already explained, I believe we can draw from the material of a poet's images definite information about his personality.

In working out this line of thought, we are justified, I suggest, in assuming that a poet will, in the long run, naturally tend to draw the large proportion of his images from the objects he knows best, or thinks most about, or from the incidents, among myriads he has experienced, to which he is sensitive, and which therefore remain within his knowledge. . . .

This reflection of the personality in the images can perhaps best be made clear by comparing those of different poets. . . .[8] [p. 13] My survey shows that, quite apart from style and method of forming the images (a study in itself), each writer has a certain range of images which are characteristic of him, and that he has a marked and constant tendency to use a much larger number of one or two kinds. Thus, to give the simplest kind of example, with Shakespeare, nature (especially the weather, plants and gardening), animals (especially birds), and what we may call everyday and domestic, the body in health and sickness, indoor life, fire, light, food and cooking, easily come first; whereas with Marlowe, images drawn from books, especially the classics, and from the sun, moon, planets and heavens far outnumber all others. . . . Indeed this imaginative preoccupation with the dazzling heights and vast spaces of the universe is, to-

[8] See p. 110—the editors.

gether with a magnificent surging upward thrust and aspiration, the dominating note of Marlowe's mind. He seems more familiar with the starry courts of heaven than with the green fields of earth, and he loves rather to watch the movements of meteors and planets than to study the faces of men.

A Synopsis of Caroline Spurgeon's "A Detailed Chart of the Images grouped under 'Daily Life' in Shakespeare and five Contemporary Dramatists: Showing their Proportion and Distribution"[9]

	Shakespeare	Marlowe	Ben Jonson	Chapman	Dekker	Massinger
Sport and Games	51	10	31	33	47	22
Classes and Types	39	12	33	37	40	37
Trades and Crafts	20	6	30	32	18	43
War and Weapons	18	13	25	48	49½	36
Substances, Metals	17	22	29	20	30	19
Money, Merchandise	13	6	24	12	17	20
Topical	10	0	18	0	12	0
Roads and Travel	7	2	3	1	8	3½
Buildings	4	1	0	0	5	1
State and Royalty	3	0	8	8	8	4
Town Life	0	0	8	6	8	0

[9] The original chart, a horizontal bar graph, is chart IV in *Shakespeare's Imagery* (New York & Cambridge, 1935). On it are the following legends: "In each case, except that of Marlowe, the images are taken from five selected plays. The Marlowe images are from the whole of his work: i.e. Tamb. I and II, Ed. II, Hero and Leander, and the better authenticated parts of four other plays." " 'Birdsnaring' and 'Falconry' are included here in the images listed under 'sport.' "

No matter what he is describing, the pictures he draws tend to partake of this celestial and magnificent quality. . . .

[p. 14] With Shakespeare it is far otherwise. His feet are firmly set upon 'this goodly frame, the earth', his eyes are focussed on the daily life around him, and he misses no tiny detail of a bird's flight, a flower's growth, a housewife's task, or the emotions written on a human face.

* * *

[p. 15] Thus, by examining their imagery alone, we can see how entirely different were these two men, in mind, temperament and outlook. We see, among much else, that Shakespeare was intensely interested in and observant of everyday concrete things and events, especially in outdoor country life and the homely indoor routine, and that his senses were abnormally acute and responsive; while for

Marlowe, concrete things had little interest; indeed, he hardly saw them, for he lived almost wholly in a world of ideas. . . .

[p. 16] I have . . . largely indulged my own curiosity in my choice of the other writer I have selected for comparison with Shakespeare in . . . their general use of imagery as a whole—Francis Bacon. Shakespeare and Bacon are the two greatest men of their day, and the claim that Bacon is in truth Shakespeare and wrote his plays is still held to be a serious and well-founded one by a large number of people. It is natural, therefore, that one should be eager to ask, 'What does an examination of their images tell us?'

* * *

We find, in the first place, that the proportion of the subject-matter of their images is entirely different. With Shakespeare nature images are always the most frequent, especially those relating to growing things in a garden or orchard: trees, plants, flowers and fruits; the weather: the sky, clouds, rain, sunshine, and the seasons. Next in frequency to these are animal images, and of these, especially images from birds. With Bacon . . . nature definitely takes the second place and his animal images are peculiarly few. Bacon's greatest number of images are drawn from subjects which may be grouped together under 'Domestic Life', that is everything touching the house and daily life indoors, such as light and fire, furnishings, hangings, textiles, needlework, clothes, jewels, marriage, birth, death, parents, children and human relations generally.

[p. 17] One reason why the 'Domestic Life' group of Bacon's images is so large is that it includes the many images drawn from light and darkness, the contrast between artificial and natural lights, and other 'light' effects, which constantly recur in his writings.

* * *

When thinking of mental activity, some picture of light seems nearly always to come before him, as when (in Book I of the *Advancement of Learning*) he points out that the schoolmen, with their 'verbal points and niceties', broke up the solidarity of the sciences, and asks, 'For were it not better for a man in a fair room to set up one great light, or branching candlestick of lights, than to go about with a small watch candle into every corner?' . . . .

[p. 18] Light, indeed, to Bacon, very noticeably represents all good things, enlightenment of every kind, both mental and spiritual: truth, virtue, knowledge, understanding, reason, and even the essence of God himself. . . .

* * *

Shakespeare shows no sign of this great interest in light, nor of Bacon's almost passionate association of light with intellect, although in *Romeo and Juliet* we find a beautiful 'running' or constantly recurring image which shows that Shakespeare there imaginatively conceives of love as light in a dark world.

Just as Bacon seems continually to see and reflect on [p. 19] human nature in the terms of light and shade, so Shakespeare seems to think most easily and naturally in the terms of a gardener. He visualises human beings as plants and trees, choked with weeds, or well pruned and trained and bearing ripe fruits, sweet smelling as a rose or noxious as a weed. . . .

Next to light and darkness, we find Bacon, in common with many Elizabethans, drawing most of his images from the body and bodily action. Here he resembles Shakespeare; but where he once more noticeably differs from him is in the quantity and range of his Biblical images, which are very numerous, and come next in this respect to those of light and the body. Bacon's mind is steeped in Biblical story and phrase in a way of which there is no evidence in Shakespeare . . . [p. 20] which is indeed totally foreign to Shakespeare. Shakespeare's Biblical comparisons and references—which are few—are practically all to well-known characters and incidents, familiar to any grammar-school boy: Adam and Eve, Cain and Abel, Solomon, Job and Daniel, Herod, Judas and Pilate, the fall of Lucifer, the serpent in the Garden, the Flood, and the Red Sea.

Whereas the mind of Bacon, one feels, is absolutely at home in the whole of Biblical story, Old and New Testaments alike, and moves there naturally, drawing easily and readily for illustration upon lesser as well as generally known incidents, often visualised and pondered upon, and thus vivid and familiar to his imagination.

* * *

[p. 21] One set of images which reveal very definite differences between Bacon and Shakespeare are those on astronomy. Both writers are interested in the subject, both have a fair number of astronomical references; and the imagination of both men is held by the old Ptolemaic system. . . .

This . . . , especially, fires Shakespeare's imagination, and his references to the movement of stars in their spheres, especially in imagery, are very many. Bacon does not refer to this, but he, on the other hand, is particularly attracted by the conception of the *primum mobile,* the great outer tenth sphere, which, according to Ptolemy, communicated its movement to all the lower spheres. . . .

* * *

[p. 23] Their nature images are another group which have a very different character. Bacon not only draws far fewer images from nature than does Shakespeare, but [p. 24] these are of a different type: they are more general, dealing with larger tracts of country, the lie of the land, hills and valleys, coppices and woods; and they show little first-hand observation of *appearances*. As a whole, Bacon's interest, unlike Shakespeare's, seems to lie in the practical processes of farming rather than of gardening, and his reflections are noticeably often made from the point of view of the owner of the land, pondering how to preserve and improve it. . . .

The difference between the sea images of the two writers is the exact contrary of that between their nature images; Shakespeare's are the more general, Bacon's the more concrete and particular. Shakespeare's sea images are (i) chiefly of storms and shipwrecks.

* * *

[p. 25] Shakespeare's other most constant sea images are (ii) the ebb and flow of tides, (iii) the action of currents, (iv) a tide rushing through a breach, (v) a ship being dashed on the rocks, and (vi) the infinite size, depth and capacity of the ocean (generally likened to love). These last three I never find in Bacon. But the great and constant difference between the sea pictures of the two writers is that Shakespeare's are chiefly concerned with the general character, quality or aspect of the sea, [p. 26] usually in storm, *as it might be viewed by a landsman,* whereas Bacon's are noticeably vivid little pictures of episodes or incidents on the sea *as experienced by a man in a ship or boat.*

* * *

The images from sport and games form another sure [p. 27] indication of a writer's tastes and individuality. Shakespeare has a great many, chiefly from falconry, shooting with bow and arrow, deer hunting, bird-snaring and fishing, and in games, chiefly from bowls, football and tennis, but his images from bowls, which he clearly knew and liked best, are about three times as many as from any other game.

In all the works of Bacon I have examined, I find three 'game' images only, one each from tennis, skittles and bowls, so there is no indication which game, if any, he himself preferred. His 'sport' images are comparatively few, and he draws upon archery, falconry, fishing, bird-snaring, wrestling, and rowing, in that order.

The differences of their attitude towards animals are also worth noticing. Shakespeare's attitude, as seen in his images, is unique among the dramatists of his time, for he shows a sympathy with and understanding of the animal's point of view and sufferings which no one else in his age approaches.

* * *

[p. 28] Bacon, compared with Shakespeare, has very few 'war' images, but he definitely asserts that he strongly approves of war, and believes it to be as necessary to a State as healthy exercise to a man's body. . . . Shakespeare hates war and condemns it . . . but a surer indication of his view is [p. 29] that he constantly symbolises it by and associates it with loud and hideous noises, with groans of dying men, with 'braying trumpets and loud churlish drums, Clamours of hell'. . . .

I could instance many other examples of significant differences between the two writers, but space does not permit. I have said enough however, I hope, to prove my point, which is this: that in addition to the very distinct differences in gifts and temperament easily to be seen in the matter and tenour of their writings, on a study of their imagery alone other noticeable differences emerge. We see, on examining their images, that the writers of these two sets of works viewed the world from a different standpoint, had had different experiences and were interested in and familiar with a different range of objects in everyday life, that even when interested in the same subject (as astronomy), different aspects of it appealed to their imaginations. We see that their tastes in sport and games were different, . . . and that moreover, on certain abstract subjects (such as the action of time), they held diametrically opposite views.

These facts all point one way, and all seem to support the view that we have here, behind these two sets of writings, not one mind only, but two highly individual and entirely different minds.

1946 Paul H. Kocher. *Christopher Marlowe: A Study of his Thought, Learning, and Character*. Chapel Hill: The University of North Carolina Press, 1946.

[p. 4] Even Shakespeare's plays are not, of course, just anybody's plays, fatherless and unrelated to one another; they are *Shakespeare's* plays, all bearing the general stamp of one personality, however difficult that personality may be to delimit. Marlowe's plays are Marlowe's not only in this general sense but also as projecions of some of his more particular ideas and passions. Criticism of Christianity, for example, appears in all the biographical documents as the most absorbing interest of his life. And likewise in his plays it is the most anxiously, skillfully, and passionately reiterated theme [p. 5] of dramatization. . . .

That these aspirations and sorrows [over the desires for power and knowledge, expressed by Marlowe's protagonists] are the poet's own is indicated by their superb eloquence, the highest of which Marlowe was capable, and, more conclusively, by the manner in which the same type of character—I had almost said the same character—is evoked over and over again. Marlowe was never able really to visualize any other. Many critics have noted that Tamburlaine, Faustus, Barabas, Gaveston, Mortimer, and Guise are but the embodiments of a craving for illimitable power in varied forms, and few have hesitated to attribute this passion to the dramatist him-[p. 6]self. Ambitions so gigantic were not known on the stage before the coming of Marlowe, and were, of course, anathema to the Elizabethan moral code.

* * *

[p. 27] There are too many such charges [against Marlowe of atheism], some by reputable, others by disreputable, men, and too many points of agreement between them. Baines and Kyd[10] cannot be shown to have colluded with each other in any way, yet their accounts possess a sameness which is the guarantee of truth. In turn, they both receive support from two Harleian manuscripts, undated but probably written in 1593, itemizing the dangerous sayings of Richard Cholmley. This was the same Cholmley who, according to Baines, "hath confessed that he was perswaded by Marloe's Reasons to become an Atheist." In one manuscript Cholmley is quoted as saying "that Marlowe is able to show more sound reasons for atheism than any divine in England is able to give to prove [p. 28] divinity, and that Marlowe told him that he hath read the atheist lecture to Sir Walter Raleigh and others."[11] The emphasis again is on Marlowe's gathering of arguments against divinity and his labors to disseminate his views, this time by laying them before

[10] Shortly before Marlowe's death, a Richard Baines sent a note to the Privy Council and in it denounced Marlowe as an atheist, citing particular atheistical and anti-Christian statements that Baines claimed Marlowe had made. Soon after Marlowe's death, Kyd made similar accusations against Marlowe to Crown Officials.—Editors' note.

[11] Both Harleian manuscripts are published in full by F. C. Danchin, "Etudes Critiques sur Christopher Marlowe," *Revue Germanique,* IX (1913), 566-87. The first MS likewise is printed by Tucker Brooke (*Life,* pp. 64-66).

Raleigh and others. As before, Cholmley cannot be connected personally with either Baines or Kyd.

A second manuscript, in the same handwriting as the first, ascribes to Cholmley many of the specific blasphemies ascribed by Baines to Marlowe, together with some new ones:

> His seconde course is to make a ieste of the Scripture with these feareful horrible & damnable speeches, that Ihesus Christe was a bastarde St. Mary a whore & the Aungell Gabriell a Bawde to the holy ghoste that Christe was iustly persecuted by the Iewes for his owne foolishness. That Moyses was a Iugler and Aaron a cosoner the one for his miracles to Pharao to prove there was a god & the other for takinge the eareringes of the children of Israell to make a golden calfe with many other blasphemous speeches of the devine essence of God which I feare to rehearse.

The language about Christ, the Virgin, the Angel Gabriel, and Moses is almost identical with that of the Baines note. . . .

* * *

[p. 68] He [Marlowe] became one of the spokesmen of a tendency. For free thought was stirring in England in a vague, unorganized way during the last fifty years of the century. Underneath the intonations of the orthodox writers, one can hear it rising, this mutter of revolutionary dissidence. For the most part it was scattered and anonymous. But in Marlowe we can see the quintessence of it drawn together and revealed. This is the unique historical importance of the Baines note, to which we have never sufficiently awakened. Of whom among the Elizabethans have we such another record? Not Raleigh, not the scientists, nor any of Marlowe's fellow dramatists, nor any other literary Englishman whose work we know. For revolutionary impact and scope it stands alone, an extraordinary document in the history of English free thought.

* * *

[p. 136] His [Marlowe's] struggle with Christianity was, indeed, one of the purest fountains of his literary inspiration. It was the occasion of his greatest play, and of many of the greatest passages in his lesser dramas. The depth of theological learning it evoked is astonishing. I do not think it too much to say that Marlowe's plays show both a more extensive and a more profound knowledge of Christian doctrine than those of any other Elizabethan playwright, including Chapman. There are whole scenes in which scarcely a line does not contain some allusion to the Bible or to didactic and controversial literature.

* * *

[p. 325] Marlowe was a far more learned man than the other university wits, Lyly, Greene, Peele, and Lodge, who had equal opportunities for study. His information ranged widely through most of the current fields of knowledge, and was, on the whole, reasonably full and accurate. He was a specialist, however, only in the subject of divinity, where his showing is remarkable on all counts. In other subjects he is best described as a respectable amateur who makes his mistakes along with the rest. High claims have been made for his astronomical science, but we have seen reason to think them unfounded. His published work shows no knowledge of the new astronomy and does, in fact, suffer from some elementary blunders. On the authority of Boas[12] it is possible to say also that as a translator of Ovid and Lucan, Marlowe, while [p. 326] usually felicitous, does not emerge a perfect Latinist. That last, extra ounce of exactitude which makes the scholar was not for him. Likewise he was a careful and enthusiastic reader on witchcraft and military science but not, so far as appears, an expert. His acquaintance with other sciences such as physics, physiology, psychology, and medicine is that of the average well-read Elizabethan. From Plato, Aristotle, Hippocrates, Galen, Celsus, and others of the classics, and later compendiums like *Batman uppon Bartholome,* Elyot's *Castel of Helth,* Du Bartas' *Divine Weekes,* and La Primaudaye's *French Academie* the ideas which he voices on these subjects could readily be derived. His views on the physical sciences are certainly in no way out of the ordinary.

1955 *The Murder of the Man Who Was 'Shakespeare'* by Calvin Hoffman, Julian Messner, N.Y., copyright by Calvin Hoffman. Reprinted with "Postscript," 1960, Grosset and Dunlap, New York, *Universal Library* series.

[p. 122] I have earlier mentioned that my search began with my almost unconscious drawing of parallelisms between the works of Shakespeare and those of Marlowe.

Critics, of course, had long ago noted a resemblance between the works of these two writers. Ironically enough, it was in part this resemblance that gave rise to the praise of Marlowe's genius. But somehow this resemblance was never followed through to its surprising end.

[12] *Christopher Marlowe,* chap. III.

Scholars have been content to assess the bond between the works of Marlowe and Shakespeare as a literary "influence." Going from the wealth of external evidence, which forced me to the conclusions I have detailed in this book, there is an even greater wealth of internal evidence to support my case.

* * *

[p. 123] The value of parallelisms is enormous. No one, with any authority, can lay claim to having deduced an "influence" in the stylistic relationship between two authors without offering parallelisms as evidence of that influence. A writer's literary style is as peculiarly his as his fingerprint. . . .

* * *

Parallelisms are merely a measuring stick, a rough one perhaps, but still as accurate as is humanly possible, by which we can try to grasp the [p. 124] mercury of a man's soul. Since we are certain of the similarity of style between Marlowe and Shakespeare—how many parallelisms, extracted from their plays and poems, constitute an "influence"? The best we can say is that a small number of parallelisms between any two authors denotes a valid influence of one author upon another; a tremendous number of them brands one of the authors as a plagiarist.

From the almost unlimited parallelisms that I have drawn from the works of Marlowe and Shakespeare, the verdict must be that the plays and poems of these two authors were written by the same person.[13]

[p. 203] [A selection from the approximately 204 parallelisms given by Hoffman.]

Marlowe	Shakespeare
Tamburlaine: The glory of this happy day is yours.	*Julius Caesar:* To part the glories of this happy day.
Tamburlaine: Ah, Shepherd, pity my distressed plight.	*Titus Andronicus:* Comfort his distressed plight.

[13] Mr. Hoffman's position is defended most completely in the Grosset and Dunlap edition of his book; *see* the "Postscript." Since it is impossible to present all of Mr. Hoffman's evidence and argument in this text, the editors have presented part of the material dealing with parallelisms. The use of parallelisms is an accepted scholarly technique.

Marlowe	Shakespeare
Tamburlaine: And angels dive into the pools of hell.	*Titus Andronicus:* I'll dive into the burning lake below.
Jew of Malta (end of play): . . . for come all the world To rescue thee, so will we guard us now, As sooner they shall drink the ocean dry Than conquer Malta, or endanger us.	*King John* (end of play): Come the three corners of the world in arms, An we shall shock them. Nought shall make us rue, If England to itself do rest but true.
Jew of Malta: These arms of mine shall be thy Sepulchure.	*Henry VI,* Part II: These arms of mine shall be thy winding sheet; My heart, sweet boy, shall be thy sepulchure.
Elegies (Marlowe's translation of Ovid): The Moon sleeps with Endymion every day.	*Merchant of Venice:* Peace, ho! the Moon sleeps with Endymion.
[p. 204] *Tamburlaine:* Holla, ye pampered Jades of Asia. What, can ye draw but twenty miles a day?	*Henry IV, Part II:* And hollow pampered jades of Asia, Which cannot go but thirty miles a day.
Tamburlaine: O, Samarcanda, where I breathed first . . .	*Julius Caesar:* This day I breathed first.
Passionate Shepherd to his Love (Marlowe's poem): By shallow rivers, to whose falls Melodious birds sing madrigals. And I will make thee beds of roses, And a thousand fragrant posies.	*Merry Wives of Windsor:* To shallow rivers, to whose falls Melodious birds sing madrigals: There will we make our beds of roses And a thousand fragrant posies.

Marlowe	Shakespeare
Edward II: Weep not for Mortimer That scorns the world and as a traveller Goes to discover countries yet unknown.	*Hamlet:* The undiscovered country from whose bourn No traveller returns.
Dr. Faustus: Was this the face that launched a thousand ships?	*Troilus and Cressida:* She is a pearl, whose price hath launched above a thousand ships.
[p. 205] *Dr. Faustus:* I was no sooner in the middle of the pond, but my horse vanished away . . .	*Merry Wives of Windsor:* . . . they threw me off, from behind . . . in a slough of mire; and set spurs away, like three German devils, three Doctor Faustuses.
Jew of Malta: Poppy and cold mandrake juice.	*Othello:* Not poppy, nor mandragora Nor all the drowsy syrups of the world.
[p. 206] *Hero and Leander:* Who ever loved that loved not at first sight.	*As You Like It:* Who ever loved that loved not at first sight.
Dido, Queen of Carthage: Did ever men see such a sudden storm, Or day so clear so suddenly o'ercast?	*Macbeth:* So foul and fair a day I have not seen.
Hero and Leander: Gentle youth, forbear To touch the sacred garments which I wear.	*Epitaph* (on William Shakepeare's grave at Stratford, said to have been written by William Shakespeare): Good friend, for Jesus' sake forbear To dig the dust enclosed here.
[p. 207] *Jew of Malta:* I count religion but a childish toy And hold there is no sin but ignorance.	*Twelfth Night:* I say there is no darkness but ignorance.

Marlowe	Shakespeare
Dido, Queen of Carthage: Then from the navel to the throat at once He ripped old Priam.	*Macbeth:* And ne'er shook hands, nor bade farewell to him Till he enseamed him from the nave to the chaps, And fixed his head upon the battlements.
Edward II: King Edward: Who's there? Convey this priest to the tower. Bishop: True, true!	*Richard II:* Bolingbroke: Go, some of you, convey him to the tower. King Richard: O good!—convey! Conveyers are you all!
[p. 208] *Jew of Malta:* Now, gentle Ithinore, lie in my lap.	*Hamlet:* Lady, shall I lie in your lap?
[p. 209] *Edward II:* Stand not on titles, but obey . . .	*Macbeth* (Lady Macbeth, to seated Lords): Stand not upon the order of going, But go at once.
Edward II: Shape we our course to Ireland, there to breathe.	*Richard II:* . . . To-morrow next We will for Ireland; and 'tis time, I trow.
[p. 210] *Edward II:* I arrest you of high treason.	*Henry VIII:* I arrest thee of high treason.
[p. 211] *Tamburlaine:* Blush, blush, fair city.	*Macbeth:* Bleed, bleed, poor country.
[p. 212] *Hero and Leander:* . . . she, wanting no excuse to feed him with delays . . .	*Titus Andronicus:* He doth me double wrong to feed me with delays.
Elegies (Marlowe's translation of Ovid): Hates any man the thing he would not kill?	*Merchant of Venice:* Whom we fear, we wish to perish.
[p. 213] *Dr. Faustus:* Ugly hell, gape not!	*Hamlet:* . . . though hell itself should gape . . .

Marlowe	Shakespeare
[p. 216] *Tamburlaine:* Ah, cruel brat, sprung from a tyrant's loins!	*Henry VI, Part III:* O, tiger's heart, wrapped in a woman's hide!
[p. 217] *Jew of Malta:* A fair young maid, scarce fourteen years of age, The sweetest flower in Cytherea's field.	*Romeo and Juliet* (Juliet, also age 14): Death lies on her like an untimely frost, Upon the sweetest flower of all the field.
[p. 220] *Edward II:* These looks of thine can harbor naught but death.	*King John:* For I do see the cruel pangs of death Right in thine eye.
[p. 223] *Massacre of Paris:* . . . breakers of the peace!	*Romeo and Juliet:* . . . disturbers of the peace!
[p. 231] *Tamburlaine* (beginning of scene): Black is the beauty of the brightest day!	*Henry VI, Part I* (beginning of scene): Hung be the heavens with black, yield day to night.

1954 "The Murder of the Man Who Was William Shakespeare," by Robert L. Heilbroner. *Esquire Magazine,* XLII, 6 (December, 1954), 114-122.

[p. 115] The 30th of May, 1593, dawned uneventfully in the small town of Deptford, England, a few miles outside of London. In the river, Sir Francis Drake's fabulous caravel, the *Golden Hind,* lay at anchor; a major tourist attraction, it had pulled so many visitors, including Queen Elizabeth herself, that the master's cabin had been converted into a saloon where refreshments were served. The townspeople of Deptford arose that morning, congratulated themselves anew on the fact that the plague which was devastating London had as yet spared their community, and prepared themselves for a fresh influx of visitors.

Hence little notice was taken of the arrival of four men, three of them of rather dubious repute. One, with a dagger at his belt, was a gentleman sharper and spy by the name of Ingram Frizer. A second was one Nicholas Skeres who often acted as a decoy for Frizer when not engaged in skulduggery of his own. A third was an adulterer and government secret agent, by name Robert Poley, by reputation unsavory. A fourth made up the group, a young man whose name was often spelled Marlin or Morley or Marlo, but whom we know as Christopher Marlowe, the greatest and most renowned poet, dramatist and literary genius until the emergence of William Shakespeare.

The four repaired to a small house, perhaps a tavern, on Deptford Strand, owned by one Dame Eleanor Bull. . . . There at ten o'clock of the morning they assembled and, according to the later report of William Danby, coroner, they "passed the time together & dined & after dinner were in a quiet sort together there & walked in the garden belonging to the said house until the sixth hour after noon of the same day & then returned from the said garden . . . & in company supped."

After supper Marlowe lay down in their room, while the other three—again according to the coroner's report—sat side by side on a bench, with their knees under a table and their backs to Marlowe on the bed. Ingram Frizer was in the middle, Poley and Skeres sitting tightly against him. A dispute arose; Frizer and Marlowe "uttered one to the other divers malicious words for the reason that they could not . . . agree about the payment of the sum of pence, that is, *le recknynge* there."

Frizer's dagger dangled from his belt before Marlowe's grasp. Infuriated, the poet snatched it from its sheath and struck at Frizer—probably with the hilt—giving him superficial cuts on his head. In self-defense, Frizer grabbed his hand and "in that affray . . . with the dagger aforesaid of the value of 12d. gave the said Christopher then & there a mortal wound over his right eye of the depth of two inches and of the width of one inch; of which mortal wound the aforesaid Christopher Morley then & there instantly died."

Queen Elizabeth was staying within twelve miles of Deptford and the town therefore was "within the verge" and fell under her sovereignty. William Danby, the royal coroner, was appointed to look into the facts. He called at the House of Dame Bull and there he noted the circumstances of the crime and made mention of the fact that Frizer did not flee but pleaded self-defense; he allowed the body to be identified by those present and threw Frizer in jail. Marlowe was buried on June 1st, in an unknown, unmarked grave, with only the epitaph of a vicar's registry in the little church at Deptford: "1st June 1593. Christopher Marlow slain by ffrancis ffrezer." The "ffrancis" was clearly an error. The vicar did not know that there was at stake another error of staggering proportions.

Thus exits the most towering and promising literary genius up to the year 1593. And thus enters Calvin Hoffman, three hundred and forty-three years later, to begin one of the most exciting and fantastic literary detective stories of all time.

* * *

[p. 116] The tiny suspicion began when Hoffman was struck by the astonishing parallelisms between Marlowe's "mighty line" and the soaring words of another well-known English writer, William Shakespeare. He made a few casual notes, for example that Shakespeare had only once used the phrase "rose-cheek'd Adonis," and so had Marlowe. The notes grew to encompass a volume; the suspicion grew to a conviction.

Hoffman's conviction was that Shakespeare's works were not written by William Shakespeare. As everyone knows, the authorship theory is not a new one. At least half a dozen substitutes for Shakespeare have been put forth with varying degrees of persuasiveness and sincerity: Edward de Vere, the talented Earl of Oxford; Francis Bacon, the great philosophic genius of his day; the Countess of Pembroke, the only candidate for a female Shakespeare; "another man by the name of William Shaksper," and still others. The theories range from the near sublime to the ridiculous. . . .

. . . [T]he theories stem, all of them, from some very obdurate and disquieting facts about William Shakespeare himself. Or perhaps one should say from a *lack* of facts. . . . [T]he actual documented knowledge of Shakespeare is astonishingly small.

As a matter of fact, until 1593 when *Venus and Adonis* was published with a dedication signed by William Shakespeare, what we actually know about Shakespeare is just exactly this and no more:

He was born of burgess folk in the small town of Stratford and baptized on April 26, 1564. He was married on November 27, 1582. He became a father the following year and again (to twins) in 1585.

* * *

Thereafter we know not much more. We have records of his joining various theatrical companies and becoming a sharer in the famous Globe and Blackfriar Theaters. We have records of his appearing in court as a witness and as a litigant. We have records of his purchasing a house and grounds. We have his will and his date of death. And we have his plays.

But even his plays are not direct evidence of his authorship. There is no manuscript in Shakespeare's handwriting, so that by "Shakespeare's plays" we mean those plays with Shakespeare's name on the title page. Most of these did not appear in print until seven years after his death, in the *First Folio,* published in 1623—in fact out of the thirty-six plays in the *Folio* only eighteen had been previously published, and some of these were not attributed to any author. In addition, a few plays which appeared after the *First Folio* have been credited by some scholars to his name, while others, published before his death with his very name on the title page, have not. Most Shakespeare authorities credit other men with collaboration in at least some of Shakespeare's work; in fact, some concede collaboration in eighteen plays. Thus "what Shakespeare wrote" consists in the final analysis of what scholars *think* he wrote—a perfectly respectable method of judgment, but one falling far short of absolute certitude.

Hence, the *known* facts about William Shakespeare tell us only that he was the son of small-town middle-class folk, that he was married and a father, that he was an actor, litigious, reasonably affluent, and that he died. They also tell us that plays and poems of the most magnificent depth and breadth ever achieved in the English language were printed under his name—along with some others that "do not merit serious consideration."

Is this not enough to establish his uncontestable authorship? It might be, were it not for some very puzzling negative facts. Here are some of the many questions which have provoked other scholars besides Calvin Hoffman into skepticism and doubt:

First, how was it possible for Shakespeare to achieve his unparalleled scope, vocabulary, and learning? Not only did he possess and wield one of the largest arsenals of words of which we know, but his detailed knowledge included legal terminology of a considerably refined sort, medical knowledge and apothecaries' lore, and a close and easy familiarity with the courtly uses and courteous ways of noble life.

Could William Shakespeare, the son of a Stratford tradesman, have had access to such circles? Perhaps, if he went to a university. But he did *not* go to a university (there is no record of his name on the detailed lists) nor is there a record of his attendance at grammar school. Then vicariously, by reading? But where was he to get the books? In Cambridge University [**p. 117**] at that time, one of the finest libraries in England consisted of a few hundred books, so precious they were locked up and even chained to the shelves. There were no libraries for the public, nor were there cheap books to be readily bought. Books were rare and expensive to accumulate. And when Shakespeare made his will—an immensely complicated will in which, aside from his famous "second-best bed" left to his wife, he allocated his clothes, small sums, and household objects to various beneficiaries—he made no mention of either books or manuscripts. Yet if he had had his own library, surely this would have been one of his most valuable possessions.

Hence Hoffman began with the puzzle of how Shakespeare acquired his learning. Where did he learn to read Greek and Latin —"the small Latin and less Greek" which Ben Jonson gave him credit for? And if he read only scantily in Latin and Greek, how did he achieve a familiarity with Ovid, Lucan, Plautus—the last of which was not available in translation at his day, although it is the basis for *The Comedy of Errors?* Shakespeare scholars do not know. . . .

Secondly, Hoffman faced the puzzle of geography. A whole group of the Shakespearean canon is set in Italy—and set there with a knowledge of the geography that argues familiarity. The points of the compass, the location of mountains at one's back or left on setting out from a town, the relation of towns to each other, the routes of travel, all these are baffling to ascribe to a man who—so far as we know—never left England and who had but the most rudimentary maps with which to work. It used to be said that his geography was rudimentary, too, and that this was a point in *favor* of Shakespeare's authenticity. Shakespeare, for example, makes his Prospero embark at Milan, and causes travelers to go from Verona to Milan by water! Ridiculous, of course—except that recent research has shown that in the Elizabethan day one *did* go from Verona to Milan by way, first, of the River Adige, and that Milan *did* have a network of canals which allowed embarkation from the city.

But something puzzled Hoffman even more than the matter of geography. We know that some of Shakespeare's works must have been written as early as 1590. Yet at a time when Kyd, Nashe, Peele, Marlowe, Chapman, and others were constantly referring to one another, *no one mentions William Shakespeare*—until after 1593! In the entire literature of the day there is only one speculative reference to Shakespeare's name—in the deathbed testament of Robert Greene (his *Groatsworth of Wit* published in 1592) where he benignly rails at Marlowe and other playwrights, and then, in a line parodying a quotation from *Henry VI,* flays an "upstart crow" who thinks himself the only "Shake-scene" in the country. Scholars have pounced on this sole reference to something resembling Shakespeare's name before 1593, in disregard of what Hoffman insists is the clear fact that "Shake-scene" was only a common epithet for any actor who could shake a stage with passion. On such slim stuff is the Shakespeare legend built.

After his death, of course, the stories multiplied. His portrait was engraved for the *First Folio* by a lad who was just fifteen when Shakespeare died. His "wit-combates" with Jonson were recalled no less than forty-six years after his death, the recorded examples not being particularly witty. The Shakespeare myth began—not right away, for almost no one at the time thought of these plays as masterworks—but after fifty, a hundred years: forged signatures, fantastic stories (including one forged letter telling of how a housewife in rummaging through an attic threw into the flames quantities of old manuscripts signed William Shakespeare), anecdotes, surmises, attributions, reconstructions—and doubt.

For while no one doubted that the actor William Shakespeare lived or that the plays signed William Shakespeare were written by a great genius, the shape of the *actor* Shakespeare constantly rubbed against the outlines of what the *writer* Shakespeare must have been.

And so there began the search for someone whose profile would more nearly fit the bill—Bacon, Oxford, Rutland, Pembroke. Each was a more satisfactory personality: learned, familiar with courtly ways, traveled, equipped with a motive for publishing in disguise. There was only one trouble for each theory. No other candidate wrote like a dramatic genius. There was only *one* person—the root of Hoffman's theory—whose plays and poetry, whose grandiloquence and fire measured up to Shakespeare's, and that was Christopher Marlowe—the father of blank verse, the great experimenter, the most beloved, respected dramatic writer of his day. The trouble was that Christopher Marlowe—as we know—was dead.

Nevertheless, the more Hoffman read Marlowe and Shakespeare, the more struck he was by the astonishing parallelisms between the two. A list begun in a moment of idle curiosity grew to number 150 examples, then to touch 1000. Research revealed that most Shakespeare authorities "gave" Marlowe full or partial credit for anywhere from one to twelve of Shakespeare's plays—often necessitating a backdating of their original composition to some time before that fateful day in 1593 when Marlowe met Frizer in Dame Bull's tavern.

But many of Shakespeare's plays that were undoubtedly written *after* Marlowe's death also had suspicious similarities. Not only were phrases borrowed wholesale, but in many instances Shakespeare actually quoted Marlowe, although his borrowing from other playwrights was conspicuous largely by its absence. In Hoffman's mind, one creative imagination could be seen through the whole protean sweep of both Marlowe's and Shakespeare's work. If only Marlowe were not dead!

And so Hoffman began to look into Marlowe's life.

Like Shakespeare, Christopher Marlowe was born of humble parentage: his father was a cobbler. Like Shakespeare, he was born in a small town, [p. 118] Canterbury, and, like Shakespeare, he was born in the year 1564. . . .

But there the similarity between their early years ceases. Shakespeare, if the records are accurate (and they have been searched with idolatrous thoroughness) never went to college. Marlowe on the other hand must have been an outstanding student, for at age fifteen he obtained a scholarship to King's School, attached to the Canterbury Cathedral—a school of brilliant reputation where he met the scions of illustrious families: Lyly, Sidney, Dobson, Bentham. He must have done well, for he received in 1581 a scholarship to Cambridge where he entered Corpus Christi College.

Here Marlowe was to remain for seven years, translating both Ovid and Lucan, probably writing (at age twenty-two!) his epoch-making *Tamburlaine*. His associates were literary figures and noblemen: Gabriel Harvey, Thomas Nashe, Thomas Heywood, and John Fletcher.

Then a strange thing happened. In 1587, when Marlowe was due to get his M.A. (the highest academic achievement in Elizabethan England), the college authorities demurred. He had been absent unaccountably for long stretches of time, he was even suspected of Catholicism (which was tantamount to treason). Not until an accidental discovery of papers in 1925 did we find out the reason for this. During his years in college Marlowe had worked as a secret agent and spy for Elizabeth and her spy-master, Sir Francis Walsingham. He had actually gone to Rheims to make contact there with a group of Catholic Englishmen suspected of plotting to put Mary of Scotland on the throne. [Marlowe was in good company, at least. Raleigh and Bacon also took Walsingham's orders—along with other literati, gentlemanly adventurers, and gentlemanly ruffians.] Hence when his degree was in doubt, the Privy Council intervened: ". . . it was not her majestie's pleasure that anie one emploied as he had been in matters touching the benefitt of his Countrie should be defamed by those that are ignorant in th' affaires he went about." Needless to say, Marlowe was speedily given his degree.

He graduated, Hoffman's research revealed, to a position of worldly brilliance. . . . [H]e had access to the huge estate of Thomas Walsingham, a cousin of Sir Francis Walsingham, and Thomas Walsingham became both his patron and his intimate friend. In London he hobnobbed with the most famous writers of the day (actually sharing a room for awhile with Kyd), engaged in long discussions with Walter Raleigh, with the mathematician Hariot, with the poet Chapman. As a playwright he was an immense success. *Tamburlaine* was a sensation (it went through seven editions) and set a fashion—a trend is more accurate—which would culminate in the saga of Shakespeare's historical tragedy. It was followed (we think, for the chronology is obscure) with the even more popular *Doctor Faustus*, which contained these deathless lines concerning Helen of Troy:

"Was this the face that launched a thousand ships
And burnt the topless towers of Ilium?"

There followed *The Jew of Malta* (the source of Shakespeare's *Merchant of Venice*), *Edward the Second*, *Dido, Queen of Carthage*, and others.

He had, as well as success, more adventure. He was involved in a fracas . . . in which a friend of his accidentally killed his opponent. Marlowe was jailed for thirteen days, then released when his friend pleaded self-defense and Marlowe was relieved of complicity in the affair.

Then—at the peak of his fortune—tragedy struck. On May 12, 1593, Thomas Kyd was arrested on charges of atheism, meddling in dangerous matters of state, and publishing seditious libel. Tortured on the rack, he said that three pages of atheist documents found in his study he had had from Marlowe, and that they were "shufled with some of myne (unknown to me) by some occasion of our wrytinge in one chamber twoe yeares since."

The charge was exceedingly grave. Only a short while before, one Francis Kett, whom Marlowe had known at Cambridge, had been tried, not for atheism but for merely advocating a Unitarian doctrine. Kett had been burned at the stake. . . .

Worse yet, Marlowe was to be charged with atheism, with believing that the "Indians and many Authors" wrote over 16,000 years ago, while the Biblical age of Adam was only 6000 years; with believing that "the first beginning of Religion was only to keep men in awe"; with stating that "all protestantes ar hipocriticall Asses"; and with a score of other sins including a defense of homosexuality. The accuser was one Richard Baines [it is pleasant to note that Baines himself was hanged the following year for a "degrading" offense] who claimed to have taken notes at the free discourse of Marlowe, Raleigh, and the other intellectuals of the day.

Six days after Kyd's arrest—before "Baines' libel" had yet come into its hands—the Privy Council ordered that Marlowe be arrested at Thomas Walsingham's estate at Scadbury where he was staying.

He was released pending trial on condition of reporting daily to the Council—a lenient treatment which can only be ascribed to his close connection with the Walsinghams.

But his position was desperate. Regardless of whether the charges were true or false, he faced the example of Kett burned at the stake and Kyd stretched on the rack. Convicted, any one of the charges against him could have meant death; at the least he was sure of torture and imprisonment. Hence it was with this threat of imminent peril that on May 30, 1593—twelve days after his arrest—Christopher Marlowe went to his fateful rendezvous at the house of Dame Bull in Deptford, in the company of Ingram Frizer, Robert Poley and Nicholas Skeres.

To Hoffman's mind, it was a very strange meeting.

What was Marlowe doing all day long with three men who were polished desperadoes, men who had formed part of the network of spies with which England gathered its intelligence abroad? One explanation is that these men, like himself, owed an allegiance—as far as *they* could maintain one—to Thomas Walsingham. In fact, they were his employees! Evidently Marlowe knew them for, as the coroner's report says, they walked and talked for many hours. *What were they talking about?*

[**p. 119**] Then he was killed. But it was a very strange murder. The blow, as described by the coroner's report, would not serve to kill a man instantly—at least such is the evidence given by a number of present-day eminent doctors who have been questioned about the wound. . . . Secondly, it is very doubtful that such a blow could have been effectively struck by a man who was—according to the testimony—wedged between two other men and with his *back* to Marlowe. Thirdly, it is odd in the extreme that an argument about *"le recknynge"* would be carried out by a man with his back to the man he was disputing.

And then there is the matter of the coroner's report. Why were no witnesses called besides Skeres and Poley? Why was Dame Bull not called? Why did not Skeres or Poley break up the fight? Why was Marlowe hurriedly buried in an unmarked grave? All strange facts indeed.

And now comes the strangest and most inexplicable fact of all. Ingram Frizer went to jail. One month after the crime he was pardoned by Queen Elizabeth, on the grounds that the crime had been committed in self-defense. *And one day after he was released from jail, Thomas Walsingham, Marlowe's friend and patron, re-engaged his services!* That a man should hire again a servant who had killed his illustrious protégé while the memory of his death was still fresh is nothing short of incredible. Nor did Thomas Walsingham stop short at Frizer. Soon we find that Poley also was in his employ again. Even more amazing, when Frizer exposed himself to a disgraceful financial-fleecing operation a few years later, Thomas and Audrey Walsingham retained his services nonetheless. The man obviously had more than a perfunctory claim on their good will.

Was Marlowe actually killed in order to prevent his talking, to block his exposure on the rack of higher-ups, including perhaps Walsingham himself? It is certainly a possibility and must be reckoned with. But it is difficult to believe that Marlowe, who was hardly an innocent in the ways of the world, would have permitted Frizer, Poley, and Skeres to spend the day in his company if he had not known their designs.

Finally, Hoffman extricated still another odd fact from the archives. For many years none of Marlowe's friends knew that he had been murdered. It was assumed in London, where his fellow writers to a man mourned his loss, that his demise was due to the plague; even Gabriel Harvey, whose brother was a vicar at the Walsinghams' church in Chislehurst, did not know—or report—the truth. *Evidently no one talked.* Surely this was one of the most enigmatic murders of all time.

Hoffman's research had now given him several threads, tangled in a knot. There was the fact of the extraordinary parallelism of Shakespeare's work and Marlowe's. Even such experts as John Bakeless (who stated in his definitive two-volume work that Marlowe had been killed) admitted that "certain plays ordinarily included in the Shakespeare canon reveal definite traces of Marlowe which can hardly be due to mere imitation. . . . The traces of Marlowe consist first of whole lines or short passages from plays known to be Marlowe's; second, of words typical of Marlowe's vocabulary, not typical of Shakespeare's . . . and third, of obvious examples of Marlowe's structure, mood, and style."

There was the extraordinary vacuum of facts concerning Shakespeare's life, which made his authorship of "Shakespeare's" works an *hypothesis,* rather than an established truth.

There was the known genius of Christopher Marlowe.

And there were the strange circumstances surrounding his death.

Hoffman wove the threads together into a single rope. When Marlowe met his three desperadoes that 30th day of May in Deptford, it was for a very well-thought-out purpose. Faced with death or torture in England, Marlowe was to make his escape—and he was to do so with the connivance of Thomas Walsingham and with the assistance of his servitors. Probably some poor wretch was brought up to the tavern after dark, and there in the small room he was done to death. The coroner was undoubtedly bribed by Walsingham not to inquire too thoroughly into the causes of death; Frizer was provided with an excuse of self-defense (which had recently proved effective when Marlowe's friend was arrested on a similar charge). The Marlowe murder was trumped up, the corpse hustled to an unknown grave and Marlowe was spirited overseas.

And there—and perhaps later back on the vast 1000-acre estate of Thomas (by then Sir Thomas) Walsingham, he wrote his works, always under the awful danger of exposure (now for complicity in a murder, as well as for atheism), condemned to eternal anonymity.

Once the escape was made, reasoned Hoffman, the great imposture began. *Venus and Adonis,* the first of "Shakespeare's works, was actually registered with no author's name at the stationer's office only six weeks before Marlowe's death. When it was published four months after Marlowe's death, it was still unsigned, and dedicated, without authorization, to the Earl of Southampton—a lad of twenty to whom over a dozen works had already been addressed in hope of winning patronage. The dedication called the work "the first heir of my invention," and it was signed, as we know, "William Shakespeare." But note, by the way, that there is not a jot of evidence that the Earl of Southampton ever knew, met, or financed William Shakespeare.

Thus part of the plot was the use of William Shakespeare, a fairly well-known actor, as the front man for the plays and poems which Walsingham had copied from Marlowe's originals and sent to him. Is this incredible? Hoffman found in Walsingham's will a bequest to a "scrivener"—the only bequest to a scrivener he came across in an examination of more than 50 Elizabethan wills. Shakespeare himself, Ben Jonson tells us, delivered manuscripts so perfect that "he never blotted out a line," a performance to whose difficulties any writer will be glad to testify. Could not this scrivener have copied Marlowe's works? Note, too, that Shakespeare's [p. 120] name itself does not appear on any *title* page until *Love's Labour's Lost* in 1598—a delayed acknowledgment of authorship that has continued to baffle scholars. And remember that of the thirty-six plays in the posthumous *First Folio,* eighteen were printed there for the *first* time. Why, one wonders, this reticence?

Add to this what we know of Shakespeare's rather unimpressive background, his rather unimpressive *known* career, and picture the possibility of such a man achieving renown in a way which could never have been detected, and the idea, while admittedly fantastic, loses its character of being absolutely *unbelievable.*

Shortly after Marlowe's disappearance comes the first of the

"Italianate" plays—*Two Gentlemen of Verona*—generally dated 1593-94. Such plays as *Titus Andronicus, Henry VI,* and *Richard III*—all highly imitative of Marlowe's *Edward the Second* and *Tamburlaine*—had (we believe) already been written. Then followed the vast flood of comedies and tragedies—a flood which, as we have seen, was largely secret until the *First Folio* appeared.

Some time in the late 1590's the famous sonnets must have been written: a contemporary, Meres, refers to Shakespeare's "sugr'd sonnets among his private friends" in 1599. The content of the sonnets has always been a mystery to Shakespeare scholars. If they are taken metaphorically, they baffle the imagination; if taken literally, they spell out a story which has nothing to do with the known William Shakespeare. But if Hoffman's theory is accepted, they tell an astonishingly confirmatory story.

The story they tell is one of crime, guilt, exile, fraud, and despair. The tale begins at Sonnet 25 where the poet laments his fate; in Sonnet 26 he says he dare not show his head; in Sonnet 27 that he must abide far away, in Sonnet 28 that he is "debarr'd the benefit of rest." In Sonnet 29 he beweeps his "outcast state." In Sonnet 36 he cries to his patron:

> I may not evermore acknowledge thee
> Lest my bewailed guilt should do thee shame,
> Nor thou with public kindness honour me,
> Unless thou take that honour from thy name.

In Sonnet 44 he speaks of "injurious distance"; in Sonnet 45 of "swift messengers" who bring him tidings from abroad; in Sonnet 48,

> How careful was I, when I took my way,
> Each trifle under truest bars to thrust,
> That to my use it might unused stay,
> From hands of falsehood, in sure wards of trust!

In Sonnet 71 he abjures his patron not to mourn him, "Lest the wise world should look into your moan and mock you with me after I am gone." In Number 72, he asks that his name be buried with his body; and two sonnets later come these startling lines (my italics):

> My spirit is thine, the better part of me:
> So then thou hast but lost the dregs of life,
> The prey of worms, *my body being dead,*
> *The coward conquest of a wretch's knife.*

Finally, in Sonnet 76 he speaks of the disguise through which "every word doth almost tell my name."

Now what do such outcries mean, coming from William Shakespeare who was riding the crest of fame and fortune in London all through these years? No one has ever provided a satisfactory answer —other than "poetic imagination."

Then there is the endlessly argued question of the dedicatee, "the onlie begetter of these insuing sonnets." His initials are W. H., and he is referred to in the sonnets in terms of passionate intimacy. Unfortunately the initials of the Earl of Southampton are H. W. (Henry Wriothesley), and he as well as other suggested dedicatees all reveal a singular lack of intimate connection with the poet. But Thomas Walsingham's name, Hoffman discovered, was sometimes spelled Walsing-Ham (W. H.), and there is concrete evidence that Marlowe was exceedingly close to him—a coincidence to be sure, but a coincidence coming on top of a hundred startling others.

But surely Marlowe must have writhed under his imposed anonymity. Surely he must have been tempted to poke fun at Shakespeare and to peep out from behind his intended disguise. What artist could bear watching another usurp his fame?

Hence it was with special interest that Hoffman noted that four of Shakespeare's plays were registered at the stationer's office (in 1600) with the caveat, "a booke to be staid." One of the plays was *As You Like It;* it was not published until 1623, and in it Hoffman looked for some reason for its curious concealment from the public.

One obvious fact struck him at once. This was the only play in which Shakespeare quoted indirectly the lines of another contemporary—and the quotation, "Dead shepherd, now I find thy saw of might: 'Whoever loved that loved not at first sight?' " was directly lifted from Marlowe's *Hero and Leander.*

But there were more clues. In the play for example is the only character named just "William" in the 1000 characters Shakespeare invented. William is a fool and a simpleton, and he is taunted for his ignorance and his small-town upbringing by Touchstone, who—as his name implies—reveals the true worth of those with whom he comes into contact. Says Touchstone to poor William, "For all your writers do consent that *ipse* is he: now you are not *ipse,* for I am he." (*Ipse* meaning I, myself.)

But Touchstone says something even more provocative. Talking to Audrey, a country maid, he says:

> "When a man's verses cannot be understood, nor a man's good wit seconded with the forward child, understanding,

it strikes a man more dead than a great reckoning
in a little room."

"Great reckoning in a little room"—what could be a more direct allusion to Marlowe's death? And how could William Shakespeare have known the facts of Marlowe's death, when *no one* knew them? And short of this interpretation, *what sense does the line make?*

[p. 121] Yet another curious hint. In studying the *First Folio* of *As You Like It,* Hoffman noted that one character was called Sir Oliver Martext—a name not to be found in any list of English genealogy and hence a contrived name. But in the *First Folio* the name is spelled Mar-Text—a pun, Hoffman believes, on "Marlowe's Text" —and it might be noted that Mar-Text says in the play, "Ne'er a fantastical knave of them all shall flout me out of my calling."

But all these hints, allusions, curious coincidences, and possible interpretations are still no more than that, and no one realizes this more clearly than Hoffman himself.

"There are only two real proofs of my idea," he says. "One would be external incontrovertible documentary evidence. The other lies in the *internal* evidence of Marlowe's and Shakespeare's works. To my mind, one imagination, one creative genius clearly lies behind the whole magnificent sweep."

To document this contention Hoffman has collected nearly a thousand parallelisms—words, ideas, classical allusions, and the like. . . .

Shakespeare scholars—who are probably apoplectic by now—are undoubtedly pointing in speechless rage to a famous study of Shakespeare's imagery by Caroline Spurgeon. Miss Spurgeon classified hundreds of Shakespeare's images—his metaphorical references to sports, nature, clothes, etc.—and concluded that his imagery was significantly different from Marlowe's. But as Miss Spurgeon's thesis reveals, Shakespeare himself was not a consistent imagist—compare *King John* and *Twelfth Night.* Nor was Marlowe, as Marion Bodwell Smith pointed out in a similar study of his imagery. Nor would we expect Marlowe, "dead" at twenty-nine, to mirror "Shakespeare" in his forties. That the selection and interpretation of imagery is at best a highly subjective study can be seen from this portrait of Shakespeare, "deduced" by Miss Spurgeon from her study of his images: "He is indeed himself in many ways in character what one can only describe as Christlike; that is, gentle, kindly, honest, brave, and true . . . ," thus conveniently forgetting about Shakespeare's bloody fantasies, his homosexual allusions, his incest motif.

More intriguing to Hoffman's mind is . . . a study carried out in 1900 by a Dr. T. C. Mendenhall [published, of all places, in *Popular Science Monthly,* December, 1901]. Dr. Mendenhall had evolved the theory that when a writer's prose or poetry was analyzed to determine the number of times he used words of different lengths, each writer would reveal a separate and unique pattern. He tested his theory . . . and found in each instance that the graph produced a unique and consistent pattern—each writer "agreeing" with his own graph and not with that of any other writer.

The work . . . might have languished, had it not come to the attention of a wealthy Baconian enthusiast. He forthwith engaged Dr. Mendenhall and staff to count some 400,000 words of Shakespeare and to compare them with a count of Bacon. . . . As "controls" Mendenhall also counted Beaumont, Fletcher, Milton, Jonson, Marlowe, and a few modern authors.

The results, for the Baconian backer, were disastrous. Bacon consistently used longer words than Shakespeare and their two graphs were utterly unlike. So were the graphs of every other writer, compared with either Shakespeare or any other. But then something happened which, in Dr. Mendenhall's words, created "something akin to a sensation." When they analyzed Marlowe they found that "Christopher Marlowe agrees with Shakespeare about as well as Shakespeare agrees with himself."

* * *

[p. 122] In the summer of 1953, a student walking through the old court of Corpus Christi College at Cambridge noticed a bit of painted wood sticking out of a pile of rubble. The rubble came from the plaster in the master's room, which was in its first process of renovation since having been plastered up after Marlowe's residence at Corpus Christi. And the painted panel was a portrait.

The portrait was of a rather sad-faced, sensitive, romantic young man. In the upper left-hand corner it read, in Latin, Age 21, and the date, 1585. Beneath it a Latin couplet read, *"Quod me nutrit, me destruit"* ("That which nourishes me, destroys me").

Who could it be? Marlowe was in Cambridge in 1585 and was twenty-one that year. Furthermore he was several years older than most of the students, and there were only a dozen in his class. And the quotation? It appears as *"Quod me alit, me extinguit"* ("that which lights me, extinguishes me") in Shakespeare's *Pericles,* and in English in Sonnet 73: "consumed with that which it was nourish'd by."

"From the moment I saw that portrait," says Hoffman, "it

haunted me. Where had I seen that face before? Then I knew—it was the Droeshout engraving in the Shakespeare *First Folio*.[14] Of course I wouldn't trust my own conclusion. So I showed the portrait and the engraving to a whole group of English portrait specialists, without telling them of my hunch. To a man they said it was the same person."

Since then Hoffman has asked various police identification experts to comment on the resemblance of the portraits. After making technical facial measurements, they told him that the eye configuration was the same, the jaw and jowl the same, that there was a marked general resemblance and specific similarities in detail. The difference was as one might expect between a man of twenty-one and one of fifty.

What does this make of Ben Jonson's famous lines facing the Droeshout engraving:

"This figure that thou here see's put,
It was for gentle Shakespeare cut."

Neither Hoffman (nor anyone else) knows. There is trouble enough about these lines, since the Droeshout portrait is utterly unlike the bust of Shakespeare at Stratford, executed shortly after his death by the brothers Johnson whose establishment was within a few feet of the Globe Theatre. Was [Ben] Jonson in on the imposture? Or—as seems more likely—did he pen these lines before he saw the engraving they were to face? We do not know.

But there is still one hope in Hoffman's mind, greater than all others. The majority of Shakespeare's manuscripts must have been preserved by someone from the time of their composition until their printing posthumously in the *First Folio*. If that someone was Thomas Walsingham, what did he do with them subsequently? Burn them? Bury them in his chest? . . .

But Hoffman has a hunch—admittedly a thousand-to-one shot. He thinks there is a possibility that Walsingham had the papers buried with himself. Hence his first order of business has been to open up Sir Thomas' tomb in Scadbury Chapel.

Or at least to try to. In the Summer of 1953, in England, Hoffman went to the Bishop of Rochester and expounded his theory and his hopes. The bishop reflected that the Dean of Westminster Abbey had given permission for Spenser's tomb to be reopened fifteen years ago on a similar hunch, and he gave his consent—subject only to the approval of the local vicar. . . . The vicar hemmed

[14] See inside front cover—the editors.

and hawed. He could not, he averred, act without the approval of his church council. Hoffman rounded up the church council and told his story for the thousandth time. They signed. "Ah," said the vicar, contemplating the signatures, "but they signed, of course, knowing full well I had the ultimate power of veto."

And veto he did, on the grounds of desecration. . . .

But the quest is not totally blocked. The newspapers in England are on the scent and the pressure on the canon is increasing. The last word that Hoffman has had from Thomas Bushell, chairman of the church council, read, "The canon is weakening."

What will the tomb reveal? In all probability, as Hoffman himself admits, nothing at all. But probabilities are not certainties, and there is just the off chance, the thousand-to-one shot, that there in the dark tomb will molder papers, one of which will read:

The Tragedie of Hamlet, Prince of Denmark
by
Christopher Marlowe

1955 *The New York Times Book Review,* Vol. CIV, No. 35, 568, June 12, 1955, pp. 1, 10-11, "Sweet Will and Gentle Marlowe," by Alfred Harbage.

[p. 1] This season's candidate as "the real Shakespeare" is Marlowe of the mighty line. . . .

The case for the gentle Marlowe is simple. He was not slain in 1593 as the records attest, but whisked out of circulation by his compromised lover Sir Thomas Walsingham. He lived on incognito to write the plays of Shakespeare. . . .

It is a bright idea, springing full-armed from the head of Calvin Hoffman, a writer and drama critic. . . .

At least Marlowe was a true poet, and a resuscitated corpse seems little less plausible than the other "real Shakespeares". . . .

A sketch of the backgrounds of this queer business should prove more useful than a refutation of the case of a sure loser like Marlowe. Refutation is futile anyway. Odd notions are dignified by solemn discussion and faddists win adherents the moment they flush out adversaries. . . .

More than twenty candidates have been named as the "real" Shakespeare. One might say that their claims cancel out, but their claims were all nil in the first place, without need of this or any other form of cancellation, and the effect of the unilateral series of refutations has been almost to cancel out Shakespeare. Whoever the plaintiff he is always the defendant, and no reputation could survive these constant appearances in the dock. Each "case" has eased the way for the next, until the one thing most people now think they know about Shakespeare is that he is a doubtful item.

To understand the implications of the authorship controversy one must first dismiss the notion that it has a rational basis. We have more reliably documented information about Shakespeare than about Aeschylus, Sophocles, Euripides, Aristophanes, Plautus, Terence, all medieval English playwrights combined, and all but a few of those of the Renaissance. Midway in his career he was the leading writer for one of the three popular London troupes. The leading writers for the other two were Thomas Dekker and Thomas Heywood, who between them wrote nearly three hundred plays, a fair number of which were printed along with copious nondramatic works complete with dedicatory epistles. Yet all that is known of Heywood's birth, parentage and marriage is conjectural, and nothing is known of Dekker's. No playwright's life was then written up, and the most remarkable thing about Shakespeare's is that our record of it is as full as it is.

So with his creative activity. The identity of playwrights then, like that of screen, radio and television writers now, was a matter of public indifference. Of the millions who watch Hope, Gobel, and the rest, how many can name their writers? In Shakespeare's time the question would have been, "Who can name the writers for Tarleton and Burbage?" No "front" was needed for anyone who wished to feed the virtually anonymous torrent of plays. The most popular single piece, "The Spanish Tragedy," went through eleven editions without mention of the author, and only a late casual allusion lets us assign it to a scrivener's son named Thomas Kyd. The now-famous "Tamburlaine" is assigned to Mr. Hoffman's Marlowe on circumstantial evidence; no one troubled to put his name on its title page. Again Shakespeare is exceptional in that his superiority was spotted in the reading as well as play-going milieux so that the record of his authorship is uniquely full.

His social background was precisely what literary historians would surmise, even if there were no confirmation. The popular playwrights as a class were humbly born, with the standing of the Shakespeares somewhat above the average. In fact, most of the great literary art in the Renaissance (and since) proves to have emanated from the emergent middle classes. Chaucer was the son of a vintner, Marlowe the son of a shoemaker, Spenser the son of a linen draper,

Donne the son of an iron-monger, Milton the son of a scrivener, and so it goes. Some of the sires were more prosperous than others, but few indeed were aristocrats. To be the son of a Stratford glove-maker was not poetically disabling. . . .

Finally it must be pointed out that Shakespeare's education was also quite typical. Most of the popular authors were products of the Latin grammar schools, and when we cannot find their names in the registers it is because we cannot find the registers. Of over twenty playwrights who first emerge with Shakespeare in the Fifteen Nineties, only three or four had university training. The learned Ben Jonson was self-taught during a youth spent in bricklaying, **[p. 10]** soldiering and acting. George Chapman could translate Homer, and Michael Drayton poetize a vast body of English lore without benefit of advanced formal education. . . .

If we look then for the basis of doubt about Shakespeare's authorship, some small bit of evidence however exaggerated, some tiny point of departure, we find no basis, no evidence, no point of departure whatever. His claim to his works is of the same nature and validity as Hemingway's claim to his, and although there is a mathematical chance that "The Old Man and the Sea" was really written by Einstein or the Duke of Windsor, it seems scarcely worth gambling upon. Neither about Shakespeare nor any of his contemporaries is there a hint of the kind of hoax that has been postulated, and although "ghost-writing" has now become prevalent, the occasions are fairly predictable: our statesmen and generals do not write the pieces signed by our journalists.

The score of elaborate "cases" presented in hundreds of thick treatises may be summarized in a single sentence: "The plays are learned and aristocratic, and must therefore have been written by a scholar like Bacon or an aristocrat like Oxford, not by an ignorant peasant like Shakespeare." The charm of the statement is that it is equally false in all its parts.

Shakespeare's plays are not *learned*. They were viewed as the reverse in their own day and for a century later. For Jonson Shakespeare "wanted art" (that is, lacked the training now commemorated in the term "Bachelor of Arts"); for Milton he was "fancy's child"; for Dryden he was *naturally* learned—"he needed not the spectacles of books." The myth of his vast learning arose in the eighteenth century when his mounting prestige made him seem a desirable member of any man's club and the scholars got in first with their bid—not the great scholars like Dr. Johnson or Edmond Malone but the pseudo-scholars like Charles Gildon (1665-1724) or the narrow ones like John Upton (1707-1760). By claiming for

Shakespeare all sorts of recondite learning they displayed their own, until the myth exploded of absurdity.

For instance, it was finally demonstrated that Shakespeare's Roman plays derived from a popular translation of Plutarch, abiding even by its misprints of place-names, as compared with Jonson's "Sejanus" and "Catiline," which derived from a fund of classical knowledge fortified by research. . . . So far as booklearning is concerned, the dispute of the eighteenth century led finally to the endorsement of the earlier opinion, that Shakespeare was a reasonably well-read man but far from being a scholar, and the impulse to bid him in passed to other professions and sects. (He has since been claimed by all, not excluding the sexual psychopaths. Lawyers have been especially diligent, and a fair number of physicians have even conferred upon him the diseases in which they specialize.)

When the myth of learning was abandoned by the scholars, it was taken up by the less literate general public, and we can understand the reasons why. The plays *looked* learned. Their classical allusions were imposing to those with education more limited than that provided by the Stratford grammar school, and their poetic idiom seemed increasingly esoteric as the Elizabethan age receded. More important, however, is the fact that the age of idolatry had dawned. Idolatry may be defined as veneration of an object without reference to its nature or value. In non-primitive societies it often takes the form of adulation by hearsay. Shakespeare was venerated. Learning was venerated. Shakespeare had been edited and discussed by learned men. The situation favored the germination of a cult, and an idolatrous fusion occurred.

In 1769 someone said that the plays must have been written not by any actor but by the most learned man of their time. In 1848 the claim was reasserted. A decade later books began to appear on the subject and the floodgates opened. The hundreds of Baconian treatises and thousands of Baconian converts, actually organized into societies and issuing periodicals, can be explained only in terms of the *Zeitgeist*. The late nineteenth century was peculiarly linked to the spirit of Francis Bacon, apostle of scientific progress and composer of moral maxims. Surely a predisposing sentiment, some underlying emotion, was working in favor of this particular candidate at this particular time. The rise and fall of the Baconian cult should alert us to the implications of its successor. That rival candidates would be named might be taken for granted; the interesting question is why the favored candidate should now be an aristocrat instead of a scholar.

Shakespeare's plays are even less *aristocratic* than learned. They are noble in a metaphoric sense but no other, as may easily be determined by comparing them with contemporary plays written by such authentic noblemen as the Earl of Stirling, the Earl of Rochester, Lord Brooke, and others—neo-classical works of a uniformly dignified dullness. . . . [p. 11] Of course, Shakespeare's plays feature kings and noblemen; they may *look* aristocratic, but the decisive factor is that for many they remain simply a detached symbol of value. Let the aristocrat succeed the savant as a twin object of veneration and the situation favors a new cult, a new fusion of idolatries.

In 1907 the Earl of Rutland was nominated as the "real" Shakespeare, in 1919 the Earl of Derby, and in 1920 the Earl of Oxford. There have also been a countess, several barons, and sundry knights. . . . If a nobleman is wanted, the Earl of Oxford is about the best one can do. . . . Seventeenth in descent from the ancient nobility, he was almost a museum piece among the "new men" of the day; he was also humorless, bigoted, and morally confused. . . .

The book in which Oxford was first nominated (J. T. Looney, "The Real Shakespeare," 1920) is much cleverer than Mr. Hoffman's, but otherwise true to type. After denigrating Shakespeare, his relatives, his town and all its ways, it applies the Conan Doyle technique of inverted deduction, although without Doyle's charming awareness of charlatanry. When the mud-spatter on the trouser-cuff leads Holmes to the inspired conclusion that his visitor must have sat at the side of his hansom cab instead of in the center, and must therefore have left a companion waiting in it down there on Baker Street, Doyle knew that he was giving Holmes back-stage assistance. He knew that the mud-spatter might be explainable in less relevant ways, but he also knew that Watson (and the reader) would accept its validity as a clue the moment the companion was produced. "Holmes, this is marvelous!"

The Earl of Oxford, of course, is *produced*. Was he not, as the author of these plays must have been, familiar with music, with Italy, with falconry, with this and with that? Above all with *aristocratic ways!* By this process it would be boringly easy to prove that the plays were written by Winston Churchill. All such books are riddled with factual misrepresentation such as the casual reader is ill-equipped to detect, but one would suppose that anyone educated enough to be interested would be able to detect critical incompetence and the elementary non sequitur.

The thinning ranks of Baconians are desperately asserting that their candidate was of *royal* blood, but no one—certainly not Mr. Hoffman with poor Marlowe—will stem the Oxfordian groundswell.

Societies are organizing, periodicals being launched, and an amazing number of people sagely remarking that "there must be something in it." Just what underlying emotion, what predisposing sentiment, in such bulwarks of democracy as England and America is making it easier to associate any kind of excellence with the son of an earl, rather than the son of a glove-maker, must be left to the social analysts to decide.

In the face of all this it is becoming fashionable in some quarters to say that it doesn't matter who wrote the plays. It does matter. The truth always matters, and the habit of playing games with it is contagious. The Holmes technique is being used and tolerated in fields of literary research that were formerly marked by a quiet reliability. . . . Most important of all, we cannot look with complacence upon things of beauty being debased into clues, cryptograms, and puerile topicalities. Under such erosion what happens to our precious heritages? Questioning their origin is halfway to questioning their existence, or at least their claim to one's attention. . . .[15]

1955 *The Saturday Review*, "Was Marlowe the Bard?" July 9, 1955, No. 28, Vol. 38, p. 16, by G. B. Harrison.

[p. 16] Calvin Hoffman's purpose in "The Murder of the Man Who Was 'Shakespeare' " is to "prove" that Christopher Marlowe wrote the works attributed to William Shakespeare.

* * *

It can hardly be expected that in a work of fictionalized approximation the author should be so pedantic as to provide page references to his authorities, a list of works consulted, or even an index, but if Mr. Hoffman expects to be taken seriously by students he must at least play the game according to the rules. Until he can produce some definite and verifiable evidence that someone saw Marlowe alive after May 30, 1593 his case for Marlowe's authorship of Shakespeare's plays is not worth examination.

However, Mr. Hoffman does add by way of appendix thirty pages of parallelisms between Marlowe and Shakespeare. Some are very slight and far-fetched; others quite striking. They confirm the

[15] Mr. Hoffman's rebuttal to the statements made above by Mr. Harbage will be found in the "Postscript" of the 1960 Grosset and Dunlap edition of Calvin Hoffman's *The Murder of the Man Who was 'Shakespeare.'*

known fact that William Shakespeare belonged to the Magnificent Race of Borrowers, and that he had a keen sense for the value and the use of a telling phrase.

1956 *Time* Magazine, May 14, 1956, Vol. LXVII, No. 20, p. 37.

[p. 37] Empty Theory

To many a zealous amateur scholar it is unthinkable, for reasons not always clear, that Dramatist William Shakespeare should have written his own plays. Some have preferred to credit Sir Francis Bacon, others the Earl of Oxford, the Earl of Rutland or the Earl of Derby. Some 20 years ago a Broadway press agent named Calvin Hoffman dug up another old theory: the true author was the dissolute young genius Christopher Marlowe. Marlowe, so this one goes, was not killed in that famous tavern brawl; he simply went into hiding and as an outlaw wrote the plays since credited to Shakespeare. Proof of this theory, Hoffman figured, might well be found in the tomb of Marlowe's benefactor Sir Thomas Walsingham, who was laid to rest some three centuries ago in the parish Church at Chislehurst, Kent.

For three years Hoffman plagued church authorities and Sir Thomas' descendants for permission to open the tomb. Last year, amid the storm of controversy that followed publication of Hoffman's book *The Murder of the Man Who Was "Shakespeare,"* consent was reluctantly given. Last week Sir Thomas' tomb was opened. "We found sand. No coffin, no papers—just sand," reported the crest-fallen Hoffman. Added the London *News Chronicle:* "Alas, not even poor Yorick."

Anne Whateley as Shakespeare

Introduction

Queen Elizabeth, Mary Queen of Scots, Anne Hathaway, Anne Whateley, the Countess of Pembroke, and the Countess of Rutland have all been offered either as the sole author or as one of a number collaborating on the writing of the Shakespeare poems and plays. A female Shakespeare is one way of explaining the uniquely feminine qualities some theorists have perceived in the works. Such qualities can be achieved, proponents of Shakespeare-as-female argue, only by one who was a woman, since men are not capable of understanding the complexities of the female mind.

One of the most recent studies, George E. Sweet's *Shake-Speare the Mystery* (1956), offers Queen Elizabeth as the author, though she (like Oxford) died some years before a number of the Shakespeare plays are thought to have been written.

One of the most interesting theories is that Shakespeare was written by Anne Whateley, the Englishwoman who was entered on the Register of the Bishop of Worcester, on November 27, 1582, for a marriage license with a man identified in the Register's Latin only as one "wm Shaxpere."

1939 *The Story of Anne Whateley and William Shaxpere* by William Ross, W. and R. Holmes, Glasgow.

[p. 9] It is now over eighty years since doubts were first expressed that William Shaxpere, or Shagspere, of Stratford-on-Avon wrote the poems and plays published under the name of William Shakespeare.

* * *

[p. 10] Construed along with the known facts of William Shaxpere's life, the story that emerges is self-evident proof of the existence and identity of [a] "concealed poet". . . . [p. 11] The great unknown genius . . . was Anne Whateley of Hillborough in the Parish of Temple Grafton, Warwickshire.

Her name is preserved in Bishop Whitgift's register at Worcester. An entry, dated 27th November, 1582, records that a licence was granted for a marriage between William Shaxpere and Ann Whateley of Temple Grafton. The marriage had been arranged, but did not take place. Instead, William Shaxpere married Anne Hathaway of Shottery in the Parish of Stratford, in December, 1582.

The events preceding and subsequent to Shaxpere's marriage are told by the "Sonnets to Mr. W. H." The key to the correct understanding of the story implicit in them is the sex of the writer. The text, as first published in 1609 and extant in modern English to-day, conveys that the sonnets were written by a man to a youth. This is incorrect. The truth is that they were written by a young lady, Anne Whateley, and that the youth to whom they were addressed, and whose beauty and worth are immortalised by them, was William Shaxpere of Stratford.

For a proper understanding of "The Sonnets" it is necessary, therefore, to revert to their original wording as written, not as published. Certain verbal changes have accordingly been made in eight of the sonnets reprinted in this book, viz., 32, 34, 38, 73, 89, 118, 145, and 151. The changes, for the most part, consist of the substitution of "she" and "her" for the masculine equivalents "he," "him," and "his."

Out of the events related by "The Sonnets" came, as an ultimate sequel, "The Works of William Shakespeare" with Shaxpere as the reputed author. The "concealed poet," Anne Whateley, remained concealed. The publication [p. 12] of her work under masculine authorship meant that her genius was able to achieve its own freedom of expression, which, in the sixteenth century, would have been hampered by convention had she attempted to write under her own name. In addition to this difficulty, the special circumstances of her life, circumscribed by bitter religious antagonisms, made concealment imperative. Afterwards, her selfless devotion to Shaxpere brought the solution of the problem into harmony with her most cherished desires.

The change of name from Shaxpere, or Shagspere, to Shakespeare was significant. The new name represented two people, and on one occasion at least, appended to "The Phoenix and the Turtle," it was spelt with a hyphen—"single nature's double name." While the conception and story of "The Sonnets" remain as originally written, it was necessary, when publication was in contemplation, to change the sex of the writer in order to maintain the masculinity of the Shakespearean authorship.

"Mr. W. H." was Shaxpere, and the "black" woman was Anne Hathaway, his wife.

The sonnets are Anne Whateley's record of the "triangle" in which all three were involved. "A Lover's Complaint," which was included in the original volume containing "The Sonnets," is Anne Hathaway's story of how she was wooed and deserted by Shaxpere. It, too, of course, was written by Anne Whateley. She was the listener on the hill who overheard and recorded Anne Hathaway's "Complaint." The reason why "The Sonnets" and "A Lover's Complaint" were published together is now clear. The same events are depicted from the viewpoints of two of the principle [*sic*] persons concerned in them.

* * *

[**p. 13**] In examining the sonnets individually, it seemed impossible that 36, beginning—"Let me confess that we two must be twain," or 39 should have been written by one man to another. Both sonnets seemed to imply that a contemplated marriage had been abandoned. If this were so, the writer must have been feminine and the person addressed masculine, or vice versa. The fourth line of 86 ["Making their tomb the womb wherein they grew?"] contains a metaphor which would not suggest itself to a man, but which would not be strangely unnatural coming from a woman. The exact meaning of the last line of 26 ["Till then, not show my head where thou mayst prove me."] was very puzzling, until its implication of the veil was caught by a comparison with the conversation between Isabella and Francisca the nun in "Measure for Measure," Act I. Scene v. 13. The various religious allusions in "The Sonnets" then began to assume importance. The writer was apparently a religieuse, and "Mr. W. H." was most probably Shaxpere. Their identity [**p. 14**] with the "sister sanctified, of holiest note" and the youth in "A Lover's Complaint" became a distinct possibility.

With this information it was not difficult to interpret the sonnets, so far, in terms of Shaxpere's early life already known.

At 127, however, the person addressed abruptly changes to a woman:—"my mistress' eyes are raven black." Was this a break in the story, a new theme from a masculine point of view? The mixture of pleading and condemnation in the succeeding sonnets, too, was bewildering. At this stage, the significance of "the marriage of true minds"—116—became clearer. Anne Whateley was writing of Anne Hathaway. Shaxpere she worshipped with all the intensity of her being. The spiritual marriage had sealed her oneness with him, therefore his wife was her "mistress." Her sense of identification with Shaxpere was so dominant that she writes, in sonnet 136, "my name is Will." She was endeavouring to create a friendship, or at least a state of tolerance between herself and Anne Hathaway, that would permit of unconstrained contacts with Shaxpere. She pleads and condemns, however, in vain. The antipathy between the two women was too great to be overcome. They were poles apart. The experimental "marriage of true minds" was at first a failure, and resulted in estrangement. "The Sonnets to Mr. W. H." end on this note.

Many of the sonnets were sent or given to Shaxpere as explanations, answers, or love-letters as they were written. One or two, specially selected, may even have been read to Anne Hathaway as a gesture of friendship. The series as a whole, however, was Anne Whateley's private reaction, stage by stage, to the events concerning her as they occurred, and, when Shaxpere decided to leave his wife and Stratford, the complete set of sonnets was given to him, "the well-wishing adventurer in setting forth."

* * *

[p. 15] The idea of a lady living the life of a nun in England, forty years after the complete dissolution of the monasteries in 1540, is, perhaps, at first sight rather surprising. It must be remembered, however, that under the reign of Mary I there had been substantial restoration of Catholicism as the national religion. The anti-Catholic measures of Elizabeth's reign were at first largely inoperative. . . .

Towards the end of Elizabeth's reign, in spite of the severe persecution, or, indeed, it may be because of it, the Catholic faith, especially in the North and Midlands of England, had recovered something of its former prestige. . . . Half the population was recusant or openly Roman Catholic. The active renaissance of the old faith culminated [p. 16] in the Gunpowder Plot of 1603. Catesby and his confederates made use of Clopton House, near Stratford, for their meetings. The residence of Anne Whateley and her sister nuns in the parish of Temple Grafton was thus situated at the very heart of Roman Catholic England.

The discipline under which they lived does not appear to have been rigid and strict as in the heyday of monasticism. The minoresses, however, were generally veiled when meeting or speaking to members of the opposite sex; there were fixed hours for meals, devotions, and absence from the house. The ladies lived in accordance with the rule of their order, and had taken the usual vows of chastity, poverty, and obedience.

Anne Whateley's sonnets, however, show that she was not an ardent believer in religious form, e.g. 125. She was a Roman Catholic because she, to all intents and purposes an orphan, had been brought up under its influence. Nevertheless, the decision, afterwards revoked, to forswear her vows taken in the ignorance of early years and to marry Shaxpere, must have meant for her a tremendous mental strain. The fact that she was under vows suggests that she was educated in some convent school abroad, the cult of the nunnery having become illegal in England.

* * *

[p. 18] In the year 1581, William Shaxpere, a youth seventeen years of age, was employed in his father's business. His schooldays at Stratford Grammar School were over. His father, John Shaxpere, according to the accepted tradition, was a butcher, a wool dealer, or a glover. Probably his business combined all three callings.

William, as his father's representative, travelled the countryside around Stratford collecting orders and delivering goods previously ordered. . . .

One of his places of call was a secluded country house in the parish of Temple Grafton, a few miles west of Stratford-on-Avon.

* * *

[p. 19] It was then the home of a small coterie of nuns. The sisterhood may have belonged to the Order of St. Clare. . . .

The nuns were interested in their youthful visitor. His personal beauty, cheerful smile and ready wit, came into their secluded lives like sunshine. Behind the veils, feminine eyes appraised his good looks and engaging ways. With one of the sisters especially, conversation had become easy [p. 20] and interesting. . . .

One day, in the spring of 1582, when he was making his usual call, this sister handed him a note. It was for himself; something she had written for him. At leisure Master Will pondered over the written message. Slowly and with some difficulty he read it; it was a very surprising communication, and consisted of a verse of poetry:—

I

From fairest creatures we desire increase,
That thereby beauty's rose might never die,
But as the riper should by time decease,
His tender heir might bear his memory:
But thou, contracted to thine own bright eyes,
Feed'st thy light's flame with self-substantial fuel,
Making a famine where abundance lies,

Thyself thy foe, to thy sweet self too cruel.
Thou that art now the world's fresh ornament
And only herald to the gaudy spring,
Within thine own bud buriest thy content
And, tender churl, mak'st waste in niggarding.
  Pity the world, or else this glutton be,
  To eat the world's due, by the grave and thee.

The thoughts expressed by the sonnet were no doubt in accord with his own secret inner urgings. He was on the verge of manhood, and vague, alluring dreams of the future had begun to colour his thoughts. . . . The veiled lady was a surprising creature. He was pleased and flattered that a woman of a serious way of life should think it worth her while to compose a poem for him.

* * *

[p. 22] A confidential friendship thus having been begun, more sonnets followed, and were given to him from time to time as he revisited the house on his father's business. The theme is always the same, himself, his beauty, and his obligations to himself and humanity to leave an heir, or better still, ten children that will leave him "living in posterity."

* * *

[p. 41] One morning in August, 1582, Anne Whateley left her home to meet Will Shaxpere. The meeting was a prearranged one. They met in the warm mellow sunshine of early Autumn, but later the sky became overcast and rain spoiled the earlier promise of the day. That occasioned some temporary discomfort. Worse was to follow.

Will confessed that he had been untrue to her, and also to himself, as she knew him. In the course of his travels round the countryside he had made the acquaintance of Anne Hathaway, daughter of a farmer at Shottery, about one mile from Stratford. She was considerably older than he. He was interested, led on, attracted, and, in a moment of passionate dalliance, the hot blood of youth prevailed over every consideration except that of the immediate present. In the reaction that followed, he confessed his fault with tears and remorse. His listener, wiser than he, faced the situation with tender understanding. She was not entirely blameless. Had she not, in her self-considered aloofness from the temptations of the flesh, advised him in seventeen sonnets to beget an heir? He had acted on her advice unwisely and too well.

* * *

[p. 60] He was aware, however, of the power he exercised over her [i.e., Anne Whateley]. If he married her, the marriage with Anne Hathaway could not take place.

Apparently he succeeded in persuading her to revoke her sworn allegiance to the Church in order to save him from the consequences of his own folly, because, on 27th November, 1582, a licence was granted sanctioning the marriage of William Shaxpere and Anne Whateley of Temple Grafton. . . .

The Hathaway family and sympathisers, however, were on the alert. On the very next day a bond was executed, under penalty, by Fulk Sandells and John Richardson, indemnifying the Bishop of Worcester and his officers against any lawful impediment to the marriage of William Shagspere and Anne Hathaway of Stratford in the Diocese of Worcester, maiden.

* * *

[p. 61] Faced with this situation, the idea of marriage with Anne Whateley had to be abandoned. Anne Whateley was filled with despair and suffered a deep sense of injury. In Shaxpere's union with Anne Hathaway she sees all her values reversed. She is dismayed at what the future holds in store for him—his soul corrupted in a squalid domesticity. Death would be welcome, but for the fact that he would be left to face life, and such a life, alone.[1]

* * *

[p. 66] Shaxpere has been married to Anne Hathaway. Anne Whateley recovered from the illness that resulted from, or was aggravated by, the marriage and the strain that had preceded it.

The next group of sonnets—75 to 96—was written during the year 1583. Shaxpere apparently was lost to her. She left Temple Grafton shortly after the marriage and moved about from place to place. She appears to have paid a visit to Spenser in Ireland. It is possible that she may have lived at Polesworth for part of the time and that there she made the acquaintance of Drayton.

A phase of dissimulation followed. Anne Whateley hid the sorrow in her heart by assuming an outward gaiety of demeanour. Her circle of friends grew. She was in close touch with the members of the Areopagus Club of which Sir Philip Sidney was president; she added verses to their efforts, and mended the style of many an aspiring poet. The one supreme subject of poetry at the time was love, and many of the young poets fell in love with their fair

[1] Ross quotes sonnets 66, 67 and 68 as expressions of Anne Whateley's despair —the editors.

mentor. They wrote of her and to her in the sonnet sequences that became the fashion. They sang the praises of her beauty and brilliance of mind, and bewailed the coldness of her invincible chastity at the same time. . . .

While absent from Temple Grafton she wrote for Spenser, one of her oldest friends. During this time and later Sir Walter Raleigh, Drayton, Marlowe, and many others also secured feathers from the wings of the Phoenix.

* * *

[p. 100] Anne Whateley's first contact with Mistress Shaxpere did not leave a favourable impression. In ancient times, black was not considered beautiful, she writes, or, if it were, it was known by some name other than beauty. Now, however, black has succeeded in taking possession of Beauty. Beauty, in the person of Will Shaxpere, has been slandered in the birth of his daughter, Susanna. Mistress Shaxpere attempts to improve on Nature by painting her face. She is ambidextrous in the art of making-up. In her countenance sweet beauty has no sanctuary, if, indeed, it is not disgraced. In harmony with this sad state of affairs, Mistress Shaxpere's eyes are raven black. They are like mourners for those plain-born ones, who do not miss the good looks that were never theirs. Her mournful black eyes falsify everything they behold with an affectation of esteem. Notwithstanding this merciless first analysis of Mistress Shaxpere, Anne Whateley admits that she was everywhere considered prepossessing. The contrast between Shaxpere and his wife in Anne Whateley's eyes, is extreme—he, "a man in hue, all hues in his controlling" (sonnet 20), she, black.

127

In the old age black was not counted fair,
Or if it were, it bore not beauty's name;
But now is black beauty's successive heir,
And beauty slander'd with a bastard shame:
For since each hand hath put on Nature's power,
Faring the foul with Art's false borrow'd face,
Sweet beauty hath no name, no holy bower,
But is profan'd, if not lives in disgrace.
[p. 101] Therefore my mistress' eyes are raven black,
Her eyes so suited, and they mourners seem
At such who, not born fair, no beauty lack,
Sland'ring creation with a false esteem:
Yet so they mourn, becoming of their woe,
That every tongue says beauty should look so.

* * *

[p. 122] Shaxpere was "the only begetter" of the sonnets, because he was Anne Whateley's lover and consort in their spiritual union. The sonnets were first written without thought of publication. When it was decided to print them, a dedication to "Mr. W. S." was incompatible with the policy of concealment. The second letter of "Shaxpere" was therefore substituted for the initial letter of the name. By a singular coincidence, "W" and "H" happen to be the surname initials of the two women concerned with Shaxpere in the story told by the sonnets. The initials, therefore, represent all three, and no better selection was possible. . . .

A Group Theory: Bacon, Oxford, and Shakespeare as Shakespeare

Introduction

The most popular general theory of the anti-Stratfordians is that the works of Shakespeare were composed by a group of collaborators. Some group theorists assign Shakespeare a role as partial author or editor of the works; others insist he provided only a name. But in each case, the theory is based on the assumption that no one man could have possessed all the literary and intellectual gifts necessary to write the poems and plays. A group theory, for example, that Bacon provided the legal knowledge in the plays, while Raleigh, Marlowe, or others provided the literary genius, thereby accounts for the impossibly diverse styles, the differing methods of expression, the massive vocabulary, and the wide legal, medical, theological, scientific, and psychological knowledge that group theorists find in Shakespeare.

One group theory has suggested that the Jesuits wrote Shakespeare, an explanation which accounts for what its author identifies as unmistakable Roman Catholic elements in the Shakespeare plays. Perhaps the most extreme, and certainly the most difficult to refute, is Percy Allen's theory that Shakespeare was written principally by Oxford with assistance from Shakespeare, Bacon, Beaumont, Fletcher, Raleigh, and others, a theory Allen has based on evidence he took from voices beyond the grave.

No Date (1945 or 1946)

Talks With Elizabethans Revealing the Mystery of "William Shakespeare," by Percy Allen, Rider & Company, 68 Fleet Street, London, E. C. 4, pp. 98, 120-1, 131.

[The following selection from Percy Allen's book records his conversations with the spirits of a number of dead Elizabethans. *"P. A."* is the author, Percy Allen. *"F. B."* is Francis Bacon, *"W. S."* is William Shakespeare, *"OX."* is Lord Oxford, and *"Johannes"* is a spiritual intermediary who passed information from the Elizabethans to a medium named Mrs. Dowden, who recorded the conversations for Mr. Allen—the editors.]

[p. 98] *First Conversation with Francis Bacon, Lord Verulam*

October 5, 1944.

Johannes. I have made an arrangement by which Bacon can speak to you. I have been able to be sure he will send the message personally. . . .

P.A. Thank you for coming. I ask permission to put to you some questions which have arisen during the course of my Shakespearean studies. First of all: Did you, or did you not, write any or all of the plays of Shakespeare?

F.B. I wrote none of the plays; but I was fortunate in being consulted frequently. A circle of interested persons was formed; and I had the honour of being one of those. I also acted as critic and adviser. You understand. It was a case of joint authorship.

P.A. Can you name the principal author of the plays?

F.B. I must make it clear to you that William Shakespeare, the actor, was also author, in some cases; but he collaborated with others; and in some cases the plays were suggested by literary men, who were outside our circle.

P.A. Had Lord Oxford any share whatever in writing any of the plays?

F.B. Oxford was largely the author; and he had a lively and original mind; *but* you must bear in mind that he always collaborated with Shakespeare.

P.A. By *Shakespeare,* I understand you to mean Will. Shakspere of Stratford?

F.B. The name he bears, which has made him famous, was deserved.

P.A. Was there, then, an understanding concerning collaboration between Lord Oxford and Shakespeare?

F.B. Yes, there was friendship and sympathy between them. Shakespeare would suggest a plot—as a rule he chose the subject matter —and Oxford would construct and elaborate. Then my opinion was asked, but accepted in only a few cases.

* * *

[p. 120] *First Conversation with William Shakespeare*

February 26, 1945.

Johannes. What do you wish for today?

P.A. First I wish to thank you warmly for having obtained for me the talks with Lord Verulam, which have been most interesting and valuable. Last time you said, though it would probably be difficult, you would, if possible, get me through to William Shakespeare of Stratford-on-Avon, with a view to obtaining a message from or a talk with him.

Johannes. The Shakespeare who heads the company in name was very unwilling to come. He consented finally, and will answer questions. He is not at all a stupid man, remember.

William Shakespeare (*sic*). Why should I be called to answer for the company?

P.A. Thank you for consenting to come. The reason why I asked you was that, having obtained information direct from Lord Verulam, I much wished to have some corroboration from you. Not that I doubt, at all, the truth of *F.B.'s* statements; but "in the mouths of many witnesses truth shall be established". We want *only* truth!

W.S. I am willing.

P.A. First, do you concur in *F.B.'s* statement that you are personally responsible for, and actually wrote, certain parts of certain Shakesperean plays?

W.S. I am responsible for parts of the plays, and for suggestions as to production of the plays.

P.A. I was told by *F.B.* that, in addition to S-n plays, you also wrote a part of *Sir Thomas More*. Do you concur?

W.S. Sir Thomas More. I took a small part in this, and much interest.

P.A. Many of our scholars here think that a part of that play, which we possess in *MS.*, is in your handwriting. Do you concur? *F.B.* told me that it *was* your handwriting.

W.S. No. I know many of the group believed it was in my writing, but it remained a mystery; and I assert it is *not* my handwriting.

P.A. Concerning your will and other documents still extant purporting to be signed by you, are these your own signatures?

W.S. Yes, these are; but I had to use a writing which was a copy of another's. [p. 121]

P.A. Why had you to do this?

W.S. It was but reasonable that the signature of my will should correspond with the signature of the writer of the plays.

P.A. Who *was* this mysterious writer?

W.S. I hesitate here; but I may perhaps describe him as an older brother playwright.[1]

P.A. Well, I will not press that question further at the moment. You tell me that you helped to produce the plays, as well as to write them. At what theatre did you do this?

W.S. I refer to the Globe, and other theatres.

P.A. Did you work with Lord Oxford?

W.S. *Yes,* undoubtedly. I was quick at knowing what would be effective *on* the stage. I would find a plot, consult with Oxford, form a skeleton edifice which he would furnish and people, as befitted the subject.

* * *

[p. 131] *First Conversation with Lord Oxford*

April 9, 1945.

Johannes. The man Shaxpere is here again! Do you want him, or do you prefer to speak to Oxford?

P.A. Delighted to speak with either; but in the circumstances I must give preference to Lord Oxford.

OX. Very willing; but embarrassed by difficult conditions. O!

P.A. Is this Lord Oxford communicating now?

OX. Yes; but speaking through a cloud. I am glad to come, if I can make matters plainer for you.

P.A. I am delighted to have the opportunity. Lord Verulam and Will Shakspere have been talking with me about the *Shakespeare* mystery. Some corroboration from you will be most valuable and interesting.

OX. Verulam does not lie; nor does the actor Shaxpere, a good friend of mine. I am glad to corroborate what they have told you; and I understand you have questions to ask? I am not a strong and forceable man like Shaxpere; but I have love on my side—love of the theatre and love of words.

P.A. Your work has won you much love here, including long and deep affection from myself.

OX. Now my work was but the filling of a frame, in most cases. I

[1] There is often, at first, some reluctance to mentioning names. *W.S.* means Lord Oxford. [Author's note.]

would have you know that I never wrote a play from the beginning to the end. I filled in the framework.

P.A. That framework, I take it, being supplied, in most cases, by Will Shakspere of Stratford—the trained actor, and man of the theatre?

OX. Yes, in most cases. He was an entertaining rogue. He was filled with tales and stories, which were not all given out as he had heard them first, but embellished for his hearers.

Edward de Vere, the Earl of Oxford, as Shakespeare

Introduction

The most popular anti-Stratfordian theory of the twentieth century is that "Shakespeare" was written by Edward de Vere, the Earl of Oxford. The idea first appeared in print in 1920 in *'Shakespeare' Identified in Edward de Vere,* a book by an English schoolmaster named J. Thomas Looney, who believed that only Oxford had the necessary birth, breeding, learning, and experience to qualify as the man of broad genius who wrote the plays and poems.

Since then, Oxfordians have produced a vast number of books and articles in support of their candidate, and many have joined the Shakespeare Fellowship, a society devoted to investigating and publishing information on the authorship controversy.

Most effective—and longest—of the arguments for Oxford is Dorothy and Charlton Ogburn's *This Star of England* (1952), which devotes 1300 pages to examining the "Shakespeare hoax" and presenting evidence supporting the Oxford theory.

Most prominent in the evidence which Oxfordians have arrayed in favor of their candidate are answers to the major objection made by orthodox Shakespeare scholars: that *Macbeth, King Lear, Antony and Cleopatra, The Tempest,* among other plays, were written after 1604, the date of Oxford's death.

1940 *Harper's Magazine,* Vol. 181, July, 1940, "Shakespeare Himself," pp. 172-185, by Oscar James Campbell.

[p. 172] "Who was Shakespeare?" The question is spread as a banner across the cover of *The Scientific American* for January,

1940. The answer, though not explicitly stated, is clearly to be inferred from an article by Charles Wisner Barrell. "Shakespeare," Mr. Barrell would say, "was Edward de Vere, the seventeenth earl of Oxford." His proof is contained in an essay entitled "Identifying Shakespeare." By way of giving a new identity to the greatest poet in the English tongue, the author describes the disclosures of x-ray and infra-red photography as applied to one of the so-called portraits of Shakespeare—the picture generally known as the Ashbourne portrait. His investigations have revealed the fact that at some "remote period" an inferior artist painted over or altered many details of the original picture. This botcher raised the forehead by an inch or so, retouched the hair to make it match the synthetic forehead, greatly reduced the size of the neck ruff, and scraped out the original inscription in order that he might scrawl in its place *"Aetatis Suae 47. Anno 1611,"* a date that could be neatly fitted into the facts of Shakespeare's life.

But these revelations serve only as the prelude to others much more important; for the camera uncovered also two insignia which identify the subject of the original portrait as Edward de Vere, seventeenth earl of Oxford. The first of these clues is an armorial device appearing on a ring worn on the man's left thumb. It proves to be the head of a wild boar, an emblem worn by the Earl in one of his authentic portraits. A second piece of evidence, heretofore hidden beneath the daubs of the bungling workman, is a crest of the Trentham family, to which Oxford's second wife belonged. In providing that his wife's crest and shield be painted into his own portrait the noble lord followed an approved convention.

Mr. Barrell's x-ray photography has uncovered also the monogram of the original artist, a "C.K.," which proves to be identical with the monogram used by Cornelius Ketel, a famous Dutch painter of the late sixteenth and early seventeenth centuries. Fortunately we know from excellent contemporary sources that Ketel painted a portrait of the Earl of Oxford. . . .

Mr. Barrell's evidence is so clear and so cogent that it is impossible to question seriously the truth of his main contention. It seems probable that at some time before the middle of the nineteenth century an unknown painter altered a number of details in a portrait of the Earl of Oxford in order to pass it off as a likeness of William Shakespeare.

Granted that this is true, has the fact of the alteration any value as evidence of [p. 173] Oxford's authorship of Shakespeare's works? Mr. Barrell's logic, stated succinctly, runs somewhat as follows: The Ashbourne portrait of Shakespeare is really a likeness of the Earl of

Oxford. Therefore the Earl of Oxford wrote Shakespeare's plays.

But Mr. Barrell's argument is not so straightforward as this. He wishes us to believe that the alterations in Oxford's portrait were made soon after Shakespeare's death, as part of an elaborate program of concealment and roguish mystification. According to his theory, someone who knew Oxford to be the real author of Shakespeare's works had the picture doctored in order that it might serve as a model for the Stratford bust. In this way the earliest and most authentic of the supposed likenesses of Shakespeare was made half to reveal and half to conceal the identity of the true author of the plays. The weakness of Mr. Barrell's contention lies in the fact that the Ashbourne portrait came to light only in the year 1847. . . . [Its discoverer] expressed himself as having not "the slightest doubt of its genuineness." He did not, however, present a scrap of evidence to support his belief beyond the character of the painting itself and the fact that he owned it.

No competent authority on Shakespeare iconography has ever shared . . . [his] confidence in the authenticity of the Ashbourne portrait. They all agree that it belongs to what the late H. H. Spielman described as "portraits of persons known or unknown which have been fraudulently faked into a resemblance of Shakespeare." No authority has doubted that the Ashbourne portrait, which now proves to be a likeness of the Earl of Oxford, was doctored for the express purpose of cheating a gullible enthusiast . . . .

The fact seems to be that when, in the latter part of the eighteenth century, enthusiasm for Shakespeare was raised to idolatry, many of the devout were willing to pay a large sum for any sort of likeness of their divinity. Yet almost no one was able to distinguish between a genuine portrait of Shakespeare and a fraud. Such conditions are certain to tempt the unscrupulous; so it is not surprising that various art dealers in London hired hacks to doctor sixteenth-century portraits into some resemblance to the Stratford bust. This illicit trade seems to have lasted into the nineteenth century. The Ashbourne portrait is almost certainly one of those spurious works. That it proves to have been originally a portrait of the Earl of Oxford painted by a distinguished artist is an interesting fact; we now know that by the middle of the nineteenth century a faked likeness of Shakespeare had a much greater market value than a portrait of one of the proudest earls of Elizabethan England. But interesting though it may be, the discovery has no bearing at all upon the question of Edward de Vere's authorship of Shakespeare's plays.

* * *

[p. 175] We know that, besides being a successful author of comedies, Oxford was the patron of a number of companies of actors during the 1580's, and that he was also the patron of John Lyly during the years in which Lyly was writing his successful court comedies. Indeed, if we must find extant plays for Oxford to father, the most likely ones would be those attributed to his secretary, John Lyly.

* * *

II

Stratford was no collection of illiterate boors and yokels. It was an important center of trade, the business metropolis of a large and fertile area, and so of much greater relative importance than it is to-day. The grammar school there was one of the best in England, and during many years of its existence had been generously supported by the Guild of Merchants, of whom John Shakespeare, the poet's father, was one [p. 176] of the most influential members. The elder Shakespeare was a manufacturer of leather, a member of what was in those days a very important craft. We know that his business success gave him a position of social importance in the community, for in a catalogue of the gentlemen and freeholders of Warwick County John Shakespeare's name appears as sixth. He was also a man of prominence in local politics for he was a member of the common council and one of the two chamberlains, or treasurers, of the borough. Later he served as bailiff, or mayor, of the town. . . . Today a man who makes a cross instead of signing his name gives manifest proof of his illiteracy. But in the sixteenth century this was not so. When we first find a cross serving as a signature on legal documents it was used because of its significance as a religious symbol. As a representation of the Holy Cross it afforded proof that the man who made it was giving religious sanctity to the ceremony of affixing his name. It was regarded as the written equivalent of an oath. Far from being a device resorted to by men who could not write, we find that in the English charters it was used by abbots, bishops, and even kings. This religious usage continued from the Middle Ages into Queen Elizabeth's time, particularly in the villages. We know that it persisted in Stratford. For example, Adrian Quiny, the grandfather of one of Shakespeare's sons-in-law, followed this custom, in spite of the fact that he had considerable education. Numerous letters which he wrote to his son are extant, and so is a letter in Latin sent to him by his lawyer. Yet Quiny, like Shakespeare's father, signs local documents with a cross.

There is also some positive evidence to establish the literacy of

John Shakespeare. In January, 1564, the financial report of John Taylor and John Shakespeare was entered in the records of the town of Stratford. The clerk endorsed their document as follows: "John Taylor and John Shakespeare have made a true and lawful account for their time being Chamberlains." This statement surely means just what it says, that the two men had kept the public moneys and had rendered a satisfactory account of them. Apparently they did their job unusually well, for they continued to keep the accounts during the following year, although two other men held the office of chamberlains. This surely can mean nothing except that John Shakespeare and his colleague for two years kept the accounts of the town in their own handwriting.

During his son's youth John Shakespeare clearly prospered in business. In 1580 he fell into some difficulty with the law, probably because he refused to attend the services of the Church of England. Twelve years later his name definitely appears on a list of such recusants. He failed to appear in court to answer the summons, as did a friend for whom he gave security. Consequently he was fined forty pounds, a large sum in those days, and one which the court would never have named unless it had known the man to be well off. If a citizen of such importance did not send his son to the local school, from what families, pray, did the three hundred grammar schools in England draw their students? At the Stratford school the boys read much more Latin than even the best classical students in an American college of to-day. Since we know that Greek also was taught there, we may be sure that if Shakespeare stayed in school through the fifth form—or until he was fifteen or sixteen years old—he would have read Demosthenes, Isocrates, Hesiod, Heliodorus, and Dionysius Halicarnassus.

Ben Jonson, in the lines which he wrote **[p. 177]** to preface the First Folio editions of Shakespeare's plays, spoke of his friend's "small Latin and less Greek." The phrase, by the way, could not have been appropriately applied to the Earl of Oxford or to any of the other noble gentlemen accused of being ghost writers for the bard. Though Jonson had trained himself to be a good classical scholar, he would, nevertheless, have thought that any man who had never attended a University could have only a small knowledge of Latin. The extraordinary fact about Jonson's famous line is that it does not read "small Latin and *no* Greek." The phrase "less Greek" suggests strongly that Shakespeare stayed in the grammar school long enough at least to begin a study of that language.

Shakespeare's relations with Anne Hathaway cannot be entirely excused. . . . Troth plight was then a pre-contract of marriage performed before witnesses, and after it the pair could live together as man and wife without much scandal. It is possible that Shakespeare and Mistress Anne may have gone through the ceremony of troth plight, but on this subject we have no information. It is even possible that Anne Hathaway's first child may merely have been born prematurely.

It is very difficult to discover what Shakespeare did before he went to London about the year 1588. By far the most famous and the least credible story is the tale of his stealing deer. It appears first in a curious nondescript collection of memoranda left by Richard Davies, a clergyman, at his death in 1708. . . .

The unreliability of this tale can be read in almost every word which recounts it. Its source is unknown and it did not become a part of the Shakespeare tradition until about a hundred years after the poet's death—both strong reasons for considering it suspect. . . .

The whole story is probably the invention of some fertile-minded reader of "The Merry Wives of Windsor." In the first act of this play some jests about luces and louses on a coat of arms are closely followed by Shallow's accusation of Falstaff, in which he says, "You have beaten my men, kill'd my deer and broke open my lodge." To convert these lines into satiric allusions to Sir Thomas Lucy, some nameless critic created the story of the deer stealing in all its picturesque detail. It has no legitimate claim to be regarded as fact.

The most authentic tradition about Shakespeare's life before going to London is one that came from the Restoration actor William Beeston. He was the son of Christopher Beeston, who had been a member of Shakespeare's company and so his familiar associate for years. The report is set down by John Aubrey in his *Lives of Eminent Men* in these words: "Though as Ben Jonson says of him that he had but little Latin and less Greek, he understood Latin pretty well for he had been in his younger years a schoolmaster in the country." It will undoubtedly produce a revolution in the minds of most laymen to have the wild young man of legend subside into a serious-minded school teacher. Yet a son of one of Shakespeare's closest busi-[**p. 178**]ness associates was a much more reliable source of information about the dramatist's life than the senile old clerk at Stratford who seventy-seven years after Shakespeare's death told John Dowdall that Shakespeare was a butcher's apprentice who ran away from his master to London, and more reliable than other Stratford gossips who later still gave currency to the story of Shakespeare's prosecution by Sir Thomas Lucy for poaching on his estate. Besides, certain facts give this story of Beeston's a kind of innate probability. Certainly among the first plays that

Shakespeare wrote were "The Comedy of Errors" and "Titus Andronicus." The first is an imitation of Plautus, the second of Seneca. The works of both those Latin authors were studied in grammar schools, and plays written for the boys to act at school and at the University were modeled on those classics. Therefore, if a schoolmaster were to try his hand at dramatic composition, he would not be unlikely to begin with the sort of imitative work that we find in "The Comedy of Errors" and "Titus Andronicus."

* * *

III

He [i.e. William Shakespeare] had already become interested in new developments taking place in the vigorous young drama of the 1580's, and the leisure he could steal from his duties as pedagogue he devoted to writing plays. When he had finished two dramas to his satisfaction, a comedy in imitation of Plautus and a bloody tragedy in the approved Senecan manner, he took them up to London in the hope of selling them to one of the companies playing there. The actors, finding them to their liking, bought and produced both works. Indeed, they were so favorably impressed with these first heirs of his dramatic invention that they attached Shakespeare to their company. He became an assistant to their "bookkeeper," an official who combined the duties of librarian, prompter, and producer. This position gave Shakespeare all the practical experience a playwright could have wished. It enabled him to find out what Elizabethan audiences wanted and what parts the members of his company liked best to take. His next plays showed how well he had learned these lessons. In "Henry VI, Part I," he wrote the kind of patriotic drum-and-trumpet play that was just then enormously popular. His "Two Gentlemen of Verona" was a comedy in the familiar Italianate manner, with a good fat part in it for Will Kempe, the clown of the company and its [p. 179] most famous member. He pleased the actors so well that by 1592 Robert Greene complained that the young Warwickshire schoolmaster was taking the bread from the mouths of the University men engaged in making their living by writing for the stage. If the companies could get their plays from men who, like Shakespeare, were attached to the actors' organizations, Greene and his friends would lose their jobs. That is the reason for Greene's contemptuous reference to a fellow who thought himself "as well able to bombast out a blank verse line" as Greene and his friends, and "being an absolute Johannes Factotum" [that is, a Jack of all trades, assistant to the

Librarian and Producer, actor and playwright] "is in his own conceit, the only Shakescene in the country."

This passage, by the way, is applicable only to a man of the theater, and to no one of the noble gentlemen put forward as the author of Shakespeare's works. By 1598 our Johannes Factotum had advanced from imitator so far on the road to originality that Francis Meres considered him to be the greatest of the contemporary writers for the stage.

Such an account of Shakespeare's antecedents and early career is more in accordance with the facts as we now know them than is the old-fashioned tale of the illiterate runaway butcher's boy. It does not explain Shakespeare's transcendent qualities of poetic skill and imagination. The ways of genius have always been inexplicable. Ben Jonson began life as a bricklayer; John Keats was born in rooms above a livery stable; Johannes Brahms spent the formative years of his youth among the brothels of Hamburg. Shakespeare's career began much more auspiciously than the life of any one of these great artists. His early environment, far from being utterly mean and uncouth, was one which might easily have nourished a man of literary genius. Certainly there was nothing about it to start a horde of attorneys-at-law, mathematicians, and retired army officers, with their camp followers drawn from the ranks of the intellectually unemployed, upon a hot search for a substitute for the illiterate "Stratfordian."

* * *

[p. 180] Students familiar with the intellectual life of Elizabethan England know that Shakespeare's knowledge was not exceptional. On the contrary, his ideas on every subject seem to have been fairly conventional. He echoes the views held by the vast majority of his contemporaries in ethics, psychology, political theory, and practical politics. For example, the scheme of social organization and every one of the political principles which form the base of his history plays, whether of English or classical times, are presented in a collection of sermons which were ordered read "by all Persones, Vicars or Curates, every Sundaye in their Churches, where they have cure."

The sermons were crammed with the ideas which the Tudor monarchs determined to have their subjects believe. The two discourses which the clergymen most frequently dinned into the ears of the congregations were "An Exhortation Concerning Good Order and Obedience" and "An Homily against disobedience and wilfull rebellion." These sermons drove home the conception of a society stratified according to divine plan and ruled over by an absolute monarch. To accept the Tudor doctrine a writer did not need to boast a line of ancestors who had suffered for the Lancastrian cause. He need not have read even one of the many contemporary volumes which set those ideas forth. He need only have gone to church in his native village with the regularity required by law. There he could not have escaped hearing the reiteration of ideas which the king and his counsellors tried to force upon every man, woman, and child in Elizabethan England.

Similarly, the rest of Shakespeare's "learning" can be shown to be no more than the knowledge in the possession of all intelligent persons of his day. Even his lavish use of legal terminology was a popular poetic convention as old as Petrarch. Two of Shakespeare's immediate predecessors in the sonnet vogue, Barnabe Barnes and Samuel Daniel, whose works he seems particularly to have admired, were addicted to this particular form of imaginative decoration. Shakespeare need not have been a lawyer or even a resident of one of the Inns of Court in order to display this smattering of legal lore. It was enough for him to have observed and admired the literary manner of some of his fellows.

His acquaintance with the customs **[p. 181]** and atmosphere of foreign lands can be explained in similar fashion. There is much less of it than any bookish child would show to-day. Everyone who steps out upon the ramparts of the castle at Elsinore feels that this is the platform where the sentinels were pacing when the ghost of Hamlet's father appeared, that this sea below is the flood into which Horatio feared the apparition would tempt Hamlet to hurl himself. The similarities in setting and atmosphere between the castle in the play and the castle at Elsinore seem, one might say, too striking to be the result of chance. Yet Shakespeare surely never visited Denmark. Must we then deny him the authorship of "Hamlet" and search the records for some Elizabethan gentleman who did go to Denmark, and, having found him, shall we then father the tragedy upon him? Certainly not. It is easy to guess how Shakespeare was able to work up his Danish local color. At least two of the actors in his company, Will Kempe and Thomas Pope, had played at the Danish court for two months during the summer of 1586. When Shakespeare needed a few facts from which his imagination could evoke the very presence of the gloomy castle by the sea, he had only to stir the memories of two of his closest friends.

The Italy which Shakespeare drew is in superficial respects like the Italy of the Novelle, which furnished the plots of many of his plays. But his imagination has transformed all the facts into something rich and strange. The Venice of "The Merchant of Venice" is no more a realistic picture of the Rialto and its denizens than the Illyria of "Twelfth Night" is a dirty seaport on the Dalmatian Coast. The travels of Shakespeare's mind brought home a much richer harvest than the diaries of gentlemen back from years of travel on the Continent; more golden than the tales of adventures among the farthest islands of strange and perilous seas. What might he not have seen of truth and beauty if he had himself fared widely afield!

IV

All this anxiety about the discrepancy between the narrow personal of Shakespeare and the wide range of life reflected in his plays is the result of the most unwarranted of all the assumptions of the anti-Stratfordians. Axiomatic to them is the notion that the work of every writer of imaginative literature is a faintly disguised history of the author's own life. In fact, they regard literary criticism as the discovery of the private life of an author as it may be ferreted out of his own work. . . .

As a matter of fact, the Elizabethan audience had no more interest in the author of a drama than we have in the men who write our movie scenarios. To them the play was emphatically the thing. The marvel is, then, that we know as much as we do about the details of Shakespeare's life. It so happens that the facts at our command are almost exclusively those which concern his life as man, actor, and business man. Most of them did little to shape his artistic career. For this reason our literal-minded friends are hard put to it to find in the conventional accounts of his life events which would seem to have furnished material for the plays. . . .

The method employed in these investigations is simplicity itself, as the following examples will show. Edward de Vere's father, one of these critics explains, was a man highly respected, par-[p. 182]ticularly by his tenants. He was also a keen sportsman. He died when his son was but twelve years old. To a lad of that age such a father must have been an ideal, a hero who ever after dominated his son's imagination. To confirm this theory they have only to turn to the works which they believe Oxford to have composed. Is not father-worship the prime motive for the hero's action in "Hamlet," the greatest of the tragedies? Does not Hamlet describe his dead father in a cry of almost religious ecstasy?

> He was a man, take him for all in all
> I shall not look upon his like again.

A passage in the opening scene of "All's Well that Ends Well" offers them even stronger confirmation of the identity of Oxford and Shakespeare. It runs like this:

> *Countess:* In delivering my son from me I bury a second husband.
> *Bertram:* And I in going, madam, weep o'er my father's death anew; but I must attend his majesty's command, to whom I am now in ward evermore in subjection.

Edward de Vere, like Bertram, not only wept for a father's death, but also was a royal ward. In fact the story of Bertram is Oxford's own story under a transparent disguise! The aristocrat Oxford married under pressure Anne Cecil of the newly emerging middle class; Bertram was forced into a union with humble Helena, who like Mistress Anne was "little" and "sweet." Later Oxford, like Bertram, refused to live with his wife. Most extraordinary likeness of all, there is a legend that the father of Lady Anne contrived by stratagem that her husband should sleep with her under the impression that she was someone else and, the story goes, that as a result of this trick she bore him a son. Helena resorted to exactly the same stratagem in order to fulfil the impossible conditions for reunion which Bertram had laid down. Therefore the Earl of Oxford wrote all of Shakespeare's plays.

Behind all such collections of correspondences is the quaint notion that only a man who idealized his father would have been able to put into the mouths of his characters such expressions of paternal admiration as Hamlet and Bertram are made to utter. Similarly naïve is the assumption that only a man estranged from his wife could have been able to depict Bertram's scorn for Helena or Othello's jealous anger at Desdemona. And most specious of all is the argument that no one could have been capable of the invention of the most extravagant feature of the play—the substitution of the wife for a mistress in Bertram's bed—unless he himself had suffered the same humiliating experience.

It is hardly necessary to say that such assumptions are ludicrous in the extreme. Many authors without superstitious reverence for their fathers have been able to present filial love and admiration convincingly. And the substitution of a wife for a mistress in a man's bed is an exceedingly common narrative device in folk tale. It was an important part of Boccaccio's story which Shakespeare dramatized.

No more convincing are the inferences which the Oxfordians draw from similarities between de Vere's twenty-two published poems and passages in Shakespeare's works. The likenesses which exist are not nearly so striking as the partisans of Oxford assert. For example, these critics quote the following stanza from one of de Vere's poems which reveals his hidden suffering:

I Hannibal that smile for grief
And let your Caesar's tears suffice,
The one that laughs at his mischief
The other all for joy that cries.
I smile to see me scorned so
You weep for joy to see me woe.

This, they say, "is at once suggestive of the lines in 'Lear' ":

Then they for sudden joy did weep
And I for sorrow sing.

Only an enthusiast would believe that weeping for joy was the private discovery of one sole poet. And only a convinced partisan could fail to remark the enormous difference in poetic power between de Vere's stiff lines and the most pedes-[p. 183] trian of Shakespeare's verses. But the Oxfordians silence such objections by crying, "Ah, these are but the noble Lord's first efforts at verse. As soon as he wrote good poetry, he called himself Shakespeare." One wonders why he was ashamed of the good poetry but proud of the bad.

V

More interesting, it must be admitted, are the inferences which the Oxfordians draw from similarities between the emotional tone of many of Shakespeare's sonnets and the inner life of Edward de Vere. These critics remind us that in the sonnets Shakespeare often strikes a note of melancholy and profound discouragement. Such expressions of distress have been recognized by critics of almost every sort as coming from the heart of a personal and private grief. Clearly the author was deeply dissatisfied with his circumstances, chiding fortune for not providing for him something better "than public means which public manners breeds." Thence, he says, his name has received a brand

And almost thence my nature is subdued
To that it works in, like the dyer's hand.

In another sonnet he speaks of the impression "which vulgar scandal stamped upon my brow." These are but two of the more specific expressions of a sense of shame and disgrace which pursues the author through many of the sonnets.

We know of no events in Shakespeare's life, so runs the Oxfordian argument, that could have produced such devastating emotions. But these moving expressions of despair and shame form a natural commentary on some of the events of Edward de Vere's life. Because he had had the misfortune to lose his father in boyhood he came in his youth under the control of Cecil, who was master of the Court of Royal Wards. He even went to live with other fatherless young nobles in Cecil's house, and was reared in its somewhat institutionalized atmosphere. The unhappy substitute for home life which this little court provided was, in Oxford's opinion, to blame for what he calls his "public manners."

Moreover, the conduct of Oxford's wife, Anne Cecil, Burleigh's daughter, stamped him with disgrace. Sometime during the years 1575-76 while he was in Italy, a member of his household insinuated suspicions of his wife's fidelity. As a result, when summoned by Burleigh to return to England in 1576, he refused to see his wife and, in spite of all Burleigh's efforts to effect a reconciliation, refused for a long time to live with her. The gossip provoked by their prolonged estrangement aroused in him a deep feeling of disgrace, emotions which he expressed in a poem written at this time. Its essence can be discovered in these two lines from it.

> Fram'd in the front of forlorn hope past all recovery
> I stayless stand to abide the shock of shame and infamy.

The note struck here, assert the Oxfordians, is the same that is sounded again and again in the sonnets and undoubtedly is the cry of the same spiritual agony.

Their assurance is hardly warranted. Even if the correspondences between de Vere's experience and the poems of Shakespeare were much closer than the Oxfordians think, their hero's authorship of these works would be highly improbable. None of the reasons advanced for keeping his composition of the plays a secret applies to the poems. Elizabethan gentlemen were honored, not disgraced, by writing such works. Wyatt, Surrey, Lord Vaux, Sir Philip Sidney, all felt that in composing and circulating their verses they were revealing one of the approved graces of a gentleman. Oxford's desire to father his poems upon a semi-illiterate actor must have been a sign of rare idiosyncrasy.

He clearly did no such thing. The man who wrote the humble dedications of "Venus and Adonis" and "The Rape of Lucrece" to the Earl of Southampton was certainly not one of the great lords of [p. 184] England addressing one of his peers. "I know not how I shall offend," begins the dedication of "Venus and Adonis," "in dedicating my unpolished lines to you . . . only if your Honour seem but pleased, I account myself highly praised." And the writer ends his obsequious lines as follows: "Your Honour's in all duty William Shakespeare." These are obviously the words of a commoner addressing a gentleman out of his sphere, in the hope of gaining him as a patron. That he succeeded in so doing is clear from the writer's dedication of "The Rape of Lucrece" to Southampton in the following year. . . . [There,] making delicate reference to the accustomed financial reward which Southampton evidently provided in return for the dedication, the author [writes]: "The warrant I have of your honorable disposition, not the worth of my untutored lines, makes it assured of acceptance"—that is, of another gift of money.

These two poems must surely be crossed from the list of the works composed by the very proud seventeenth Earl of Oxford. And not even his most enthusiastic partisans have yet denied that all three of Shakespeare's longer poems were written by the same man.

As to the sonnets, the passages supposed to reveal Oxford's personal drama certainly adumbrate the situation of a sensitive actor at least as clearly as they do the sorrows of Edward de Vere. For example, "the public means which public manners breeds" can be made to refer with as much propriety to the stage career of William Shakespeare as to Oxford's education at court. For the public manners of an Elizabethan courtier were regarded as the last word in *savoir vivre*. And the lines

> And almost thence my nature is subdued
> To what it works in, like the dyer's hand

describe effectively that loss of personality which every actor feels who must spend his life impersonating one character after another. They are much more apt in such a connotation than they would be in describing the disappearance of the man Edward de Vere in the courtier. Even the "vulgar scandal" might refer as well to Shakespeare's "o'er-hasty marriage" as to the suspected infidelity of Anne Cecil.

The most original feature of the sonnets is their dramatic story of man, mistress, and friend. No counterpart of this situation has been found in Oxford's career. But the same struggle between love and friendship had already been the theme of "The Two Gentlemen of Verona." Surely the dramatist who had used this plot would have had no trouble in devising all the details of the story of a man's loss of an unworthy mistress to a dear friend.

The conception of literary composition upon which the reasoning of the Oxfordians is based is invalidated by the little we know about the ways of the creative mind. The greater the work of art the more remote it is from raw biographical fact. Direct observation of the lives of others and knowledge gained from books furnish the starting point of a process of literary creation more often than does any part of the author's life history. Between the sowing of this seed and its flowering into artistic creation an interval must elapse, during which the original fact is transmuted by the imagination. The process obliterates most of the points of resemblance between the literary work and the actual facts which served as its inception. Maxwell Anderson's "Winterset" may serve as an excellent illustration of what usually happens. The play is the author's imaginative reaction to the arrest, trial, and execution of Sacco and Vanzetti, events in which he played no part whatever. The plot of the drama, written years after the actual tragedy, is so different from what really happened that no one would be able to re-create the historical facts from the story or from the characters who enact the play.

[p. 185] The ways of Shakespeare's imagination were surely as unpredictable as those of Mr. Anderson. Facts upon which his imagination worked must have been even more incalculably transformed than those associated with the careers of Sacco and Vanzetti. . . . He was a dramatist able to create hundreds of characters utterly unlike himself and to drive them into experiences utterly unlike his own, endowing them with passions as far from his own emotions as the east is from the west. To search in his plays for realistic reports of his personal experience is to misunderstand completely the nature of effective dramatic composition and to misconceive the character of genius. . . .

None of the skeptics would have loosed his wayward ingenuity upon the problem unless he had made at least one of the assumptions which have been shown to be false. . . .

1948 "Letters to the Editor," *The Saturday Review of Literature,* Vol. XXXI, No. 40, October 2, 1948, p. 22.

Pseudonym, Shakespeare

[p. 22] Sir: In the review of G. B. Harrison's "Shakespeare: 23 Plays and the Sonnets" [*SRL* June 5] there is a misstatement so gross as to vitiate any claims to scholarship. Mr. Redman speaks of "those who hold fuzzily to the notion that 'we know nothing about him' [Shakespeare] instead of realizing that we know more about him than about 'any other Elizabethan dramatist'."

The most meager knowledge of the Shakespeare mystery cognizes the fact that all we know of the Stratford Shakespeare, Shacksper, or Shakspe, could easily be printed on a half-column of this page. It consists of perhaps a score of often sordid facts—baptisms, marriage, real estate deals, lawsuits, fines, etc. Not one of these records indicates in the slightest way that the Stratfordian was a writer. Nor do the few recorded items regarding the actor Shakespeare (who may or may not have been the Stratfordian) give any such evidence.

While there were many laudatory references to the *author* "Shakespeare" by his contemporaries, not one of them identifies him as the man of Stratford. The name was as much a pseudonym as Mark Twain or O. Henry, and it was a common practice in Elizabethan times to use stooges, often ignorant, whose names were put on title pages, even by the clergy. The anonymity of several important Elizabethan works has never been pierced.

What Mr. Harrison and Mr. Redman "know" about Shakespeare is a fictitious biography based on hearsay, conjecture, and old wives' tales collected by the actor Betterton seventy years after the Stratfordian's death, and, in Mr. Harrison's case, inflated by inferential interpretations of topical subjects in the "Plays and Sonnets." The assertion that Shakespeare of Stratford was the author was not asserted in print until many years after his death.

On the other hand, what we know about "other Elizabethan dramatists" is considerable. Of such writers as Edmund Spenser, Marlowe, Ben Jonson, Nash, Lyly, Peele, and others we have a good picture of their education, the books they owned, and their artistic interests which qualified them as writers.

While many of the best-known and most influential scholars in England—such men as the Dean of St. Paul's Cathedral in London, the Canon of Chelmsford Cathedral, principal of Victoria College, University of Liverpool, head master of the Charterhouse School, the professor of English at the Royal Naval Academy, etc.—have publicly attested to their belief that the true author was Edward De Vere, seventeenth Earl of Oxford, hardly a single important professor of English literature in the United States has been willing even to consider the new historical evidence that has changed the whole Elizabethan picture. They rest content, like the Encyclopedia Britannica, with historical data derived from sources no later than 1897. Many of the college faculties have been invited to refute, if possible, the new evidence that has accumulated since then. All have refused.

It is true what Mr. Redman says, that we know more about Shakespeare than about any other Elizabethan writer—but the

"Shakespeare" is not the Shakespeare of Stratford. He was the brightest star in the firmament of talent in that splendid era. A royal ward, brought up at Court, he was familiar with its usages. Highly educated, with degrees from both Oxford and Cambridge, familiar with the Greek and Latin classics, he could give the plays their sophisticated touch. A student at Gray's Inn for three years, his references to the intricacies of law are easily accounted for. Traveled in Italy, a champion in the tournament, an aristocrat *pur sang,* an expert falconer, a musician, a poet praised as the best, and excellent in comedy, and above all, as Lord Great Chamberlain in charge for years of the company of players who performed Shakespeare's dramas, he had every possible qualification for the authorship, while the dummy of Stratford had not one.

New York, N.Y. Gelett Burgess.

1948 "Letters to the Editor," *The Saturday Review of Literature,* Vol. XXXI, No. 45, November 6, 1948, pp. 21-2.

[p. 21] Sir: Mr. Gelett Burgess's discovery that there are ignoramuses who, after all the evidence presented to the contrary, still believe the plays attributed to Shakespeare were actually written by that unlettered lout of a horse-holder, has alarmed me. I am now convinced that any further delay in arousing the reading public's attention regarding certain facts about George Bernard Shaw, as he is called, may make it more difficult to establish the true authorship of the plays bearing his name.

It will be seen from the evidence I am presenting that it is just as unlikely that the real Shaw wrote the plays attributed to him as that Shakespeare wrote the plays of Edward De Vere.

Let us consider that the facts about Shaw's life are no better established than that "perhaps score of sordid facts," as Mr. Burgess puts it, we have about Shakespeare. We are dependent upon birth and marriage records, reports in the notoriously unreliable press, and biographies which disagree throughout, and which are questionable on other grounds. For example, we know that the so-called biography of Shaw by one who supposedly knew him, Frank Harris, was written by one Frank Scully, who never saw Shaw and therefore could not prove Shaw ever lived! In other cases, Shaw, as he is called, when mysteriously given access to the U.S., changed the original text of the author to suit his purpose. (We shall show what the purpose was!)

From the small body of uncontestable fact about Shaw, it is certain that he was not of royal blood, or even lordly lineage. His father was no more than a corn merchant. George Bernard Shaw, as he is called, never had any formal schooling after the age of fourteen. Indeed, it is questionable whether he had much schooling earlier, because of his apparent inability to spell or punctuate correctly. Any who have seen his letters know them to be studded with "thru," "dont" (without the apostrophe), etc.

How could one who never went to college or even high school have possibly written such a masterpiece as "Candida"?

There is no evidence whatever that the real Shaw even tried to write anything in his youth. He was certainly content to work for five years in, of all places, a real estate office. It's simply incredible that the author of "Pygmalion" could have existed five years in such a stultifying atmosphere. However, we do not have to believe our senses; for staring us in the face is indisputable evidence of the man Shaw's ineptitude as a writer when he did try to make his living with a pen. In nine years after he left the real estate office (under circumstances which we can conjecture), he earned exactly £6. Four novels, as they were called, were rejected one after the other by publishers. One was about prize-fighting, which is only further evidence of what low tastes he had. Try to couple that with the authorship of "Saint Joan"!

His family had to struggle for existence. "I did not throw myself into it, I threw my mother into it," Shaw said. That sufficiently characterizes the man who some persons believe, oddly, wrote "Mrs. Warren's Profession."

The real Shaw did, it seems, work in the lowest type of literary endeavor, criticism, but drifted from publication to publication—*Pall Mall Gazette, The Star, The Saturday Review,* apparently unable to keep a job. It is well known that any person capable of creating first-rate plays (such as "The Apple Cart," "On the Rocks," etc.) devotes himself to creative work and does not resort to making a living as scavenger among other men's ideas; the critic at best is one who knows how but cannot do it himself.

Realization of this might have made him disposed to allow his name to be used on another man's work. He practised such deceit himself, as those aware of the relationship of Shaw and Carnatto Di Bassetto know. But that is another story.

And now for a conjecture.

The other man with great plays in his mind and heart was in a position that required deceit, as De Vere was. He was an aristocrat, son of a lord and grandson of a duke. He had the education, background, and ability for his chosen profession of playwright, such as De Vere had. But playwriting was no occupation for one of his social position. Persons of the theatre were not acceptable in his set. Also, the kind of plays he was determined to write would, he realized, inevitably compromise the political career for which he was destined by his family and its traditions—if presented in his own name.

The circumstances demanded that the plays bear another's name. A nom-de-plume would be more easily penetrated. So a deal was made, I conjecture. How wise the playwright must have regarded his decision when [p. 22] he rose to high office—the highest office! How embarrassing it might have been for him then if Backbenchers had quoted lines he put in John Tanner's mouth in "Man and Superman." Or for him to have had to receive an ambassador from Bulgaria who was aware the prime minister was the author of "Arms and the Man."

That reference gives you a hint as to the true identity of the author of George Bernard Shaw's plays. You will find stronger hints in a comparison of the literary styles of a recent autobiographical work of an exalted personage in Great Britain. But I now present, for the first time, plainer evidence of the true author of Shaw's plays. His name is concealed in the titles of the plays! Look:

"*W*idower's Houses"
"Sa*i*nt Joan"
"Ma*n* and Superman"
"Arm*s* and the Man"
"*T*he Philanderer"
"To*o* Good to be True"
"A*n*drocles and the Lion"

"Mr*s*. Warren's Profession"
"*P*ygmalion"
"Ov*e*r-Ruled"
"O*n* the Rocks"
"Ba*c*k to Methuselah"
"G*e*tting Married"
"G*r*eat Catherine"

"The Do*c*tor's Dilemma"
"*H*eartbreak House"
"Yo*u* Never Can Tell"

"Major Barbara
"Caesar and Cleopatra"
"The Man of Destiny"
"Candida"
"Misalliance"
"John Bull's Other Island"

New York, N.Y. Clark Kinnaird.

1949 "Good Frend for Iesvs Sake Forbeare: Was Shakespeare Really Shakespeare?" By Bergen Evans. Pages 7-8, 39-40. *The Saturday Review of Literature* for May 7, 1949. Vol. XXXII, No. 19.

[p. 7] Dissertations on the subject of who wrote the plays commonly ascribed to William Shakespeare of Stratford-on-Avon now exceed what could be read in a lifetime. More than 4,000 separate books and articles, in six languages (according to a bibliography prepared by the late Professor Joseph S. Galland), support and dispute the claims presented for seventeen possible alternate authors. *The Saturday Review* has recently published a number of letters excitedly for or against the various proposed pretenders. Of them, Bacon leads the field (if we overlook Shakespeare) with Edward de Vere, the seventeenth Earl of Oxford, a strong runner-up and gaining rapidly. Hard at their heels come the Earls of Rutland and Derby and scattered down the track are Sir Edward Dyer, Robert Burton, Sir Walter Raleigh, Christopher Marlowe, and, bringing up the rear amid the plaudits of the feminists, Anne Hathaway!

* * *

To the faint extent that the backers of the various entries feel any compulsion to be reasonable, their chief argument is a negative one. How, they ask, could an uneducated provincial have ever acquired the universal knowledge manifested in the plays?
Ironically, this question is founded on the hysterical claims of omniscience for their idol by the bardolators (such as Schlegel's pronouncement that Shakespeare had mastered "all the things and relations of this world"), claims which have been steadfastly refuted by informed critics from Ben Johnson [*sic*] on but which seem to have an irresistible appeal to the unscholarly. And to support their as-

sumption the various theorists have labored mightily to present the Stratford man as an illiterate oaf and his home town as a benighted spot through whose mired alleys trudged as low a group of cretins as ever gibbered in the suburbs of Dogpatch.

Actually, however, sixteenth-century Stratford was a pretty civilized place. It is true that one John Shakespeare, probably the poet's father, was fined for leaving refuse in the street, but the significance of this is surely not that refuse littered the streets but that householders were fined if it did—an indication of a civic pride considerably in advance of that of twentieth-century Chicago. The town had a grammar school and a fine church and several other buildings more substantial than one would find in most American communities of the same size today, and was probably more self-sufficient in cultural matters. All intellectual activity had not yet been sucked into the metropolis; culture was not then mass-produced in one spot and piped back into the country towns as wobbling shadows and syndicated banalities.

As for the man himself, it cannot be denied that his report cards have not been preserved, but surely the writing of the plays ought to render them unnecessary as proof of his literacy. Lincoln had practically no schooling, but the author of the Gettysburg Address and the Second Inaugural can hardly be considered uneducated. Indeed, if the Stratford man were half the ignorant boor his denigrators insist he was, it reflects very little subtlety in the true author to have selected him as a front. J. Thomas Looney, the one-eyed monarch of these blind guides, perceived [**p. 8**] this pitfall and attempted to prevent his ardent followers from making a gadarene plunge into it by begging them to remember that Shakespeare, though of low extraction and mean capacities and reduced, through Mr. Looney's researches, to a "somewhat ignominious" position, was, after all, Lord Oxford's stooge and as such entitled to at least courtesy.

As for the great Shakespeare "mystery," it consists, in brief, of our not knowing as much about the man as we wish we did. But, even so, we know more about him than we do about any of the other claimants except Bacon. He was, apparently, one of the best-known citizens of his day. Plays attributed to him were published as by him over a period of thirty years and not only was their authorship never challenged but more than a score of contemporary men of letters, at various times, mentioned him, praised him, and estimated his genius about as we do now. There are periods in his life about which we know nothing, but so are there in the lives of almost all of those who are advanced to supplant him, and when we consider the difference between his social position and that of some of them we can consider ourselves fortunate for knowing so much.

The first of all the challengers, in point of time, bulk of literature and noise, number and ingenuity of supporters, is Francis Bacon whose claim, first advanced in 1785, rests fundamentally on the assumptions that the author of the plays was omniscient and that Bacon not only knew everything but had practically a monopoly on information.

Both assumptions are false. The plays abound with errors: Bohemia is endowed with a seacoast; characters board ship at Verona for passage to Milan; Cleopatra, laced in a corset, plays billiards; Hector quotes Aristotle and Hamlet attends an as-yet-not-founded university; there are clocks in ancient Rome and cannon in the time of King John; Edgar, though a contemporary of the pre-Roman Lear, is familiar with Bedlam, and there is a king of France at a time when All Gaul was still divided into three parts. The list of such blunders could be extended through many pages. The entire subject received its definitive treatment thirty years ago in "Shakespeare's England," a symposium by a score of authorities that canvassed Shakespeare's knowledge in a dozen fields and concluded that he had no such immense and specialized information as some of his admirers had given him credit for. His vast knowledge of law, for instance, a pillar of the whole Baconian structure, proved upon examination by an expert in Elizabethan law, Arthur Underhill, to have been "neither profound nor accurate."

Bacon's omniscience has stood scrutiny no better. It is true that he boasted to have taken all knowledge for his province, but the opinion of the best scouts for several centuries now has been that he failed to occupy the entire province. His book learning is considerably greater than that of the author of the plays, to be sure, but it still falls short of the claims made for him.

There is no disgrace in that, however, for much has been claimed. He has been hailed as the author of the entire Elizabethan drama, with "The Faerie Queene" and "The Anatomy of Melancholy" thrown in. Less rational enthusiasts (for, incredible as it may seem, the distinction is possible) have also credited him with Montaigne's "Essais," "Pilgrim's Progress," the "Tale of a Tub," and "Robinson Crusoe." The first of these may have been, as claimed, a youthful exercise in French, but the last three present a biographical problem since they were published from fifty-two to ninety-three years after a body presumably his was buried at St. Albans. One explanation is that he left them in manuscript. Another is that he merely feigned death and found someone else willing (for the sake of the sarcophaus, possibly) to take his place in the tomb in order that he might e free from interruption, a convenience necessary for so volumi-ous an output. And a third is that he dictated them from the spirit vorld, as he did the particular cipher that he communicated to Mrs. . C. A. Windle of San Francisco.

Unfortunately, Bacon is a peculiarly *un*likely candidate. The xtent of his known duties and the bulk of his acknowledged works vould make the production of thirty-six such plays in addition and n secret, in or out of cipher, more incredible than their being writ-en by the most unlettered hind in the land. Then it would be diffi-ult to find two men whose styles vary more widely. Bacon is stately, rave, and condensed; Shakespeare is impetuous, sparkling, and ex-ravagant. Jonson, who knew both men, tells us that Bacon's speech vas so concise that if his listener coughed or turned aside he missed he meaning; whereas Shakespeare's volubility overflowed the ounds of decorum and stood constantly in need of restraint. pedding, one of the greatest students of Bacon, doubted whether ne could find as many as five lines together in any of Bacon's works hat could be mistaken for Shakespeare's by anyone familiar with heir styles.

The Earl of Oxford, whose cult though younger is now the most vital, is a far more likely possibility. Indeed, if the author of the plays were as unknown as the cultists assume he is, De Vere would be an interesting hypothesis. But the evidence advanced in his sup-port is weak compared to that which connects the plays with one Wiliam Shakespeare and identifies him as the leading dramatist of his day.

This is sometimes granted, in lucid intervals, by those who still vociferously maintain that there is nothing to connect this person with "the butcher boy of Stratford" other than a trifling similarity in their names. But as Mr. Hoy Cranston has pointed out [*SRL* Nov. 6, 1948]—and several hundreds before him—the Stratford man's will definitely identifies him as a "fellow" of Burbage and of Heming and Condell, the actor-editors of the First Folio; and a score of passages in the plays make it plain that their [p. 39] author was a man with a more than amateur interest in stagecraft. To be sure there is no holograph of any of the plays and no notarized assurance that so-and-so observed him, at such-and-such an hour, composing this or that scene. But the evidence for remains more convincing than that brought against the common supposition. Indeed, if it were maintained that almost any work of 200 or more years ago was really written by someone else of the same name and that all passing references to the generally-assumed authorship were parts of a conspiracy, it would be hard to *prove* the orthodox position. If the anti-Stratfordians ever tire of their game and want something *really tough* to wrestle with, let them try to prove that Swift wrote the "Tale of a Tub."

The alleged concealment of authorship, involving the most elaborate perjury and extensive subornation of witnesses ever known, is generally explained on the grounds that the writing of plays was then regarded as a base occupation, one whose public acknowledgment would have put an end to any possibility of the courtier's or statesman's career to which the true author aspired.

But this, too, has been exaggerated. Writing for the popular stage would certainly in the days of Elizabeth (as today) have been regarded as beneath a statesman's dignity. But most of those who have any serious following as challengers were known in their own day to have been at least dabblers in the drama. The Earl of Derby was known to be "penning comedies for the common players," and Meres in 1598 speaks of Oxford, the great patron of the players, as "the best for comedy among us." Burghley probably disapproved of such activities but it is questionable to what extent the Queen did and there is no doubt that James approved.

That De Vere hoped to clear his name from some vague but horrible disgrace by telling his story in the disguise of the plays would be meaningless if he did not arrange for an eventual, even if posthumous, disclosure of his identity and the pertinent parallels. And to have had any value such a disclosure would have to have been made while the generation that had misjudged him was still alive. Whereas the bulk of the plays did not appear until a generation after his death and when they did they were more firmly assigned to Shakespeare than ever before.

It is argued that if Shakespeare really wrote the plays he would have been more concerned with their publication, instead of leaving so many of them, as he seems to have, to the mercy of friends and fellow actors. But this argument has even greater force against the other claimants. If the true author went to such lengths to insure anonymity, why didn't he go to a few more to insure publication? Why did not he at least correct proofs, for all first editions of the plays have many passages more garbled than any author could endure to see ascribed to even his nom de plume.

Much of the evidence for the presumed authorships is "internal." It lies, that is, between incidents or expressions in the plays and certain facts in the life of the claimant. But deductions of this nature are particulrly dangerous when dealing with a dramatist who, to the extent that he is successful, must present sympathetically hundreds of different and even opposed points of view. If it is claimed—as it is—that because some of Othello's actions and thoughts are applicable to Oxford he must have been the author of the play, it may be asked how Iago, Edmund, and Richard III came to be so convincingly portrayed? What sort of composite monster was the man? Or—if we turn [p. 40] to consider Launce and Bottom and Gobbe [*sic*]—what sort of composite fool? Burghley may have been the model for Polonius, but Oxford was not the only man who knew Burghley and Burghley was probably not the only sententious old man then living. Once this sort of hunt is started some very wild geese get chased. Mr. Looney will have any educated reader's acquiescence when he begins by asserting that there is a resemblance between Elizabeth's chief counselor and Claudius's. But when he insists that it follows Ophelia is Anne Cecil and Oxford is Hamlet, his reader grows uneasy. And his conclusion, that Fortinbras is James I, dissolves the demonstration into laughter.

There is one form of internal evidence, however, that carries much more conviction. Where a metaphor has no particular relation to the character using it or where, as frequently happens, it is out of keeping with the character, it is not unreasonable to assume that it is the author's own. When—to illustrate—Othello says, "Were it my cue to fight, I should have known it without a prompter," he is plainly employing the language of the greenroom, not of the camp, and is speaking out of character; and but for the absurdity of underlining the obvious we would be justified in saying that whoever wrote the play was familiar with stagecraft.

The simile was plainly unconscious, a self-revealing slip of a mind to which cues and prompters were everyday matters. There are many such similes in the plays and they are highly revealing of the author's nature, of his likes and dislikes and of the experiences which had shaped him. They have been collected and examined by Dr. Caroline Spurgeon, of the University of London, whose "Shakespeare's Imagery" is probably the most significant of the many books that touch on the problem of authorship. Miss Spurgeon shows, for example, that although there are many images in the plays drawn from falconry, tennis, and other gentlemanly sports (the many references to which have been advanced as proof that only an aristocrat could have been the author), the images from the popular game of bowls "are about three times as many as from any other game." The images of the sea are such as view it from the land. The images from gardening are from the point of view of the worker in the garden not (as almost exclusively with Bacon . . .) from the point of view of the owner of the garden. The author of the plays shows *in his figures of speech* an intimate knowledge of village life, with a special sympathy for the poor and the despised. He has no direct knowledge of war. The craft with which he seems most familiar is carpentry. He is versed in cookery to an astonishing degree, while his domestic images center in a yeoman's kitchen, the one large room which would have then served a well-to-do farmer or a small burgher for cooking, eating, and general relaxation. The ill-ventilated fire, the guttering candle, the oil-dried lamp, and the mess and smell of food that has boiled over onto the stove come ceaselessly to his mind as tropes of frustration and disgust. Nor are these figures common to his times; they are highly idiosyncratic. They are not what we would expect from the lord keeper's son or the premier earl of the land. But they are what we might expect from the Warwickshire countryman.

Those who oppose the comonly-accepted authorship grant that no one point they can advance suffices to prove their argument but insist that the cumulative effect of their many points . . . is irresistible. But their own logic works as much against as for them; for the difference between a fact and a possibility is a measure of uncertainty, and the residual doubt which attends each of their surmises is also cumulative.

* * *

Take the much-publicized assertion that X-ray and infra-red photographs have revealed a portrait of Oxford underlying the "Ashbourne" portrait of Shakespeare. If it could be proved that the Ashbourne picture is a contemporary portrait of Shakespeare; if it could be shown that there is another portrait under it, and if it could be shown that this portrait is a portrait of the Earl of Oxford, it would be, to say the least, curious.

But not one of the suppositions can be established as a fact—particularly, and most strikingly, the second, upon which, of course, the third is wholly dependent. One would certainly have assumed, after all the brouhaha, that there was *some* portrait underlying the Ashbourne picture. But let any dispassionate seeker after the truth turn to the photographs of these "findings" (he may see them in *Scientific American,* January 1940, pages 4-8) and compare them with a genuine disclosure by X-rays of one portrait underlying another (such as the "Portrait of a Lady," supposedly by Franz Pourbos the Younger, reproduced in its various stages of detection and restoration on Plate I, opposite page 64F, Vol. 17 of the 14th Britannica) and ask himself if there is the slightest indication of anything except a few preliminary strokes and minor alterations underlying the surface portrait in question. Nor is the "discovery" of "Oxford's Crest" on the signet ring worn by the subject of the portrait any more convincing. Only the eye of faith could have detected the resemblance and only the effrontery of fanaticism drawn it in crudely with white paint and solemnly presented it as evidence.

Next to abuse of those who disagree with them, no term is more common in the writings of the anti-Stratfordians than "it is impossible to doubt" or "it cannot be questioned." But men who have espoused one of the most startling doubts ever conceived cannot be permitted the use of such phrases. If we are not going to doubt, then the Stratford man must be left in possession. And if we are, we can hardly accept anyone who has yet been advanced to displace him.

1949 "Letters to the Editor" *The Saturday Review of Literature,* Vol. XXXII, No. 23, June 4, 1949, p. 24.

[p. 24] Sir: Bergen Evans, when asked [*SRL* May 7] "how . . . could an uneducated provincial have ever acquired the universal knowledge" shown in Shakespeare, whips out, as a partial answer, "the writing of the plays" as "proof of his literacy." This method of proving the literacy of Shakespeare from his plays, in order to prove they *are* his plays, earns Bergen a large niche in the history of unnatural nonsense.

Chicago, Ill. William A. Klutts.

1949 "Letters to the Editor," *The Saturday Review of Literature,* Vol. XXXII, No. 23, June 4, 1949, p. 24.

[p. 24] Sir: Why must those who maintain that the plays commonly attributed to Shakespeare were actually written by the man from Stratford always act as if any opinion to the contrary were either a personal affront or else the hysterical obsession of some crackpot? As Mr. Bergen Evans points out, more than 4,000 separate books and articles in six languages support other claims. Surely there must be strong evidence on this side to have caused such a furor. Such a fiery controversy can hardly burn where there is no fuel. In the name of fair play give both sides equal and unbiased consideration!

Cambridge, Mass. Marcia M. Roof.

1949 "Letters to the Editor," *The Saturday Review of Literature,* XXXII, No. 23, June 4, 1949, pp. 24-5.

[p. 24] Sir: Since not a single one of my traditional opponents has shown any knowledge of the recently discovered historical facts indicating the Oxford authorship of the Shakespeare plays, let me state briefly the basic reasons for the Oxford cause that they may know what we are talking about. Space prevents documents, but the Shakespeare Fellowship can show proof of the truth of every one of these statements. I call them "The Oxford Primer."

1. It is unimaginable that the author of the immortal plays was not known for his literary genius by his contemporaries. Webbe, the anonymous author of "The Arte of English Poesie," Peacham, Day, and many others praised Edward de Vere, Seventeenth Earl of Oxford, for his creative "doings" in superlatives and accounted him a poet and dramatist of the highest order. He was an acknowledged leader in the literary life of the Shakesperean [*sic*] age. Many other veiled allusions to his genius, in the symbolic diction affected at the time, have been found in which Oxford is easily identified, notably in a contemporary description of the author of "Venus and Adonis" by Thos. Edwards in his "Narcissus" (1593).

2. The plays give *prima facie* evidence that the author was an aristocrat with a feudal point of view. Oxford was the premier Earl of the Realm, the head of one of the oldest families, the most loyal supporter of the Crown.

3. The author must have been familiar with the theatre. Oxford was supervising patron of several companies of actors performing Shakespearean plays. He was a lessee of Blackfriars' Theatre. He frequently acted himself in court masques and revels, and had a life-long interest in the stage.

4. The author must have been well educated and had read widely. Oxford received degrees from both Oxford and Cambridge universities. He was a well-known patron of the arts. Golding was his uncle and Lyly his secretary. Of the "source books" which Shakespearean critics agree that the author must have read, Oxford is known to have owned at least a dozen. Several of these were dedicated to him, and records have been found of his purchase of the others. He is known to have read Latin easily and to have had considerable knowledge of French and Italian.

5. The author must have been well acquainted with court life and manners. Oxford, when twelve, became a Royal Ward, was brought up in the home of Lord Treasurer Burghley, and was for some years a favorite of Queen Elizabeth.

6. The author must have had a thorough knowledge of the law. Critics have found his technical phraseology accurate; and a great many of his figures of speech have reference to legal practice. Oxford studied some years at Gray's Inn and was familiar with the intricacies of the jurisprudence of the time.

7. The author must have had a personal knowledge of Italy, its topography and customs. Oxford traveled for over a year on the Continent, and spent several months in Italy.

8. The author must have been an expert sportsman, familiar with its slang, with a knowledge of music and botany. Oxford from his youth was [p. 25] experienced in falconry, and was the winning champion in at least two tournaments. He was a composer of music of professional skill. His home, while with Burghley, had the most complete botanical garden in Britain.

9. Oxford was known to his initimates as "Gentle Master William." He had a favorite estate in Warwickshire on the river Avon. His crest as Lord Bulbec was a lion shaking a broken spear.

10. The author must have had personal knowledge of war and of navigation. Oxford fought for some time in the Low Countries and, with Sussex, on the Scottish border. At his own expense he equipped a ship and fought it against the Spanish Armada.

11. The First Folio Shakespeare is dedicated to the Earls of Montgomery and of Pembroke. One became Oxford's son-in-law, and the other was at one time engaged to his other daughter. The Earl of Southampton, to whom "Venus and Adonis" was dedicated, had been strongly urged to marry Elizabeth Vere by Lord Burghley and others. "A Midsummer Night's Dream" was given at Greenwich Palace in January 1595 in celebration of the marriage of Oxford's daughter Elizabeth to the Earl of Derby.

12. It was the custom of Elizabethan writers of noble birth to publish their works anonymously; but some, even clerics, used stooges whose names were put as authors on the title pages of the true authors' works. "And he that cannot write true English without the help of Clerkes of Parish Churches will need make himself the father of interludes." So says Greene in his "Farewell to Follie."

But Oxford had special personal reasons for desiring anonymity. He fell into disgrace through his love affair with Anne Vavasor; he dissipated an immense estate in bad investments and his maintenance of his theatrical companies, and became almost bankrupt; and he earned an unsavory reputation by preferring the companionship of writers and players to the artificiality of court life. He could not afford, while seeking a remunerative official position from Elizabeth, to acknowledge publicly that he was the author of plays revealing so many autobiographical secrets and ridiculing so many prominent personages.

13. Lastly, Charles Wisner Barrell has proved that three famous portraits of "Shakespeare," the Ashbourne and Janssen in the Folger Library at Washington and the Hampton Court portrait owned by the King of England, are all overpainted portraits of Edward De Vere, X-ray and infra-red photographs showing that the original head and ruff have been redone and identifying details changed or obliterated.[1]

14. An intimate connection has been definitely traced between members of Oxford's family surviving him and the accepted contemporary authority on "Shakespeare," Ben Jonson.

If we compare these facts with the complete lack of any similar contemporary certification of the Stratford Shakespeare's association with any literary activity, the logical conclusion is evident, *i.e.*, that Oxford used the name "Shakespeare" as a pseudonym. Not only did Shakespere possess *none* of these qualifications for authorship, but Oxford was the *only* Elizabethan writer who possessed them all. One of the happiest results of the scholarship and research that have been given to Oxford's life is the fact that a new and authentic chronology of the plays has proved that the so-called "crude" plays which Shakespeare has been supposed to rewrite and improve were actually pirated publications of memory versions of his own works, which rescues the author's name from the traditional charge of plagiarism.

Thus, in bringing to light the life, environment, and activities of Edward De Vere, a consummate genius who, though neglected and maligned heretofore by history, was the true leader of the British Renaissance, there has been revealed the man who, by all scientific standards, is the most logical and believable candidate for the authorship of the Shakespeare plays and sonnets.

New York, N.Y. Gelett Burgess.

1949 "Letters to the Editor," *The Saturday Review of Literature,* Vol. XXXII, No. 23, June 4, 1949.

[p. 24] Sir: Let us end the dreary wrangling in your columns over who or what was Shakespeare with the true facts.

The works of "Shakespeare" were actually produced by the mind

[1] *Scientific American,* January, 1940—the editors.

of Zzxxyt, a fifth-rate Martian poet of the XIV Dynasty of the Empire of Equatorial Canals. About 1500 A.D. he was engulfed by a wandering space warp, and set down on Terra, in England. Being unable to return to Mars, until the humans perfected space travel, out of sheer ennui he produced the works of "Shakespeare," "Webster," "Ford," "Jonson," "Spenser," "Lyly," "Marlowe," etc., etc.

It was simple for Zzxxyt to have these works published and produced as authentic productions of their supposed authors. He merely used the well-known Martian faculty of telehypnosis to implant the works in the minds of their putative authors.

Zzxxyt is still alive, and in residence at Glamis Castle. However, the climate of Terra, and the protracted delay in opening up interplanetary travel has [*sic*] embittered his never very equable temper. He now takes out his spite by telehypnosis of Eliot, Sartre, Kafka, Capote, *et al.*

San Francisco, Calif. G. F. Freudenberg.

1949 "Letters to the Editor," *The Saturday Review of Literature,* Vol. XXXII, No. 26, June 25, 1949, pp. 27-28.

[p. 27] Sir: While perusing Bergen Evans's article ["Was Shakespeare Really Shakespeare?" *SRL* May 7] I was particularly struck by his concluding remarks concerning the groundless and tenuous character of the anti-Shakespearian [*sic*] hypotheses. I was, however, surprised to note that while confuting each special claim, Mr. Evans fails to bring forward the mass of factual proof contained in that highly official document which could not be tampered with, the London Stationers Register, whereon seventeen of Shakespeare's plays were duly inscribed under the author's name, correctly spelled, together with mention of the theatrical company responsible for the staging of each comedy or tragedy as soon as printed. Two wardens presided over the great Register and, for the price of sixpence issued license to print, thus securing copyright, but only after they had investigated the contents of the book and were satisfied as to the identity of the author held responsible for its appearance. True, certain writers used a pen name, but this did not mean anonymous publication. Walter Raleigh was perfectly well known under the pseudonym Ignoto; just as Spenser was recognized by the public as Colin Clout.

When the sonnets of Shakespeare were inscribed on the Stationers

Register (1609) Richard Field had become master of the Stationer's company. It would be strange indeed if the man who had already printed two poems redolent of the Stratford atmosphere, landscape, and the rural sports for which the region was famous, should have confused the real actor-author he had known from boyhood with the lord chancellor of England.

Why also should doubt be cast on the general culture and knowledge of Latin possessed by Stratford school boys? There still remains written proof in the correspondence of Richard Quinney, Shakespeare's son-in-law. The grammar school handsomely endowed by the Catholic family of Clopton insisted upon having as teachers only men with degrees from Oxford or Cambridge. Their salaries paid out by Shakespeare's father were superior to those of Eton. Among the younger boys' textbooks were Lilly's Latin Grammar and his "Sententiae Pueriles," containing copious extracts from Seneca, Terence, Cicero, Plautus, Ovid, and Horace. No wonder that Shakespeare makes one of his characters say when quoting a classical couplet: "'Tis a phrase from Horace but I learned it in my Latin Grammar."

A man of exceptional learning presided over young Shakespeare's later scholastic years. This was Simon Hunt, Bachelor of Oxford, whose license to teach in the Schola Grammaticali in Villa Stratford super Avon figures on the register of the Archbishop of Worcester, where the documents concerning the poet's marriage [p. 28] are also consigned. Simon Hunt's learning is hard to question. For, when the Elizabethan persecutions obliged him to take refuge on the Continent he rose rapidly to one of the highest places in the Church of Rome so that the claim put forward by Baconians and others that Stratford grammar-school boys were necessarily boobies may be lightly set aside.

Paris, France. Clara Longworth de Chambrun.

1949 "Letters to the Editor," *The Saturday Review of Literature,* Vol. XXXII, No. 36, September 3, 1949.

A Look at the Register

[p. 26]

Sir: I have a copy of the London Stationers Register before me and seventeen of Shake[s]peare's plays are not there "duly inscribed under the author's name, correctly spelled," as asserted by the Countess of Chambrun [*SRL* June 25]. Only five plays are so recorded, namely, "Henry the Fourth," "Much Ado About Nothing," "King Lear," "The Two Noble Kingsmen," [*sic*] "A Yorkshire Tragedy." And three times out of five the name is spelt "Shakespere."

As for the reliability of that "highly official document . . . the London Stationers Register," "The Two Noble Kingsmen" [*sic*] is not included in the First Folio and is primarily the work of John Fletcher, "A Yorkshire Tragedy" is a totally spurious Shakespeare play, the "King Lear" of this first registration is an atrocious text filled with bewildering errors and misreadings. The reason is evident. It is a text hurriedly and haphazardly put together from rough stenographic notes made of an actual performance. It is a manifest "steal." It is an attempt by prior registration to deprive the purchaser of the play of his copyright.

Gelett Burgess in his itemized argumentation in favor of the Earl of Oxford [*SRL* June 4] makes no mention of Oxford's dying in 1604 and of this registration of "King Lear" occurring in 1607. It is true that the inscription of a play in the Stationers Register at a certain date is not positive proof that the play was written shortly before that date. But the wording in the Stationers Register reads, "A booke, called Master William Shakespeare his historye of King Lear as yt was played before the Kinges maiestie at Whitehall vppon Sainct Stephens night at Christmas Last," and this specification does suggest a first performance of the play December 1606. Moreover, Act I, Scene 2, Gloucester says, "These late eclipses in the sun and moon portend no good to us: though the wisdom of nature can reason it thus, and thus; yet Nature finds itself scourg'd by the sequent effects"; and in autumn of 1605 there occurred two notable eclipses of the moon and sun, that of the moon on the 27th of September, that of the sun on the 2nd of November. Oxfordians, having searched the almanacs through in vain for another instance of two close eclipses of the moon and sun, would dismiss this mathematical evidence as a mere accident of literary phrasing coinciding with fact. However, there is this more. Early in 1606 there appeared a small pamphlet translated from the High Dutch entitled "Strange fearful and true news which happened at Carlstadt in the Kingdom of Croatia." It enlarged upon "the Earth's and Moon's late and horrible obscurations." The similarities of phrase, rhythm, and sentiment indicate that the author of "King Lear" was indeed influenced by a reading of the pamphlet.

There is strong evidence that when "King Lear" was written the Earl of Oxford was dead.

Topanga, Calif. Alden Brooks.[2]

1949 "Letters to the Editor," *The Saturday Review of Literature*. Vol. XXXII, No. 36, September 3, 1949.

[p. 26] Sir: In connection with the Stratfordian-Oxfordian controversy the following dates (some conjectural, others approaching certainty) are of interest. 1605-06: "Lear," "Macbeth"; 1606-07: "Antony and Cleopatra"; 1607-08: "Coriolanus," "Timon of Athens"; 1608-09: "Pericles"; 1609-10: "Cymbeline"; 1610-11: "The Winter's Tale"; 1611-12: "The Tempest"; 1612-13: "Henry VIII," "The Two Noble Kinsmen." The dates, those of the earliest production of the plays, are given by Sir E. K. Chambers in "William Shakespeare: A Study of Facts and Problems."

The seventeenth Earl of Oxford died in 1604. If he wrote these plays in the years suggested above, he must have been the most distinguished of Elizabethan ghost writers.

Grand Forks, N. D. F. Y. St. Clair.

1949 *An Outline of Psychoanalysis* by Sigmund Freud, translated by James Strachey, W. W. Norton and Company, Inc., New York.

[p. 96] The name "William Shakespeare" is most probably a pseudonym behind which there lies concealed a great unknown. Edward de Vere, Earl of Oxford, a man who has been regarded as the author of Shakespeare's works, lost a beloved and admired father while he was still a boy, and completely repudiated his mother, who contracted a new marriage soon after her husband's death.

---

[2] Brooks supports the thesis that Sir Edward Dyer wrote the dramas attributed to Shakespeare. See his *Will Shakespere: Factotum and Agent* and *Will Shakespere and the Dyer's Hand.*

1960 Norman N. Holland, "Freud on Shakespeare," *PMLA*, June, 1960, Volume LXXV, No. 3, pp. 163-73.

[p. 164] In spite of his admiration of Shakespeare's works, Freud entertained doubts about authorship, not unnaturally in a way, for Freud was often interested in things or people not being what they seemed to be, dreams or slips of the tongue, for example. . . . For a time he flirted with the notion that Shakespeare's face "could not be that of an Anglo-Saxon but must be French, and he suggested that the name was a corruption of Jacques Pierre". . . .

About 1923, he read J. Thomas Looney's *Shakespeare Identified*. . . . A year later he reread the book, and . . . in 1930, he wrote Theodore Reik, "I no longer believe in the man from Stratford." . . . In a speech accepting the Goethe Prize, he announced, "It annoys us all that we will never know who made the comedies, tragedies, and sonnets of Shakespeare, whether it was really the untaught son of the Stratford petty bourgeois who in London achieved a certain status as an actor, or whether it was the noble, highborn, and finely cultured, the passionately disordered, the somewhat declassé aristocrat Edward de Vere."

* * *

[p. 165] Even in his last writings, Freud clung to the idea, relating Hamlet's Oedipus complex to the fact that the Earl of Oxford's beloved father had died when the supposed playwright was still a boy and his mother (whom he later repudiated) had quickly remarried.

* * *

[p. 172] Freud was indeed a lover of Shakespeare, an *amateur* in the finest sense. It is true that Freud's views on authorship were at least eccentric if not downright hostile. It is true, too, that, quoting from memory rather than from a text, he often misquoted and that he was frequently mistaken about the facts of Shakespeare's life or of the plays.

1959 *American Bar Association Journal*, "Elizabethan Whodunit: Who Was 'William Shake-Speare'?" by Richard Bentley, Vol. 45, No. 2, February, 1959, pp. 143-146, 204-208.

[p. 143] Three and a half centuries, more or less, have rolled by since the Bard of Avon "shuffled off this mortal coil". Since then

Shakespeare has become big business in Stratford, with vested interests, worth millions a year in tourist trade. He has become a "sacred cow". To question his authorship is considered "bad form", like eating peas with your knife, or even spitting on the rug. If you question it you are branded by Shakespeare scholars as either a knave or a fool, or perhaps both.

The scholars help us to understand Shakespearean language, to appreciate the content and structure of the writings and to learn the literary sources upon which the author drew. These are primarily literary questions and strictly within the sphere of scholars. But the question of the identity of the author is not purely a literary question; it is also a question of evidence. It is, therefore, properly within the province of lawyers to inquire as to the authorship and to judge of the competence and validity of the evidence.

The known facts are few. The first real biography of Shakespeare was published ninety-three years after his death and covered four pages. This and subsequent biographies are based largely upon inferences from the works and upon assumptions and guesswork. There is admittedly no direct proof of the authorship. We can arrive only at the most probable solution upon the preponderance of the evidence. And we should not reject a new conclusion merely because it may be different from an old one, long accepted.

* * *

Let us, therefore, summarize the only contemparaneously recorded and substantiated facts, carefully reviewed and checked.

* * *

William Shaksper of Stratford

A William Shaksper (*not* Shakespeare) was baptized April 26, 1564, in Stratford, a town of 1,600, a squalid and "a bookless neighborhood". Like most of the inhabitants his parents were illiterate. Nothing whatever is known of him until he was 18, when a license was issued for his marriage to Anne *Whateley* of Temple Grafton. [p. 144] The next day a bond was filed for his marriage to Anne *Hathwey* (*sic*) of Shottery. No marriage to either Anne is recorded, but a daughter was baptized barely six months later, and two years later, twins.

By 1597, at 33, he had mysteriously become wealthy and contracted to buy perhaps the most pretentious residence in Stratford. In the earliest biography it is reported he received a large payment, the modern equivalent of some $20,000, from the Earl of Southampton to help him purchase some property, but no *quid pro quo* nor date is suggested.

A letter written to him in 1598 asked for a loan, but there is no evidence he ever read or answered it, nor, indeed, any indication that he ever wrote a letter in his life.

The rest of the records in Stratford show activity in the grain and malt business, transactions in real estate and litigated matters in which he was usually the plaintiff, once suing for less than two pounds. He was godfather to an alderman's son. The only contemporary record of any conversation of his was about his proposed enclosure of common pasturelands, to deprive the poor of their rights. The town of Stratford successfully opposed this.

He signed his will in three places in March, 1616, and died a month later. His will left to his wife his "second best bed with the furniture", and disposed in detail of various articles such as a sword, a bowl, jewelry, plate, etc. It mentioned no interest in a theater, no writings, no books, nor any literary property whatever.

No public mention was made of his death. His son-in-law wrote in his diary "My father-in-law died on Thursday." These are all the known facts about his life in Stratford.

Records in London show that in 1612 he signed a deposition in a lawsuit between two men whom the court found to be low characters, with one of whom he had been a lodger in 1604. He and two others bought a house in London and he signed a deed and a mortgage. Two years later there was a lawsuit about the title. The three signatures just referred to and the three on his will are the only signatures ever known to have existed.[3] All are written in a scrawled, unformed hand, all are spelled differently, but none is spelled "Shakespeare".

London records show him as legatee of a small bequest, that he was put under a peace bond in 1596, and was a tax defaulter that year and the next.

These are all the known facts about Shaksper of Stratford. The name William Shakespeare does appear as an actor in 1598, 1603, and 1604, with no reference to any part he played. Nowhere apart from the works themselves was a Shaksper or Shakespeare referred to during his lifetime either as a playwright or a poet.

* * *

[p. 145] There is a doubtful record of a William Shakespeare, unidentified, as receiving thirty-four shillings for work on a pictorial design.

[3] See p. 80—the editors.

Nothing whatever is known of the last years of Shaksper's life. The parish register in Stratford records the burial of "Will. Shaksper(e), gent." on April 25, 1616. On a stone in the church over what is shown as his grave appears doggerel verse which it is said he himself wrote:

Good frend, for Iesus sake forbeare
To digg the dust encloased heare;
Blese be ye man yt spares thes stones,
And curst be he yt moves my bones.

The above are all the established facts about the Stratford man who is considered the greatest literary mind of all time. In the words of Hamlet, "The rest is silence."

No contemporary historian mentions either Shaksper or Shakespeare. One antiquarian published in 1656 an engraving of a monument in the Stratford church with a bust of Shaksper. It showed a sad-eyed man with a drooping mustache and bald head holding a sack of grain in his lap. In 1747 this bust was replaced with the bust seen in the church today. In the new bust the face was wholly changed to look somewhat like the portrait in the First Folio, a pen was shown in his hand and a writing tablet on a tasselled cushion replaced the grain-sack.

We find no external evidence to identify William Shaksper of Stratford, or Shakespeare the actor, as an author. What of the works themselves?

Two poems, *Venus and Adonis* and *The Rape of Lucrece,* were published in 1593 and 1594 bearing the name "William Shake-Speare."[4] This name had never previously been published anywhere. It appeared at the end of unauthorized dedications to Henry Wriothesley . . . The Earl of Southampton. The first referred to the work as "the first heir of my invention". Of the thirty-six plays attributed to Shakespeare, published in the First Folio of 1623, seven years after the death of Shaksper, only fifteen, all quartos, were published during his lifetime. Of these only nine bore the name Shakespeare as the author, the other six being published anonymously. Only three plays published in that name during his lifetime were ever registered for copyright purposes. Many of the plays were produced and pirated earlier.

Between 1595 and 1611 eight other plays were published also in quarto form, some by the same publishers, with authorship attributed to Shakespeare. Seven of these eight are rejected by Shakespeare scholars as not having been written by him. The eighth is

[4] See p. 13—the editors.

considered doubtful. The scholars thus accept as authentic six quarto plays never attributed to Shakespeare during his lifetime and reject as spurious seven quarto plays which were published under his name or initials. Clearly then they reject title-page evidence as the test of authenticity. Their test is comparison with other works they consider authentic. However, there is extant no manuscript nor any literature whatsoever proved to be Shakespeare's. . . . In 1609 *Shake-Speares Sonnets Never Before Imprinted* appeared containing 154 sonnets and also a poem which scholars reject as not by Shakespeare. The sonnets were dedicated to "Mr. W. H." It is generally thought by scholars that these are the reversed initials of Henry Wriothesley, The Earl of Southampton, the man to whom *Venus and Adonis* and *The Rape of Lucrece* were dedicated.

The sonnets are regarded by scholars as autobiographical. They refer frequently to a fair youth and to a dark lady. The Earl of Southampton, who was nine years younger than Shaksper, is thought to be the fair youth. There is no agreement as to the identity of the dark lady, for whom apparently the author had a hopelessly passionate attachment, in spite of her faithlessness to him. The sonnets indicate the author's devotion to the fair youth. They suggest some scandal about him and that a turn of fortune bars the author from public honor. They express, however, a conviction that the lines will live and give immortality to the person about whom they are written.

There are a few references to the works in contemporary writings. During Shaksper's entire life, however, not one of his contemporaries ever referred to him personally as a writer. The only references to Shakespeare were to writings with which that name was connected, and none referred otherwise personally to a writer of that name. Thus neither in the writings them-[**p. 146**]selves nor in their authorship is there anything whatsoever which identified the Stratford man with the author of any of the works, or identifies the two different names, Shaksper and Shakespeare with each other.

The negative evidence is significant. There is no record that Shaksper ever attended school; none that he ever wrote anything. There are no early writings reflecting the development of his skill. Yet he was in his thirtieth year when the first publication appeared, with the literary style fully developed. Then after prolific publication of deathless writings the flow suddenly stopped and he spent his last years in utter obscurity. If he wrote the Shakespeare works, he did so without being paid and let them be pirated freely during his lifetime, although this same man was consistently penurious, frequently suing debtors for small sums. Though twenty of the thirty-six plays were unpublished when he died, his will which made detailed disposition of his belongings, was silent as to any books or other literary property.

It does not appear this man ever travelled abroad or could have become familiar with Latin, Greek or foreign languages. Yet the author's works show familiarity with foriegn countries and languages, familiarity with Latin, especially Ovid; and he coined thousands of English words of Latin and Greek derivation. He had a vocabulary of 15,000 words, almost twice as many as the 8,000 words in the vocabulary of John Milton, the scholar.

Shaksper of Stratford did not frequent court circles so as to become closely familiar with court life and manners, chivalry, tournaments, falconry and sports of the nobility. If he was the author of the works we cannot account for his intimate knowledge of these things and of the law; nor can we understand how one of his consistently materialistic interests could soar to the heights of sublime imagery found in the poetry.

The Shakespeare scholars say that this is all accounted for by his genius. The argument seems to run like this: Shakespeare for centuries has been regarded as the author of the works. The author of the works was a man of superlative genius. Therefore, Shakespeare was a man of superlative genius, and for that reason must have been the author of the works. That is to say, the greater the ignorance and lack of preparation, the greater the genius, and hence the greater the likelihood that Shaksper was the author. This of course is nonsense. Macaulay said of Dryden:

> Genius will not furnish a poet with a vocabulary; it will not teach what word exactly corresponds with his idea and will most surely convey it to others. Information and experience are necessary for strengthening the imagination.

Ben Jonson wrote, "a good poet's made, as well as born". One would expect scholars as well as lawyers to be among the first to recognize the necessity of education, training and preparation.

Shaksper lived unknown as a literary man, and died unnoticed. There was not even sufficient interest in him for anyone to have inquired about him of any of his children or of his granddaughter, nor to write even a four page biography about him until almost a hundred years after his death. Ralph Waldo Emerson said, "I cannot marry the works to the life." Charles Dickens said, "The life of William Shakespeare is a fine mystery, and I tremble every day lest something should turn up." Others who are said to have doubted the authorship include persons of distinction in many different fields: Nathaniel Hawthorne, Lord Palmerston, Walt Whitman, Sir George Greenwood, Mark Twain, Prince Bismarck, Oliver Wendell Holmes, Sigmund Freud, John Bright, Henry James, Lord Brighton, Lord Penzance and John Greenleaf Whittier.

* * *

[p. 206] *Edward de Vere, Seventeenth Earl of Oxford*

Another who disbelieved that Stratfordian authorship was an English schoolteacher with the unfortunate name of J. Thomas Looney. His name has not helped his theory. He had no preconceived notions, except that the identity of the author was deliberately concealed, and the name Shakespeare a pseudonym. He decided to look for early works of the author, convinced the Shakespeare works were his mature writings.

He was struck with the form of the six line pentameter stanzas in *Venus and Adonis,* the earliest Shakespeare writing, "the first heir of my invention". He looked for this form in other sixteenth century verse. He found it in the poetry of Edward de Vere, the seventeenth Earl of Oxford, whose name he had not previously noted. Oxford's dates were 1550 to 1604, so that he was about forty, the right age, when the Shakespeare works began to appear. Reading all this poet's works, Looney found the form of stanza he had noted was common in de Vere's poetry and in Shakespeare, but almost nowhere else in contemporary English verse. As he studied de Vere's life he became convinced, and published his book, *Shakespeare Identified,* in 1920. Others later supplemented his research, notably Dorothy and Charlton Ogburn, the latter a lawyer, in a voluminous work in 1952, entitled *This Star of England.*

The following is a résumé of what they found.

Edward de Vere was trained by his father in riding, hunting, falconry and jousting, but his father died when he was twelve, and the boy then inherited the title as the seventeenth Earl of Oxford. His coat-of-arms bore a lion shaking a spear. As the ranking peer of England he also took the hereditary title of Lord Great Chamberlain, an office close to the Queen's person. His mother shortly remarried, and Queen Elizabeth as his guardian placed him in the household of William Cecil, the Lord Treasurer, and virtual Prime Minister. There he was tutored by his uncle, the scholar, Arthur Golding, in French, Latin and Greek, the classics and poetry. Under Golding's tutelage he made translations of Ovid, one of the principal sources drawn from in Shakespeare. Golding at this time was preparing his principal work, the first English translation of Ovid, which the scholars tell us was the translation used by Shakespeare.

Oxford was graduated from Cambridge University at fourteen and took his master's degree from Oxford University at sixteen, followed by three years' law study at Gray's Inn. There he wrote, produced and acted in plays and masques.

He entered the Queen's service at [p. 207] Court and continued to write and produce poetry and plays to entertain the Queen, who spoke six languages and had a deep interest in literature and the classics. He also distinguished himself in tournaments and became known at Court as the "Spear-shaker". He was sometimes called "Will", a sort of pun on a translation of the name, Vere.

Although the Queen, then forty, was seventeen years older, she "wooed the Earl of Oxford", as reported in state papers, and they had a love affair over several years. (The incredulous are reminded that about fifteen years later she had a love affair with the Earl of Essex, and she was thirty-four years older than Essex.)

Oxford became restive at the idle life at Court, but the Queen denied his request to enter the military or naval service. To keep him at Court she approved his marriage to Anne Cecil, the Lord Treasurer's daughter, then fifteen. She made Cecil Lord Burghley, to give his daughter adequate rank. Burghley was shrewd. He had Oxford make over to him one of his principal estates and kept a hand in the management of the others. The marriage was unhappy. Anne was dominated by her parents who disapproved of Oxford's literary activities, not then considered respectable even for one not a peer.

Oxford travelled in Europe, especially Italy, visiting the places where scenes were later laid in the Shakespeare plays. The famous seven ages of man, as described by Jaques in *As You Like It,* are portrayed with striking similarity in an allegorical mosaic in the pavement of the Cathedral at Siena, where Oxford sojourned in 1575.[5] He kept writing Burghley to send him more money, and to sell his lands for the purpose. Burghley had spies constantly watching him.

When Oxford reached the French Court, he learned his wife had given birth to a daughter. An ugly rumor reported it occurred eleven, and not not nine, months after he left England. He rushed back and refused to speak to his wife or Burghley when he landed.

Oxford kept rooms in London where he encouraged writers such as Lyly, Kyd, Marlowe, Munday, Nashe, Dekker, etc., and he helped them financially. He had his own troupe of actors, known as "Oxford's Boys". Henry Wriothesley, the Earl of Southampton, was one

[5] *Edward de Vere, 17th Earl of Oxford and Shakespeare,* by William Kittle (1942).

of this group. Oxford wrote plays for them and this troupe came to occupy a leading place in the dramatic world. Oxford became improverished in this venture. The Queen had promised to finance it but did not keep her promise until later.

In 1578, Oxford was the chief dramatist of a pageant for the Queen at Cambridge. The poet, Gabriel Harvey, hailed Oxford both as a poet and as a tournament hero. He said of him, "thine eyes flash fire, thy countenance shakes a spear".

Oxford became hopelessly infatuated with a wanton, dark-eyed and dark-haired maid of honor of the Queen, a "dark lady", named Anne Vavasor. This passionate attachment resulted in the birth of a child, and the Queen, a woman scorned, had them both imprisoned in the Tower. Oxford was released after forty-one days, but was banished from Court for two years.

The lands of Oxford were constantly being sold to pay debts. His personal fortune dwindled under Burghley's management, while the crafty Burghley himself became wealthy. Most of the records about Oxford are from Burghley's papers. They contain self-serving statements to indicate he was helping Oxford, but everything derogatory about Burghley, or favorable about Oxford, was apparently carefully destroyed.

In 1586, Oxford sat on the Court that tried Mary Queen of Scots. The same year Queen Elizabeth made him a grant of the modern equivalent of $40,000 a year, probably to fulfill her earlier promise to help finance the theater. The Shakespeare historical plays made the theater a patriotic rallying ground, as the Spanish Armada threatened. In 1588 Oxford commanded a ship against the Armada. While he was at sea, his wife died.

Three years yater, Oxford remarried. His second wife, Elizabeth Trentham, was well-to-do. They lived in London near the theater where plays later published as Shakespeare's were produced. His only son was born in 1593 and was named Henry.

* * *

Oxford was one of six peers who bore the canopy at Elizabeth's funeral, as he had borne her canopy at the Armada victory celebration. In the 125th Shakespeare sonnet is the line "Were't aught to me I bore the canopy?"

Oxford died June 24, 1604. King James caused eight Shakespeare plays to be produced at Court as a tribute to him. When Oxford's widow died nine years later, fourteen of the plays were produced at Court in tribute.

All the facts of Oxford's life are consistent with his having been the author of the Shakespeare works, and none is inconsistent. Every important fact, including familiarity with the law, which the works themselves, without [p. 208] other evidence, indicate must have been true of Shakespeare *was* true of Oxford. His writings were praised by his contemporaries, including the great poet Edmund Spenser. In a dedicatory Sonnet to Oxford, published in the *Faerie Queene* in 1590, Spenser hailed him as one "most deare" to the Muses.

Although passages in two or three of the plays are assumed by some scholars to refer to events occurring after 1604, the principal question about Oxford, if he wrote the Shakespeare works, is his anonymity. The Oxfordian argument on this point is as follows: The autobiographical sonnets refer to disgrace and loss of the author's good name. But more cogent reasons appear. An unwritten code forbade the publication during their lives of poetry written by the nobility. Furthermore, the law prohibited the portrayal on the stage of living persons. Prominent public characters, the intimate details of the lives of royalty, the foibles and sins of those at Court, and current political events and affairs of State, all thinly veiled, form a major part of the subject matter. These could be regarded as pure imagination if written by an outsider. But when written by one in Oxford's position at Court, they would take on reality and have repercussions upon the throne itself. In spite of her love of literature, the Queen could not ignore this hazard. We are told that at Burghley's instigation she herself enjoined anonymity upon Oxford as the price of his freedom to write as he chose. In his devotion to her he accepted these terms.

But the sonnets show the author chafed unhappily at his enforced anonymity. However, the pseudonym may be revealing, and perhaps there is a name-clue in one sonnet in the words "My name is Will." We know "Spear-shaker" and "Will" were Court nicknames for Oxford.

The argument is that Shaksper of Stratford took advantage of the official conspiracy of silence about Oxford's authorship, and used the resemblance of his name to insinuate his own authorship, which Oxford was powerless to deny. Later through Henry Wriothesley, the Stratford man was used as a blind. Southampton's payment to him for this service was the mysterious source of Shaksper's wealth. The two years Southampton was in prison were almost the only ones during which no publication of the Shakespeare works appeared, from the first poem published in 1593 until Oxford's death in 1604. That year *Hamlet* was completed in the second quarto, generally considered the last, best, and most autobiographical play. Oxford had a cousin, Horatio de Vere, thought to be the Horatio of the play. . . .

On Oxford's death publication of the Shakespeare plays stopped, and except for three plays and the sonnets, no more were published until nineteen years later when twenty plays were published for the first time.

After Oxford's death, Burghley's son, Robert Cecil, Francis Bacon and Ben Jonson are believed to have persuaded the Earl of Pembroke and his brother, Oxford's son-in-law, the Earl of Montgomery, and also Oxford's son, the eighteenth Earl, to preserve the anonymity. The Earl of Pembroke paid Ben Jonson the modern equivalent of $8,000 a year to supervise the posthumous publication under the pseudonym and to write the introductory poem for the First Folio, as though he had been personally acquainted with Shakespeare. The Folio was dedicated to the Earls of Pembroke and Montgomery.

There is further evidence. In 1940 X-ray and infra-red examinations of several portraits of Shakespeare showed them to be alterations of portraits of Lord Oxford. . . .

This is the gist of the Oxfordian argument, which is copiously supplemented in the books with supporting quotations from the Shakespeare works.

1959 *American Bar Association Journal,* "A Mystery Solved: The True Identity of Shakespeare," by Charlton Ogburn, Vol. 45, No. 3, March, 1959, pp. 237-241.

[p. 237] One hundred years ago two English barristers were so much impressed by Shakespeare's acquaintance with the law that each wrote a book on the subject. William Lowes Rushton in 1858 published his *Shakespeare a Lawyer;* and John Lord Campbell published his *Shakespeare's Legal Acquirements* in 1859, the year he was created Lord Chancellor, after having held the office of Lord Chief Justice. . . .

Sidney Lee, a layman, the author of a lengthy biography of the Stratford man (although all the known facts of his life can be put on less than one page), noted in the earlier editions the poet's "accurate use of legal terms which deserves all the attention which has been paid to it". Other writers . . . were impressed by Shakespeare's legal attainments.

* * *

The dramatist was obviously a trained lawyer. When this inevitable conclusion was put forward, it became obvious that "Shakespeare" must, therefore, have been a pseudonym. This would never do! Sidney Lee thereupon accomplished a quick *volte face* and wrote: "Shakespeare's legal knowledge, so far from being exceptional, is but a mingled skein of accuracy and inaccuracy; the errors are numerous and important". Lee showed his own "profound" knowledge of the law by writing that Shakespeare (*sic*) "obtained judgment from a jury" against Adderbrook for a few shillings. Lee selected Arthur Underhill to write the chapter on "Law" in the first volume of *Shakespeare's England,* the production of which was undertaken by Lee, and which was published in 1909. Underhill obligingly wrote in his chapter that "Shakespeare's knowledge of law was neither profound nor accurate". . . . Underhill gives his explanation that the Stratford [**p. 238**] man "was prone to litigation" and could have learned his law in being sued and in suing his malt customers. He was never a student at the Inns of Court; in fact, as Arthur Underhill tells us, the Inns were very exclusive in those days, admitting none except "gentlemen of the blood", and this by royal command. A Boston lawyer took up the cudgels on Lee's side, and inserted a chapter called "Bad Law in Shakespeare" in a book he published in 1900, which Lee hailed as "especially noteworthy". This was Charles C. Allen, who in 1862 had been appointed Associate Justice of the Supreme Judicial Court of Massachusetts. Allen, by the way, was answered conclusively by Sir George Greenwood, K.C., an eminent barrister and M.P., in a volume entitled *Shakespeare's Law.*

* * *

Shakespeare's Law . . . Illustrations from the Plays

Here are a few illustrations from the plays and the sonnets revealing the author's acquaintance with the law and legal phraseology:

In *The Comedy of Errors* one of the characters speaks of "fine and recovery", an expression also used in several other plays. Today lawyers scarcely know the meaning of "fine and recovery", which were collusive actions in Shakespeare's day employed to bar estates tail, to bar dower, to convey estates of married women, to enable married women to join with their husbands in selling property, etc. In this play too there is an example of *mesne process* in an action on the *case.*

In *As You Like It* there are also illustrations which, as Lord

Campbell said, present themselves rather to the mind of one initiated in legal proceedings than of one who had been brought up as an assistant to a butcher. The usurping Duke, wishing to seize the real property of Oliver, awards a writ of extent against him in the very language which Campbell wrote would have been used by Lord Chief Baron of the Court of Exchequer—an *extendi facias.*

In *King Henry VIII* there is an example of writ of *praemunire,* this very word being used by the Duke of Suffolk in addressing Cardinal Wolsey.

In *The Merchant of Venice,* Antonio was arrested on *mesne process.* The bond which had been given by him shows a distinction between a single bill and a bond with a condition. Punctual payment is indicated in the language, "Let good Antonio keep his day." When Salarino says the Duke will never grant this forfeiture to hold, Antonio replies: "The Duke cannot deny the course of law." Portia, under the authority of the Doge, acts as judge and asks if there is a plea of *non est factum.* In the Elizabethan era there was a contest between the Chancellor in the Court of Equity and the common law judges. The latter resented the Chancellor's effort to enjoin the execution of their judgments. Portia holds that under the common law "there is no power in Venice can alter a decree established. . . . This bond is forfeit." Portia, however, changes her role from judge to chancellor and Antonio is saved.

In *The Taming of the Shrew,* Shakespeare speaks of the *Leet,* which in that day was a court of criminal judicature. He understands the custom of lawyers: "And do as adversaries do in law, strive mightily, but eat and drink as friends."

All's Well that Ends Well has an interesting illustration of the law of guardian and ward, dealing with the right of the guardian to select a wife for his ward if she be of equal rank. The King of France, in requiring Bertram, Count Rousillon, a ward, to marry Helena over Bertram's strenuous objections, is here acting as the sovereign as well as guardian. Edward de Vere, the 17th Earl of Oxford, was a royal ward, his immediate guardian being Sir William Cecil, who, with the Queen's consent, required him to marry Cecil's own daughter, then fourteen; but de Vere, a lawyer, knew he was not obligated to consent, since Anne Cecil was a commoner and he was a noble. This was the law, as explained by Littleton. The obstacle was met, however, by the Queen's giving Cecil the rank of Lord Burghley. Even so, when the wedding was set for September, 1571, de Vere failed to appear and it had to be postponed until the following December.

In *Measure for Measure* we have an example of a "pre-contract", *per verba de praesenti,* being sufficient to constitute legal marriage, although there has been no wedding.

In *The Winter's Tale,* Queen Hermione was indicted for treason. The proper legal language was used as alleging an overt act committed by her "contrary to the faith and allegiance of a true subject".

In *Henry IV,* Part I Mortimer says: "And our indentures tripartite are drawn which being sealed interchangeably". Henry uses the expression, "enfeoffed". Another legal term in this play is to "sue his livery", which is a proceeding by a ward of the Crown on reaching majority to obtain possession of his land. In *Henry IV,* Part II, Shallow talks a good deal about having beer at the "Inns o' Court" with Falstaff.

* * *

In *Othello,* Iago speaks of "non-suiting" his mediators.

In *Antony and Cleopatra,* Lepidus speaks of "taking by descent rather than by purchase".

In *Romeo and Juliet,* Montague and Capulet are "bound over", as in English law, to keep the peace.

In *The Merry Wives of Windsor,* one of the characters in speaking of Falstaff says: "If the devil have him not in fee simple, with fine and recovery, he will never I think in the way of waste attempt us again."

A number of the sonnets use the analogy of legal terms, notably Sonnet 46 where almost every line draws on expressions used in sixteenth century legal procedure, especially connected with landholding and real estate. . . .

[**p. 239**] Shakespeare never makes a mistake in the use of legal terms, as a layman trying to use them would be bound to do.

1959 *American Bar Association Journal,* "The Case for the Defense: De Vere *et al.* v. Shakespeare," by William W. Clary, Vol. 45, No. 7, July, 1959, pp. 700-703, 750.

[**p. 700**] Every lover of "Shakespeare" must wish that he knew the full story of the life of this great literary genius. The skimpy and prosaic records of the Stratford man, as outlined by Mr. Richard Bentley in the February issue of the *Journal,* leave one cold. And it is not strange that many thoughtful persons have doubted whether such a man could have been the real Shakespeare. Certainly there is no impropriety in expressing these doubts, as Mr. Bentley has done in a clear and interesting manner.

But Mr. Bentley says that it is in part a question of evidence for lawyers. And he has given a summation of the "evidence" on the basis of which he asks the "jury" to retire and consider its verdict. Now if the question is to be decided on the basis of legal evidence, and if I were attorney for the Stratford man, I should think it my duty to challenge Mr. Bentley's statement that "There is admittedly no direct proof of the authorship."

I am not quite sure what Mr. Bentley means by "direct proof". All the eye-witnesses are dead so the only kind of evidence possible is written or documentary evidence. I should think documentary evidence, properly authenticated, given by persons so situated as to have knowledge of the facts, would be direct proof. I believe there is such evidence and that it does prove that my client was the real Shakespeare. This evidence is found in Shakespeare's will, which Mr. Bentley quotes in another connection, and in the First Folio.

The crucial clause of the will which enables us to identify the Stratford man is found in a bequest made in these words:

> To my ffellowes John Hemynge Richard Burbage & Henry Cundell XXVIs VIIId a peece to buy them Ringes.[6]

The three men thus remembered are shown by official records to have been members of a company of players known first as the Lord Chamberlain's Men and later as the King's Men. Thus we have documentary proof that the man of Stratford knew these three men and considered them his "ffellowes". The official records show that a man named Will. Shakespeare was a member of their company.

In 1623, two of these men, Heminge and Condell, being the last surviving members of this company (Burbage having died in 1619), issued the first collected edition of "Mr. William Shakespeare's Comedies, Histories & Tragedies" known, of course, as the First Folio.

In the dedicatory address in this volume Heminge and Condell wrote:

> We have but collected them [the plays in the Folio] . . . onely to keep the memory of *so worthy a friend and Fellow* alive, as was our Shakespeare, by humble offer of *his plays* to your most noble patronage [italics added].

[6] Several similar bequests of money to buy rings, including one to Shakespeare's godson William Walker, are made in the will. The "memorial ringe" was evidently a token of affection and esteem.

Mr. Bentley has narrowed the issue to the simple question "Was Shakespeare [the author] the same man as Shaksper [of Stratford] . . . " These documents furnish clear prima facie proof that the Stratford man who remembered Heminge and Condell in his will as "My Fellows" was the same man whom Heminge and Condell remembered as their "Friend and Fellow" and whose memory they wished to honor by publication of "his plays". **[p. 701]** The authenticity of the documents and records quoted is not questioned. In the absence of conflicting evidence *of greater weight* I think they would have to be accepted in a court of law as conclusive of this issue. There is no such conflicting evidence.

If Shakespeare of Stratford did not write the plays in the First Folio then Heminge and Condell were either (1) deceived by their friend and fellow who successfully foisted on them as his own thirty-six plays which had been written by someone else, or (2) Heminge and Condell were themselves party to this gigantic fraud. Neither assumption is tenable.

Did Heminge, Condell Lie? . . . Why Should They?

There is not a shred of evidence to support even a suspicion that Heminge and Condell were deliberately lying when they wrote the statements in the First Folio. Nor is there any basis for the supposition that they were deceived. On the contrary there are excellent reasons why their statements should be accepted at face value.

Heminge and Condell were "fellows", *i.e.*, partners with Shakespeare, (identified above as the Stratford man) in the production and staging of the very plays in the First Folio. They were with Shakespeare day and night. They knew where he lived, how he lived and how he occupied his time. They state in their address to the reader that they saw his manuscripts. Their association extended over a period of many years (scholars say at least sixteen). If Shakespeare was incapable of writing these plays it is difficult if not impossible to suppose that men like Burbage, Heminge and Condell would not have had their suspicions aroused when he handed them play after play, year in and year out, of the quality of *Julius Caesar, Macbeth* or *Twelfth Night* and represented them as his own compositions. But their suspicions were not aroused. On the contrary they testified that his "wit" (which then meant intellectual power) "can no more lie hid, than it could be lost". . . .

. . . I think the evidence quoted does settle the issue. But there are several reasons why the debate continues. One is that scholars, and lawyers too (as I know to my sorrow) have a disposition to solve problems the hard way. I have many times seen lawyers in court build up mountains of evidence, all the time getting farther and farther away from the central issue, when the answer is so easy and so close at hand that it is completely overlooked—like Poe's Purloined Letter. Of course, the evidence I have cited has not been overlooked, but I think that in general, both sides have failed to appreciate the probative value this evidence would have in a court of law.

* * *

It is not my province as a lawyer to go behind the legal evidence. But there is one aspect . . . of special interest to lawyers. . . . That is, how can we account for Shakespeare's vast knowledge of law?

* * *

Shakespeare's Law . . . Taken from His Sources

. . . let us take an example . . . of Shakespeare's legal knowledge. In Act III, Scene 1, [*Henry IV,* Part I] the three conspirators Glendower, Mortimer and Hotspur enter into a contract for the partition of all England into three parts. The transaction is described in perfect legal language. Here it is:

> *Mort.* The Archdeacon hath divided it
> Into three limits very equally.
> England, from Trent and Severn hitherto,
> By south and east is to my part assign'd;
> All westward, Wales beyond the Severn shore,
> And all the fertile land within that bound,
> To Owen Glendower; and, dear coz, to you
> The remnant northward, lying off from Trent.
> And our indentures tripartite are drawn;
> Which being sealed interchangeably,
> A business that this night may execute,
> To-morrow, Cousin Percy, you and I
> And my good Lord of Worcester will set forth
> To meet your father and the Scottish power,
> As is appointed us, at Shrewsbury.

The word "tripartite" is an unusual word, seldom used by laymen, even if they are college graduates. How did Shakespeare know this word and how did he learn to use it correctly? . . .

[p. 702] [In] Holinshed's *Chronicles,* which is the principal source of this play, . . . the "attorney-like" partition agreement is described in these words:

> Heerewith, they by their deputies in the house of the archdeacon of Bangor, divided the realm among them, causing a tripartite indenture

> to be made and sealed with their seales, by the convenants whereof, all England from Severne and Trent, south and eastward, was assigned to the earle of March: all Wales, and the lands beyond Severne westward, were appointed to Owen Glendower: and all the remnant from Trent northward, to the lord Persie.
>
> (Holinshed's *Chronicles* 1586, Volume 3, page 521.)

This makes [an] imagined scene of Shakespeare's law office experience in Stratford seem a bit ridiculous. All Shakespeare had to do, with Holinshed's book open on his table in front of him, was to turn Holinshed's language into blank verse. Being a poet, he did this easily and supremely well.

This excerpt shows not only how Shakespeare borrowed Holinshed's legal phraseology, but also how he got his knowledge of English history. Many similar examples could be cited.

William Shakespeare . . . Doctor, Lawyer, Merchant, Chief

Shakespeare's knowledge is indeed varied and covers a wide range of subjects. It has been seriously claimed not only that he was a lawyer, but that he was a sailor (his familiarity with seamanship[7]), a soldier, a physician, an apothecary, a horticulturist, a merchant, a courtier, a nobleman, etc., etc. If we pursue such claims much farther we will soon reach the point where we will have proved that nobody at all wrote Shakespeare because no such person could possibly have existed even with the aid of a university education. But an author did exist and the evidence is pretty clear that he was a professional playwriter. And the knowledge he displayed in other fields can, I believe, be explained in much the same way as his knowledge of law is explained.

Moreover, scholars tell us (and here they have a right to speak) that although Shakespeare's understanding of human nature was profound, his general knowledge in the various fields above mentioned was superficial and insular. It was the kind of knowledge a man of keen intellect and good memory would absorb from a hasty reading of "sources"; and sometimes he was guilty of absurd errors which Bacon, Marlowe or de Vere would hardly have made. So I conclude that most of his knowledge can be accounted for, and that his lack of formal education was no insuperable obstacle to his authorship of the plays and poems.

There is one other point on which a lawyer might comment. That is the absence of any reference to "literary property" in Shake-

[7] It has been computed that there are more nautical terms in the plays than there are legal terms. . . .

speare's will. The reason for this which I think would naturally occur to a lawyer is that Shakespeare sold his plays to the company that produced them. But Mr. Bentley says that if he (the Stratford man) wrote the plays "he did so without being paid". I have never seen any evidence to support this assertion. On the contrary there is a strong presumption that his company paid him for his work either directly or through his share of company profits.

This presumption is supported by what scholars say was the common practice of the time, namely, that companies owned the plays they produced. It is also supported by documentary evidence which I will not take time to quote but which may be found in *The Shakespeare First Folio, Its Bibliographical and Textual History,* by W. W. Greg, Oxford, 1955, pages 15-16.

So I conclude that by 1616 Shakespeare had parted with his literary property and there was no occasion to mention it in his will. And so too all the other arguments and inferences in Mr. Bentley's article are subject to counter arguments and inferences.

I do not expect this statement will close the debate. Indeed it would be too bad if it did, for it would put an end to the most interesting controversy in all literary history. But I believe I have shown that there are good reasons why a lawyer may rest in the belief that the much-maligned man of Stratford, notwithstanding his lawsuits and his dealings in malt, was the man whodunit.

1959 *American Bar Association Journal,* "The Shakespearean Controversy: A Stratfordian Rejoinder," by John N. Hauser, Vol. 45, No. 7, July, 1959, pp. 704-707, 765-766.

[p. 704] In the February and March issues of the *Journal* articles appeared by two distinguished lawyers, Richard Bentley and Charlton Ogburn, regarding the authorship of Shakespeare's plays and poems. The thrust of both articles is that William Shakespeare of Stratford-on-Avon did not and could not have written the works traditionally attributed to him.

* * *

The controversy is a fascinating one and it is not surprising that lawyers have been interested in it. As is true of other famous Elizabethans, only a moderate amount of evidence survives as to the facts of William Shakespeare's life. His authorship of the plays and poems probably never will be proved beyond a shadow of a doubt. . . .

I submit, however, that the preponderance of the evidence shows that the credit belongs to Shakespeare of Stratford.

* * *

[p. 705] Let us examine (1) some of the principal points on which anti-Stratfordians rely in arguing that Shakespeare of Stratford did not write the works attributed to him; and (2) the theories advanced in support of the Earl of Oxford as the real author of the works.

I. The Case Against Shakespeare of Stratford

A. *Shakespeare Spelled His Name the Wrong Way*

Anti-Stratfordians . . . point to the fact that Shakespeare was baptized as Shaksper and in the six unquestioned examples of Shakespeare's signature he signs his name Shaksper or Shakspere or Shakspeare.[8] On the other hand, the plays were published and referred to by contemporaries as having been written by Shakespeare or Shake-speare. To the anti-Stratfordian this goes to prove that the actor "Shaksper" and the playwright "Shakespeare" were different men. But a number of documents and records refer to the Stratfordian actor as "Shakespeare". There is, for example, the record of a payment to him as an actor in 1594, the deed (or "fine") to New Place in 1597, and the royal patent issued in 1603 to the King's Men, the group of players of which Shakespeare was a member.

Elizabethans were apt to be careless in their spelling and there are many other examples of variant spellings of the names of prominent people. Sir Walter Raleigh often spelled his name Ralegh. Others spelled it differently, such as Rawley, Raghley, Rawlie, etc. Christopher Marlowe's name was written, among other ways, as Marloe, Marley, Morley and Mar-low. The Marchioness of Exeter ended a letter to her son, the Earl of Devon: "by your lowfying mothar, Gartrude Exettar".

* * *

B. *Shakespeare's Father Was Illiterate*

Anti-Stratfordians evidently accept as gospel that Shakespeare's father John was illiterate. The only evidence of this is that Shakespeare's father used his "mark" in signing some documents. This mark consisted of a neatly drawn pair of glover's dividers, for John, among other things, was a glove-maker.

[8] See pp. 5, 80—the editors.

The fact is that many people in Elizabethan times used a "mark" to sign documents even though they were literate. For example, Adrian Quiney's mark appears in some of the same Stratford records which bear John Shakespeare's mark. Yet letters by Quiney prove he could write if he wanted to.[9]

John Shakespeare was a man of substance in Stratford during Shakespeare's childhood. He served as alderman, chamberlain (co-treasurer) and mayor, and those are curious offices for an illiterate man to have held.

C. *Shakespeare Was Unschooled and Illiterate*

. . . Not satisfied with claiming Shakespeare's father was illiterate because he used a "mark", the Anti-Stratfordians rely on the apparently [*sic*] illegibility of Shakespeare's signature to prove he was illiterate too.

Of the six signatures in question, three are affixed to the pages of Shakespeare's will written about a month before his death. These signatures are pretty shaky. The other three appear on a conveyance, a mortgage and a deposition in a lawsuit. . . . the signatures are mainly in the Old English script (much like German script) that commonly was taught in school in Shakespeare's time. . . . To assert that the signatures are the scrawls of an illiterate man is to confuse Elizabethan handwriting with modern handwriting.[10]

Any such illiteracy certainly would have been a great burden to Shakespeare, who even the anti-Stratfordians admit was an actor, and one of the members and owners of the most successful group of players of the time.

We must concede there is no surviving record of Shakespeare's schooling. There was a guild school in Stratford to which townspeople of substance could send their children free of charge. The masters were Oxford or Cambridge graduates. There is no reason to believe that John Shakespeare did not send William to the school. . . . there were more schools in Shakespeare's time in proportion to the population than existed in Victorian England.

It is fairly certain Shakespeare did not go on to Oxford or Cambridge. Some of his playwright contemporaries such as Marlowe were college trained. Others were not, including Ben Jonson, and Jonson's erudition and knowledge of classical literature were and still are regarded as greatly superior to Shakespeare's. There were

[9] *Shakespeare of London, supra,* page 6.

[10] S. A. Tannenbaum, *Problems in Shakspere's Penmanship* (New York, 1927), pp. 20, 117. Dr. Tannenbaum considers that Shakespeare was a skillful writer and that even the signatures to the will reveal a "good, fluent, clear, simple, legible, and even somewhat artistic hand".

plenty of opportunities in London for self-education. Thousands of books and pamphlets of all descriptions were being printed including English translation [*sic*] of Greek and Latin classics. . . [p. 706]

D. *Shakespeare Knew Too Little About Law*

The very foundation of the anti-Stratfordian dogma, as set forth forcefully in the articles by Messrs. Bentley and Ogburn, is that Shakespeare must have known too little about law, medicine, travel, seamanship, history, the classics and life at court to be able to write the plays and poems. The dogma continues that the real author must have had extensive training in most or all of these fields and particularly law because of the supposedly specialized knowledge shown in Shakespeare's work. Obviously Shakespeare had no such training and therefore he is eliminated.

Who had such training? Why of course the Earl of Oxford or Sir Francis Bacon or Sir Walter Raleigh, etc., etc. All members of the aristocracy. Oxford, Bacon and Raleigh had legal training, Raleigh sailed the seas, Oxford traveled around dissipating his estate, and Bacon was a notable scholar. More or less the same could be (and has been) said for many other aristocrats.

This sort of reasoning would classify as imposters Jonson, Dekker, Marlowe, Webster, Kyd and most of the other Elizabethan dramatists. Many of their plays are about happenings at court, foreign lands and historical occurrences. Their writings contain classical allusions, usually to a greater degree than Shakespeare's plays, and enough legal expressions to delight any present-day lawyer.

* * *

All this points up the necessity for considering Shakespeare in the light of his time, not as a superman writing in a vacuum. Thus far the only thorough study of the use of legal concepts in the plays of Shakespeare and his contemporaries is *The Law of Property in Shakespeare and the Elizabethan Drama,* by Paul Clarkson and Clyde Warren (Baltimore, 1942). The authors, both lawyers, read and indexed all the plays of Shakespeare and seventeen of the best known other Elizabethan dramatists. Their conclusion, amply documented, is that

> . . . our reading of the plays revealed that about half of Shakespeare's fellows employed on the average more [p. 707] legalisms than he did—some of them a great many more. For example, the sixteen plays of Ben Johnson [*sic*] (whose apprentice years were spent in laying bricks, and certainly not in copying deeds and drafting pleadings) have a total

of over five hundred references from all fields of the law. This surpasses Shakespeare's total from more than twice as many plays. Not only do half of the playwrights employ legalisms more freely than Shakespeare, but most of them also exceed him in the detail and complexity of their legal problems and allusions, and with few exceptions display a degree of accuracy at least no lower than his.

* * *

E. *He Went Unnoticed by Contemporary Men of Letters*

The final part of the anti-Stratfordian dogma with which I will deal is the assertion that Shakespeare of Stratford went unnoticed and unmentioned by contemporary writers. Anti-Stratfordians of course do not intend this as a literal statement of fact. There were many contemporary references to Shakespeare[11] but anti-Stratfordians endeavor to explain them all away. For example where a contemporary has written praising or mentioning Shakespeare as a dramatist or poet, we are told that the allusion is to the works and proves nothing about the identity of the man. . . .

References to Shakespeare appear, among other places, in the writings of his fellow dramatists John Webster, Francis Beaumont and Ben Jonson. It was Jonson who wrote the famous poem in the First Folio of Shakespeare's plays, addressed "To the memory of my beloved, the author, Mr. William Shakespeare." In the poem Jonson refers to Shakespeare as "Sweet Swan of Avon" and clearly links actor with author.

Anti-Stratfordians claim that this poem was a hoax perpetrated to conceal the true author of the plays. But the prime candidate as the "real author"—the Earl of Oxford—had been dead for nineteen years. Lord Burghley who supposedly imposed strict censorship on Oxford's career as a dramatist, had been dead for twenty-five years. Queen Elizabeth had been dead for twenty years, and Shakespeare of Stratford for seven years. What was there to hide?

The introduction that Shakespeare's fellow actors Heminge and Condell wrote for the First Folio also has been called a hoax, again on the purest sort of conjecture. And finally there is the poem contributed to the First Folio by Leonard Digges of Stratford, in which reference is made to Shakespeare and the "Stratford Monument".[12]

There is just too much to be explained away. The evidence of the First Folio alone should, I submit, be sufficient to convince an impartial reader that Shakespeare the actor and Shakespeare the

[11] *The Shakspere Allusion-Book,* two volumes (Oxford, 1932). This is an enormous collection of the allusions to Shakespeare from 1591 to 1700.

[12] See p. 246—the editors.

writer were the same person, and that the "real" Shakespeare did not go unnoticed.

II. The Case for the Earl of Oxford

Unquestionably the current favorite candidate among the anti-Stratfordians is Edward de Vere, the 17th Earl of Oxford. He was born in 1550 and died in 1604. . . . In a recent history of the Elizabethan period Oxford is described as

> light-headed, a fop . . . talented, with a taste for literature and the society of players, dissolute and with no head for money whatever: he was always ready to sell a manor at less than its value for ready cash; at the end, he had the mentality of a failed gambler.

What qualifications did this "light-headed fop" have for writing the Shakespearean plays and poems? Oxford was well educated, went to both Oxford and Cambridge and studied law. One of his coats of arms bore a lion shaking a spear. He travelled in Italy and other parts of Europe and is supposed to have started a fashion at Elizabeth's court for wearing Italian clothes. He was of course familiar with the sea, warfare, customs of the nobility and the Greek and Latin classics.

Oxford in his time was recognized as a writer of plays and poetry (some poetry has survived) and like other noblemen he was a patron of the arts. It has been argued that some events in his life bore a resemblance to events referred to in the Shakespearean plays and sonnets.

Why then, aside from the evidence that Shakespeare of Stratford wrote the plays and poems, could not Oxford have been their author? [p. 765]

A. *There Is No Evidence That Oxford Had the Necessary Ability*

We have seen that Oxford had all the "qualifications" that supposedly were necessary to have written the Shakespearean works. All the qualifications *except* the unique sort of genius displayed by the works. Unfortunately one cannot take an artistocrat, give him a college education, stuff him full of law, history, the "classics", knowledge of foreign lands and court life, and produce a Shakespeare. . . .

* * *

What evidence is there that Oxford had the necessary ability to write the Shakespearean works? . . . A number of Oxford's poems survive, some reasonably familiar such as the one beginning, "If women could be fair and yet not fond . . ." But the critical verdict cannot put these poems in the first rank. They are simply "good specimens of Elizabethan courtly poetry". . . .

Oxfordites assert that their candidate was recognized as the foremost poet and dramatist of his age. Their source for this remarkable statement appears to be a book by one Henry Peacham, *The Compleat Gentleman,* published in 1622. Peacham's qualifications seem to be that he describes himself as a Cambridge Master of Arts. Peacham gives his list of the outstanding poets of the age as follows:

> Edward Earle of Oxford, the Lord Buckhurst, Henry Lord Paget, the noble Sir Philip Sydney,[13] M. Edward Dyer, M. Edmund Spenser, Master Samuel Daniel, with sundry others whom (together with those admirable wits yet living and so well knowne) not out of Envy, but to avoid tediousnesse, I overpasse.

As Oxfordites proudly observe, their candidate (the ranking nobleman) is listed first. There is no mention of Shakespeare. However, the list doesn't purport to be complete: both the "sundry others" and the "wits yet living and so well knowne" are omitted, and the list says nothing about playwrights.

The scarcity of other references to Oxford as a literary giant is explained away by Oxfordites on the theory that powerful hands were "dedicated to erasing his memory from the knowledge of man". . . . [Yet] Oxford is mentioned as a writer of comedies in Francis Meres' *Palladis Tamia* (1598). But Meres also mentions William Shakespeare, praises Shakespeare highly and lists the eleven plays generally considered to have been written by that time. . . .

B. *Oxford Died Before the Later Plays Were Written*

Unfortunately for his partisans, Oxford died in 1604. Contemporary evidence, generally accepted, shows that ten of the Shakespearean plays were written after 1604, including *King Lear, Macbeth, Antony and Cleopatra,* and *The Tempest.*

King Lear, for example, is considered to have been written in 1605 or 1606. It was performed at court during the Christmas holidays in 1606. Two of the speeches in the play refer to "late eclipses in the sun and moon" which occurred in September and October, 1605. The two speeches appear to have been taken almost verbatim from a pamphlet published in February, 1606. *The Tempest* is considered to have been written in about 1611. The plot draws on

[13] Doubtless an imposter [*sic*]. The real poet's name is spelled "Sidney".

the Bermudan adventures and discoveries of Sir George Somers, no report of which reached England until September, 1610.

1959 *American Bar Association Journal,* "The True Shakespeare: England's Great and Complete Man," by Dorothy and Charlton Ogburn, Volume 45, No. 9, September, 1959, pp. 941-943, 990-996.

[p. 941] To those who can believe that the noblest works in our language—still vital and inspiring, gay, sophisticated, tragic, profoundly wise, a glory of literature—were the creation of a provincial butcher's apprentice who went up to London in his early twenties, became "a servitur in the theatre", then a minor actor, and some dozen years later returned to the dirty little village of Stratford to buy property, profiteer in grain and sue his neighbors for small sums of money, one need not appeal. They are satisfied with their miracle. They see Shakespeare as merely another playwright like the well-educated London writers who frequented the Boar's Head Tavern, and they regard his works as fiction presented in a vacuum, brilliant but with only a surface meaning, "objective". To them it is not inconceivable that the grain-dealer whose hungry neighbors wished to hang him at his own door for hoarding corn, could write,

> Who steals my purse steals trash; 'tis something, nothing . . .
>
> [or]
>
> By Jove, I am not covetous for gold . . .
> But if it be a sin to covet honour
> I am the most offending soul alive.

* * *

They are not moved to protest as Coleridge did against this concept of Shakespeare: "I speak reverently, does God choose idiots by whom to convey divine truths to man?" Nor would they agree with Carlyle that Shakespeare was "the chief of all poets hitherto: the greatest intellect who, in our recorded world, *has left a record of himself* in the way of literature".

[p. 942] It is to the others—to those who know with Emerson that you may "use what language you will, you cannot say anything but what you are": mediocrity produces mediocrity and greatness greatness—that the following . . . is addressed.

* * *

I.

Edward de Vere, 17th Earl of Oxford, hereditary Lord Great Chamberlain and Companion to the Monarch, was forced to bow to the fiat of anonymity. But in the ardent hope that his "good name" would be known to posterity, he filled both plays and sonnets with unmistakable clues to his identity. Wordsworth was right about the sonnets: "With this key Shakespeare unlocked his heart."

In Sonnet 76 the poet puns on his name, E. Vere, or E. Ver, as it was sometimes spelled:

> Why write I still all one, *ever* [E. Ver] the same,
> And *keep invention in a noted weed,*
> That *every* [E. Ver-y] word doth *almost tell my name,*
> *Showing their birth and where they did proceed?*

"Every word" almost tells his concealed name, E. Ver. The "noted weed", or garment, in which he clothes his verse is the true story that he relates in all he writes. (If the poet had been a recognized playwright named Shakespeare, this sonnet would be meaningless.)

In No. 81 he promises the Fair Youth immortality:

> Your name from hence immortal life shall have,
> *Though I,* once gone, *to all the world must die.*

It is ordained that the world must not know that Edward de Vere was Shakespeare. (There was no reason why the Stratford man's name "must die", if his work had merited immortality. Marlowe's name has lived in his work, for all of which he has received credit.) De Vere was jealous of his great name, the most illustrious in England, and he felt the obligation it entailed. His highest wish was to do it honor, as his ancestors had.

In No. 36 he says to the Fair Youth, who is his son:

> I may not evermore *acknowledge thee,*
> Lest *my bewailed guilt* should do thee shame.

When the Queen, seventeen years his senior, had seduced the young courtier, he had given her a son, "a little western flower"; the "bewailed guilt" was his, for she, an absolute monarch, preferred to pass on, "In maiden meditation, fancy free", preserving her legend. Through the machinations of the Cecils, **[p. 943]** Francis Bacon and their followers the legend has been fairly well preserved, though Elizabeth Tudor was no more a virgin than her father had been.

In No. 71 he counsels his son to forget him after he is dead:

> Do not so much as *my poor name* rehearse,
> But let your love, even with my life, decay.
> Lest *the wise world* should look into your moan
> And *mock you with me* after I am gone.

The bitterness of his sacrifice is here. His great name has been made a mockery.

No. 72 expresses the deep melancholy of renunciation:

> *My name be buried* where my body is,
> And live no more to shame nor me nor you.
> For *I am sham'd by that which I bring forth . . .*

He was shamed by being unable to acknowledge either his son or his work. Here is the final tragedy of the noble poet. His name was indeed "buried". How poignant it is when the truth is known!

* * *

II.

The motive for the enforcement of Oxford's anonymity stemmed from the autobiographical and topical content of his poems and plays, the candid revelations they contained. Like Hamlet's, his players were "the abstracts and brief chronicles of the time". He knew everything, and he told everything, as exuberant genius does, without reservation. He did this sometimes symbolically, sometimes with astonishing literalness, always fearlessly. Although working in the Queen's service and with her strong support ("I serve Her Majesty", he wrote Burghley in 1583, "and I am that I am"), he told the truth about her too. Regarding himself as his sovereign's defender—her Spear-shaker in the field of literature, as his ancestors had been on the battlefield—he wrote certain plays to warn, or to "catch the conscience of" the Queen.

No one in the kingdom except Elizabeth's premier Earl, her "chiefest courtier" and favorite, would have been allowed to portray on the stage the deposition of an English monarch, as Shakespeare did in *3 Henry VI* and in *Richard II*. . . . *3 Henry VI* was written to warn the Queen about her "too much lenity" to villains; *Richard II* subsequently stressed the warning: "A thousand flatterers sit within thy crown . . ."—both these at times when she was succumbing to the blandishments of certain wily schemers at court. Although she was angry, she admitted the imputation: "I am Richard, know ye not that?" she snapped. . . .

(It is inconceivable that Elizabeth Tudor would have permitted a common playwright such license. *This fact alone is enough to dispose of the Stratford thesis.*)

* * *

[**p. 990**] One of Oxford's most candid, literal and detailed portrayals of the Lord Treasurer is in the character of Polonius, Chief Minister at the court of Denmark. (*Hamlet* is straight autobiography, with some of the revelations made in symbolic terms. The Ghost of his father is Vere—Truth—informing his son about what is "rotten in the state of" England; Horatio and Francisco are Oxford's cousins, Horatio and Francis Vere.) Cecil, an inveterate eavesdropper, set spies upon his own son and later upon his son-in-law, Oxford, when they travelled abroad, just as Polonius employs Reynaldo to spy upon Laertes. (Cecil was called "the Fox" at court.) . . .

When Polonius cries out from behind the arras, Hamlet, exclaiming, "How now! a rat?" stabs the old busybody with his rapier. After the fashion of Elizabethan drama, this was, in one sense, a symbolic death (it was so understood by the *cognoscenti* at court, although the play was of course "caviare to the general"): Hamlet is stabbing the intruder with his rapier wit. So that when the King demands, "Now, Hamlet, where's Polonius?" he can reply with *sang-froid,* "At supper . . . Not where he eats, but where he is eaten: a certain *convocation* of *politic worms* are e'en at him. Your *worm* is your only *emperor* for *diet.*"

This would have caused much merriment at court, with the Queen shouting with laughter. For the garrulous William Cecil (whom Elizabeth had created Lord Burghley in order that his daughter might make a *mariage de convenance* with the Earl of Oxford) had often been heard to say that he had been born during the session of the [**p. 991**] *Diet* of *Worms,* when Charles V was proclaimed *Emperor:* thus a *"convocation* of *politic worms."* But there is a further allusion; for *Ver* is French for *worm,* and this Ver is dieting upon his victim, Burghley, who, as it happens has done him an irreparable wrong and is getting off lightly enough. Incidentally, it is well known that Polonius's precepts to Laertes paraphrase those given by Burghley to his own son.

(Of course no common playwright could have dared caricature Lord Burghley. It was bold even for the Queen's favorite to do so;

for the portrayal of a living person recognizably on the stage was a Star Chamber offense.)

* * *

"The great Lord Burghley", who was also represented in the characters of Shylock—"My daughter! O my ducats! O my daughter!"—of Capulet, bustling about to entertain his noble friends; of Pandarus, telling Cressida, "If my lord get a boy of you, you'll give him me"; of Cassius, the politic schemer; of Gonzalo, the old counsellor; and of others, partially or wholly—the ambitious Lord Burghley, consummate politician and arch Philistine, sanctimonious hypocrite and smooth contriver, had no intention of allowing the world to know that the dramatist was his son-in-law or the Queen's favorite either, for that matter.

* * *

[p. 992] III.

For five hundred years the Earls of Oxford had been official swordbearers to the Monarch, and they had wielded their spears ceaselessly in martial combat for the glory of England. Edward de Vere, the 17th Earl, had expected to do likewise, but the Queen was shrewd enough to recognize and make more appropriate use of his genius. Not only was he the champion Spear-shaker to Her Majesty in the three great tournaments of his maturity, he was following her demands by shaking the spear of his wit—his rapier wit—in her service, using the *words* (which he thought of as his *sword*) in her defense and for her glory, while entertaining her and her court, the foreign ambassadors and visiting dignitaries with the brilliant dramas which so delighted the scholarly and pleasure-loving Elizabeth Tudor. Incidentally, Edward's boyhood crest as Viscount Bulbeck, before he came into the earldom, was a lion shaking a broken spear, symbol of a disabled enemy. . . .

In 1578, in a Latin oration addressed to the Earl of Oxford, during the Queen's progress to Cambridge, Gabriel Harvey declaimed, "Thine eyes flash fire, thy countenance *shakes speares*." (Later he called the handsome, lively young Earl "the observed of all observers". Oxford used this phrase to describe Hamlet: it is one of the innumerable identity clues scattered throughout the plays.)

Surely "Shake-speare" was the inevitable choice of a pen-name for this Elizabethan with his insatiable zest for word-play.

* * *

[p. 993] VI.[14]

At Castle Hedingham in Essex, when Edward was a child, his father, Lord John de Vere, maintained a company of actors. At Cambridge and Oxford the young Earl wrote and acted in plays, and so he did later at court. . . . Hamlet instructing his players is Oxford training his and the Queen's actors at court. He rented the Blackfriars Theatre for a time, and he maintained three road-companies during the 1580's. In 1602 he combined his London company with that of Lord Worcester. . . . The reason there is no record of Henslowe's ever having made payment to Shakespeare, either as actor or as playwright, as he did to all the others of any consequence, is that the Lord Great Chamberlain of England accepted no money for his work. It is surely significant that the memoirs in two published volumes of the famous actor Alleyn which discuss the playwrights and actors of the time make no mention at all of Shakespeare.

* * *

[p. 994] VII.

It is impossible within the scope of this outline to quote statements about the Queen's love for Oxford or the high praise given him by writers and musicians of the day, most of which material has been discovered through research among unfiled documents in the British Museum which escaped Burghley's censorship. . . .

. . . In 1586, when England was threatened by attack from Spain, the Queen made Oxford a grant by Privy Seal Warrant of £1,000 a year ($40,000) to arouse the populace. He and the playwrights in his workshop poured out chronicle plays. When the lusty, though ignorant, people heard Henry's rousing cry, "Once more unto the breach, dear friends, once more!" they went wild with patriotism, volunteering in droves all over the country for service against Spain. Oxford and Elizabeth share the credit for England's greatness. Rowse assumes that this enormous grant was a merciful gift to an impecunious nobleman. He ought to know that Elizabeth never gave a shilling without value, and usually much more, received. . . .

In 1598 Meres was commissioned to publicize the pseudonym in his *Palladis Tamia*. . . . Meres mentions Shakespeare in various categories. In an early one he also mentions Oxford's name as a dramatist. It would have been too suspicious if he had left him out

[14] Parts IV and V have been omitted—the editors.

entirely, for there were many who knew he had written plays for performance at court.

* * *

[p. 995] VIII.

The Victorian scholars and their followers, in viewing Shakespeare's clowns and comic scenes with a kindly tolerance for Elizabethan humor, have missed many vital points. In *As You Like It* (V.1), Touchstone (Shakespeare-Oxford) encounters William, a Clown (Shaksper), in the Forest of Arden. It seems that William has laid claim to Audrey (the plays), but she assures Touchstone that "he hath no interest in me in the world". (Audrey is called a "foul slut", for the theatre was held in low repute and Oxford's name "receives a brand"—Sonnet 111—for being associated with it.) There is talk of a *vicar,* Sir Oliver *Martext* (III.3.41), who is of course the *vicar*ious writer who *mars* the *text* of the plays which Shaksper—calling himself Shakespeare?—has procured—the "stolne and surreptitious copies"—to sell to the printers heretofore unable to obtain them. Touchstone says that "all your writers do consent that ipse is he. Now, you are not ipse, for I am he." (All the writers knew Shakespeare's identity.) And in an amusing speech suited to the Clown's vulgar understanding, Touchstone orders William to leave the forest. William departs forthwith, just as Shaksper left London when it was decided to publish some of the plays at last and Meres was employed to do the publicity work.

Ben Jonson pictures this same brash pretender, whom he calls "a gull", in *Every Man Out of His Humour.* E. Ver, the Man—the knight, Puntarvolo—is irritated by the smart-aleck doings of Sogliardo, the gull, and Shift, his bohemian *alter ego,* who has secretly "set up his play-bills at Paul's" then struts around "using action to his rapier" (*i.e.,* shaking his spear). Sogliardo brags of the coat-of-arms he has obtained (everyone knows about Shaksper's hard-won coat-of-arms), and it develops that this blazons "a Boar *without a head,* . . . ramping to gentility". Oxford's crest was a Blue Boar. It is all crystal clear.

The Arguments for Shakespeare as Shakespeare

1899 *A New Variorum Edition of Shakespeare: Much adoe about Nothing*. Second edition. Ed. by Horace Howard Furness, J. B. Lippincott Company, Philadelphia, London.

[p. vii] To Shakespeare's friends and daily companions there was nothing mysterious in his life; on the contrary, it possibly appeared to them as unusually dull and commonplace. It certainly had no incidents so far out of the common that they thought it worth while to record them. Shakespeare never killed a man as Jonson did; his voice was never heard, like Marlow's, in tavern brawls; nor was he ever, like Marston and Chapman, threatened with the penalty of having his ears lopped and his nose slit; but his life was so gentle and so clear in the sight of man and of Heaven that no record of it has come down to us; for which failure, I am fervently grateful, and as fervently hope that no future year will ever reveal even the faintest peep through the divinity which doth hedge this king.

1901 "Did Shakespeare Write Bacon?" *National Review,* XXXVIII (1901), 402-6; reprinted in *Men, Books, and Mountains,* by Leslie Stephen, collected by S.O.A. Ullmann, 1956, Hogarth Press, London, pp. 74-80.

Did Shakespeare Write Bacon?

[p. 74] Were Shakespeare and Bacon identical? A new answer was recently suggested to me by a friend, and a consideration of his hypothesis led to the discovery of such corroborative arguments that it should only require a brief exposition to secure its acceptance by some people. I may briefly recall certain well-known facts. Bacon had conceived in very early youth an ambitious plan for a great philosophical reform. He had been immediately plunged into business, and at the accession of James I, when a little over forty, had been for many years a barrister and a Member of Parliament, and had moreover taken a very active part in great affairs of State. He was already lamenting, as he continued to lament, the many distractions which had forced him to sacrifice literary and philosophical to political ambition. Now that a second Solomon was to mount the throne, he naturally wished to show that he was a profound thinker, deserving the patronage of a wise monarch. Besides merely selfish reasons he hoped that James would help him to carry out his great schemes for the promotion of scientific research. He resolved, therefore, to publish a book setting forth his new philosophic ideas. He had not as yet found time to prepare any statement of them, or even to reduce them to order. He was still immersed in business and harassed by many anxieties. Now Bacon, if there be any truth in Pope's epigram or Macaulay's essay, was not above questionable manoeuvres. If he had not time to write, he could get a book written for him. We know in fact that he afterwards employed assistants, such as Hobbes and George Herbert, in preparing some of his literary work. It is plain, however, from the full account of his early life in Spedding's volumes that he had as yet no connection with the famous men of letters of his time. Not one of them is mentioned in his [p. 75] letters, though at a later time he became known to Ben Jonson, who has celebrated the charms of his conversation. Jonson's friendship with Shakespeare gives some significance, as we shall see, to this circumstance. Bacon took a significant step. He had recently incurred reproach by taking part in the prosecution of his former patron, Essex. He now (1603) made conciliatory overtures to Southhampton, who had not only been a friend of Essex, but had been under sentence for complicity in the rising for which Essex was beheaded. Why did Bacon approach a man so certain to be prejudiced against him? One reason suggests itself. Southampton was a patron of men of letters, and especially the one man whom we know to have been helpful to Shakespeare. If Bacon was desirous of hiring an author, Southampton would be able to recommend a competent person, and there was no one whom he was more likely to recommend than Shakespeare. Shakespeare was by this time at the height of his powers, and had shown by *Hamlet* his philosophical as well as his poetical tendencies. He was recognised as an able writer, capable of turning his hand to many employments. He could vamp old plays and presumably new philosophies. If Bacon wanted a man who should have the necessary power of writing and yet not be hampered by any such scientific doctrine of his own as would make him anxious to claim independence, he could not make a better choice. Southampton is said, on pretty good authority, to have made a present of £1,000 to Shakespeare. The story is intelligible if we suppose that he paid the money on Bacon's account, and for some service of such a nature that any trace of Bacon's interest in it was to be concealed.

At any rate somebody wrote a book. The famous *Advancement of Learning* appeared in the autumn of 1605. It is dedicated to James, and gives a general survey of the state of knowledge at the time; or, as the last paragraph states, is "a small globe of the intellectual world." It shows literary genius and general knowledge, but not the minute [**p. 76**] information of a specialist. Who wrote the book? I need not rely upon the probabilities already mentioned, however strong they may be, which point to Shakespeare. If Shakespeare wrote it he might naturally try to insert some intimation of the authorship to which he could appeal in case of necessity. One of the common amusements of the time was the composition of anagrams; and I accordingly inquired whether such a thing might be discoverable in the *Advancement*. It would most probably be at the beginning, and I was rewarded by finding in the first two lines a distinct claim of Shakespeare's own authorship and a repudiation of Bacon's. Naturally, when a man is writing two sentences in one set of letters he has to be a little obscure, and will probably employ a redundant word or two to include all that are required. Shakespeare's style, therefore, if perceptible, is partly veiled. The opening words are "There were under the law, excellent King, both daily sacrifices and free-will offerings, the one pro(ceeding, &c.)." To the end of "pro" there are eighty-one letters. Re-arrange them and they make the following: "Crede Will Shakespere, green innocent reader; he was author of excellent writing; F.B.N. fifth idol, Lye."[1] I won't try to explain why the reader should be called green and innocent, but the meaning of the whole will be perfectly clear when the last words are explained. F.B.N., of course, means Francis Bacon. "Fifth idol" refers to one

[1] If anyone cares to verify this, he may be helped by the statement that in both cases A occurs in four places, B in one, C in three, D in three, E in fifteen, F in four, G in two, H in four, I in six, K in one, L in six, N in six, O in four, P in one, R in seven, S in three, T in five, U in one, W in three, X in one, and Y in one. [Author's Note.]

of the most famous passages in a book hitherto ascribed to Bacon. In the aphorisms prefaced to the *Novum Organum* the causes of human error are described as belonging to *four* classes of "idols." False systems of philosophy, for example, generate what are curiously (though the word would naturally occur to a dramatist) called "idols of the theatre." Of the others I need only say that they do not include one fertile source of [p. 77] deception, namely, direct lying. Shakespeare intimates that his employer was illustrating this additional or fifth kind of idol by his false claim to the authorship. The aphorisms, however, were for the present held back. The book was published, we may presume, before Bacon had discovered this transparent artifice. Shakespeare would chuckle when calling his attention to it afterwards. Bacon would be vexed, but naturally could not take public notice of the trap in which he had been caught. His feelings may be inferred from his later action. When Shakespeare's plays were collected after the author's death, Bacon we know got at the printers and persuaded them to insert a cryptogram claiming the authorship for himself. The claim was obviously preposterous, but the fact that he made it is interesting to the moralist. It is a melancholy illustration of a familiar truth. Bacon had probably come to believe his own lie, and to fancy that he had really written the *Advancement of Learning,* or that, having bought it, he had a right to it. Then, he thought, he would make sure of a posthumous revenge should the anagram be deciphered. "If Shakespeare succeeds in claiming my philosophy, I will take his plays in exchange." He had become demoralised to the point at which he could cheat his conscience by such lamentable casuistry.

Meanwhile Bacon's fame was growing; and so was his immersion in business. In 1607 he became Solicitor-General and a comparatively rich man. In the next year he makes references to a proposed continuation of his great philosophical work. In other words, he was thinking of procuring its continuation. Probably there was some little difficulty in getting over the misunderstandings which would inevitably arise from these dark and dangerous dealings. The bargain might be hard to strike. In 1611, however, we know that Shakespeare gave up the stage and retired to pass the last five years of his life at Stratford. All his biographers have thought this retirement strange, and have been puzzled to account for the supposed cessation of authorship. No [p. 78] successful writer ever gives up writing. The explanation is now clear. Shakespeare retired because Bacon, who had grown rich, could make it worth his while to retreat to a quiet place where he would not be tempted to write plays, or drink at the "Mermaid," or make indiscreet revelations. If it be asked what he was doing, the answer is obvious. He was writing the *Novum Organum*. It was all but impossible for Bacon in the midst of all his astonishing political and legal activity to find time to write a philosophical work. No doubt he did something: he made notes and procured collections of various observations upon natural phenomena with which he supplied his co-operator. We may even suppose that he persuaded himself that he was thus substantially the author of the book which he prompted. Shakespeare died in 1616, leaving the work as a fragment. Bacon, who not long afterwards became Lord Chancellor, put the papers together, had them translated into Latin (which would obliterate any lurking anagram), and was able to publish the book in 1620. I leave it to critics to show the true authorship from internal evidence. It is enough here to note certain obvious characteristics. The book in the first place, as is generally admitted, shows that the author was not only an amateur in science, but curiously ignorant of what was being done in his own day. That was quite natural at Stratford-on-Avon, while Bacon in London had ample means for hearing of the achievements of leading men of science, even if he could not appreciate their work. In the next place the *Novum Organum* is the work of a poet. The scientific formulae are given in the shape of weighty concrete maxims—"Man is the servant and interpreter of Nature," and so forth. So in classifying the various kinds of experiments, the writer does not elaborate an abstract logical scheme, but represents each class (there are no less than twenty-seven) by some vivid concrete emblem. One class suggests the analogy of a signpost at crossroads and receives the famous name of *Instantiae crucis,* the origin of our common phrase, "crucial experiments." Bacon was not a poet—as anyone may see [p. 79] who looks at his version of the Psalms—Shakespeare certainly was.

After publishing this "magnificent fragment," as an accomplished critic calls it, Bacon was convicted of corrupt practices, and passed his few remaining years in trying to proceed with his philosophical work. The result was significant. He had no official duties to distract him, but also he had no Shakespeare to help him. His later publications added a little or nothing in substance. The chief of them was *De Augmentis*. This is simply an enlarged edition in Latin (the anagram of course disappearing) of the *Advancement of Learning*. The early book, as the same critic says, has an advantage over the "more pretentious" version from the "noble and flowing" (shall we say the Shakespearean?) "English," while the additions are of questionable value. I will only notice one point.

The *Advancement of Learning* speaks of the state of poetry at the time. "In poesy," says the author, "I can report no deficience. . . . For the expression of affections, passions, corruptions, and the customs we are beholden to poets more than to the philosophers' works: and for wit and eloquence not much less than to orators' harangues." That was a very natural opinion to be expressed by Shakespeare. In the *De Augmentis* the last sentence disappears; but a fresh paragraph is inserted upon dramatic poetry. The theatre might be useful, it says, either for corruption or for discipline; but in modern times there is plenty of corruption on the stage and no discipline.

Bacon, it may be noticed, was aiming this backhanded blow at Shakespeare in the same year in which he was inserting the cryptogram in the first folio. It may appear, at first sight, that he was inconsistent in condemning the very works which he was claiming, and it may even be said by the captious that the fact throws some doubt upon the cryptogram. A deeper insight into human nature will suggest that such an inconsistency is characteristic. Bacon wishes at once to appropriate Shakespeare's work and to depreciate it so long as it is still ascribed to Shakespeare. I omit, [**p. 80**] however, the obvious psychological reflections and will only remark that other works ascribed to this period, the *Sylva Sylvarum* and so forth, no doubt represent the collections which, as I have said, Bacon formed to be used as materials by his collaborator.

I have told my story as briefly as may be, and leave details to be filled up by anyone who pleases. Plenty of writers have insisted upon Shakespeare's logical subtlety and powers of philosophical reflection. They will be ready to believe that the author of *Hamlet* was also the author of the *Novum Organum,* and will be relieved from the necessity of accepting the old paradox that the "wisest" was also the "meanest" man of his time. The meanness may all be ascribed to one man, and the wisdom to the man from whom he stole it.

1958 Frank W. Wadsworth, *The Poacher from Stratford.* University of California Press. Berkeley and Los Angeles.

EPILOGUE

[**p. 162**] Our revels now are ended, and perhaps the author, like Prospero, may be allowed to reflect upon them for a moment. As they melt into history, the actors of our pageant leave certain ineradicable impressions behind. First, is a sense of their sincerity—with very few exceptions, the people whose writings are here chronicled have been honestly convinced that Shakespeare did not deserve his fame, and that, as a corollary, their own candidate had been robbed of the glory rightfully his. Equally strong is the impression of militant idealism—the idea of the Poet is very clear to them and very important, and they resist bitterly any invasion of that splendid concept. Closely related to the ideal, is the sensitive class-consciousness shared by all dissenters, who are attracted to Ariel and repelled by Caliban, overlooking the fact that to Caliban the author of *The Tempest* has given some of the loveliest lines in the play. Finally, they are all, no matter how much disguised by the trappings of historical scholarship, romantics at heart, romantics of an older, richer, more Keats-[**p. 163**]ian school, enamored of cloud-capped towers and gorgeous palaces, of handsome knights and lovely ladies.

It is not surprising, therefore, that certain features are common to any argument that Shakespeare did not write the plays. Inevitably, the negative case is based upon those known facts of Shakespeare's life that reveal him to have been an ordinary lower-middle-class person, possessor of all those plebeian virtues which in a poet are embarrassing, but in a people the cause of national boasting. But then it is easier, one must admit, to argue on the basis of character and environment that a man *could not* have done something, than it is to go out and find actual proof that he *did not*. Similarly, the positive case is always presented in terms of probabilities, not of actualities; and, as we have seen, without the check of factual evidence some very complex historical theories are possible. Inevitably the result is the substitution of a series of involved hypotheses in place of a disappointingly small number of historical facts.

The question is frequently asked, if, when all is said and done, it matters who actually did write the plays and poems; and the question is deserving of an answer. Whether it matters to William Shakespeare, I do not know. That it does matter, on purely emotional grounds, to a great many people who love the Shakespearean works, I do know. But the real significance of the battle over the authorship goes far beyond Shakespeare and the controversial literature, for it strikes at the heart of man's knowledge of himself. The reasons we have for believing that William Shakespeare of Stratford-on-Avon wrote the plays and poems are the same as the reasons we have for believing any other historical event—for believing that Julius Caesar was stabbed by Brutus and the conspirators, that Charles I lost his head, that Abraham Lincoln was shot watching a performance of *Our American Cousin*. We believe these things because, in the opinion of those best qualified to judge, the historical [p. 164] evidence says that they happened. In exactly the same way the historical evidence says that William Shakespeare wrote the plays and poems. If one can argue that the evidence in Shakespeare's case does not mean what it says, that it has been falsified to sustain a gigantic hoax that has remained undetected for centuries, then one can just as surely argue that other evidence is not to be trusted and that, as Henry Ford said, "history is bunk." That is why the charge that Shakespeare did not write the plays does matter. And that is why, until contradictory factual evidence is unearthed, there appears to be no valid reason to doubt that the official records, the evidence of title pages, the testimony of self-described friends and fellow writers, mean just what they appear to say—that William Shakespeare of Stratford was the author of the wonderful works that bear his name.

1959 "Shakspere Was Shakespeare," *The American Scholar,* Autumn, 1959, Vol. 28, No. 4, pp. 479-88. by William T. Hastings.

[p. 479] There is for most of us a remote and academic character in the debates on whether the Homeric poems were by Homer or by six poets or by a woman, whether *Beowulf* sprang full-panoplied from the brainpan of the folk, whether the vision of William concerning Piers Plowman was recorded by one Langland or by five successive redactors. But we take Shakespeare for granted until suddenly shocked by the discovery of disbelief near at hand. Reacting from shock, as a scholar should, by checking bibliographies at the library, one becomes aware of the steady stream of anti-Stratfordian monographs and books.

The anti-Stratfordian is annoyed or enraged by the smugness of us Shakespearians. Typically smug was Dr. Samuel A. Tannenbaum's remark to me: "I never bother about Bacon or Oxford stuff because the proponents of those theories are either insane or unmitigated liars." Somewhat to the same effect Sir Edmund Chambers observed: "Small minds are caught by, and fail to comprehend [Shakespeare's] greatness and . . . variability. . . . With these paradoxes I do not propose to concern myself. Doubtless they should be refuted, that the people be not deceived, but the task must be left to someone with a better temper for the patient anatomizing of human follies."

There is nevertheless some danger that the people will be "deceived"; for the preachers of heresy are assiduous, and the worthlessness of what they write cannot be fully understood unless one has a knowledge of Elizabethan conditions and of the ascertained facts regarding Shakespeare, and has also trained oneself to a relentless logical analysis of theories and the evidence on which they rest. The Baconian variety of the heresy has been dealt with effectively many times; replies to the other and more recent fantasies are to be found chiefly in scattered articles and reviews. They are all in some degree incomplete; and sometimes, by assumptions based on insufficient evidence, they expose themselves to the same charge of fallacy as the utterances which they oppose. It seems worth while, therefore, to attempt a general view of the whole controversy, with a small amount of analytical detail.

The Case Against Shakespeare

> It is a tale
> Told by an idiot, full of sound and fury,
> Signifying nothing.

"Orthodox commentators are perpetually on the horns of a dilemma," declares the author of *Exit Shakespeare,* B. G. Theobald. With the positing of this dilemma all the anti-Stratfordians, whatever their particular allegiance, invariably begin. They commit here a fundamental fallacy based on ignorance, which has been exposed again and again; but as their whole case rests upon it, we must listen to them and make brief reply.

The first horn of the alleged dilemma is the concept of the vulgarian from the Avon. This horn has, so to speak, four prongs. [p. 480]

Prong 1: The man of Stratford, it is charged, was an ignorant and illiterate actor, an "unlettered peasant," an "ignorant boor," who apparently received only one letter in his lifetime and was even uncertain about the spelling of his own name.

Prong 2: He was a thrifty businessman, it is said, engaged in petty transactions. "The rustic William's biographies show him," says C. W. Barrell, "to have been first a butcher's apprentice and later in life a maltster, money-lender, and land-speculator." "Is it," asks Percy Allen, "a normally probable supposition that the author of *Love's Labor's Lost* and *Hamlet* was a maltster?"

What are the facts? No evidence has been or can be adduced for the "ignorant boor" formula. The butcher's apprentice story is mere legend and is, after all, irrelevant: Marlowe probably knew shoemaking, and Ben Jonson bricklaying; Charles Dickens worked in a shoeblacking factory; William Dean Howells was a printer's devil. I myself hoed barefoot in the cornfield and played "butcher's apprentice" to my father, a country doctor. The "maltster" charge is based on Shakespeare's having once shared in an attempt to profiteer by buying up malt and holding it for a rise in price in a bad season. He was a moneylender and land speculator in precisely the same way that all of us have been and perhaps unfortunately still are.

Prong 3: Virtually nothing, it is said, is known of his life: he was probably resident in London only ten years (1587-97); he left behind him no letters, no manuscripts, no library, and numerous phony portraits.

To this charge the general answer was given long ago. What is true of Shakespeare is more true of all other Elizabethan authors who were not in the public service. Our information about Shakespeare, as a matter of fact, is unusually extensive for the time. Where, one may ask, are the manuscripts, libraries and portraits of Marlowe, Kyd, Greene, Dekker and Heywood? As to the chronological details, we have London records of Shakespeare not only up to 1597 but in 1598, 1603, 1604, 1605, and perhaps 1612-13.

Prong 4: Can any good thing, it is asked, come out of Stratford? "The conditions which must have surrounded Shakespeare in his native village [were appalling]. . . . The agricultural classes . . . were densely ignorant, brutal in their manner, almost barbarous in their customs, and incredibly filthy in their habits." As to education, "much schooling was impossible, for the necessary books did not exist . . . scholars . . . drew nothing out of the County Grammar Schools."

To the attack on the educational opportunities available one may reply by referring to the recent studies of Louis Wright, Watson, and Plimpton. The latter's *Education of Shakespeare* gives in detail the quite respectable curricula of various schools. They prepared boys for the university by the age of thirteen or fourteen; Shakespeare was fourteen in 1578, about the time he is supposed (by some) to have left school to help his father. It must be remembered that Shakespeare's father held the important town offices of burgess, alderman and bailiff, that his mother came of a good county family, the Ardens, and that his daughter Susannah married a university man.

The second horn of the dilemma emphasizes (in contrast with the ignorant actor) the superior endowments of the author of the plays. The author, it is argued, was a learned and cultivated poet-dramatist, probably a member of the nobility.

I have already in part anticipated the reply to this conception. The argument that between 1584 (or 1585) and 1592 Shakespeare could not have completed his education, got acclimated to London ways, and developed his poetic vehicle to the point exhibited in *I Henry VI* is purely arbitrary and has no factual basis; whereas there is factual support for the contrary assumption, as I shall presently show. Note, too, that Ben Jonson, the bricklayer's son, was not a university graduate but was a sufficiently learned man to condescend—like a university graduate—to Shakespeare in the matter of Latin and Greek. Thomas Dekker, Thomas Heywood and other Elizabethan dramatists who lacked the imprimatur of a university give a good imitation of [p. 481] breadth of knowledge. In the foreword to Barton's *Shakespeare and the Law,* James M. Beck reveals the fallacy behind this horn of the dilemma by showing that the works of Mark Twain, the great medievalist—who was, by the way, a violent Baconian—could not have been written by the uneducated boy from Hannibal, Missouri, the runaway, tramp printer, river pilot and mining prospector.

The theory that the author of the poems and the plays was a man of special learning has been developed in extravagant and mutually destructive claims. To one theorist he must have been a soldier because of his intimate knowledge of the methods and the jargon of war. Others label him variously a lawyer, sailor, astronomer, divine, printer, sportsman, gardener, physician, world traveler.

Close analysis shows, however, that Shakespeare's use of legal terms is often an inexact, layman's usage; that when precisely used, the terms are often derived from his sources, such as the old Chronicles; that other dramatists use legal terminology liberally, some much more than Shakespeare; that Shakespeare sometimes treats legal concepts and procedure as highhandedly as is now done in the movies, notably in the trial of Shylock. This method of analysis is valid for the other fields of Shakespeare's supposed expert knowledge and has been applied with similar results.

The difficulty of these literal-minded persons is, of course, that they have little understanding of the business of authorship. Particularly they have not understood the reality behind the remark of Shakespeare's first editors that his "mind and hand went together," that he possessed an unusual ability to assimilate, and to make easy and apt use of what he had picked up.

Having established, to their own satisfaction, this dilemma—that only a cultivated gentleman of high education could have written the plays and that Shakespeare, the actor of Stratford, was an ignorant vulgarian—the anti-Stratfordians discern between its horns, so to speak, the "Shakespearian mask"; namely, "Willm Shakspere" of Stratford is the mask behind which "William Shake-speare," the gentleman-nobleman-poet, Mr. X, conceals himself from the public gaze while engaged in the vulgar business of writing plays. The actor "Willm" (they ignorantly ascribe this spelling to his ignorance, and they love to spell his surname "Shaksper" or "Shaxpere" in contrast to the amplitude and, as they think, the symbolism of "Shake-speare") is supposed to have been a party, presumably at a price, to this most grandiose of all literary hoaxes. Evidence of the split of persons and personalities is, they believe, deducible from the rarity or absence of contemporary allusions to Shakespeare as specifically both actor and poet-dramatist or as man of Stratford and dramatist. So far as they admit that allusions to Shakespeare exist, they seek to discredit them.

* * *

Usually, however, with total lack of candor they disregard the existence of such evidence, hoping thus to deceive the uninformed. Of these allusions I shall say something later on. They endeavor to discredit the Stratford monument, arguing that it is not the original. Some argue that the portrait of Shakespeare in the First Folio is an effigy, not a human countenance, [p. 482] in spite of its acceptance by his friend Ben Jonson. Others urge that it is the portrait of a nobleman, on the strength of the style of the doublet, although both Chambers and Sidney Lee find it the normal costume "of a well-placed man."

Here the anti-Stratfordians rest their case against Shakespeare.

The Case for X

Gives to airy nothing
A local habitation and a name.

It is a curious fact that almost without exception the advocates of Mr. X are amateurs. Not professional scholars, they sneer at the academic conservatives; the failure of scholars to take their arguments seriously is evidently bitter medicine to them. Among the early Baconians, you recall, were Miss Delia Bacon, an amiable lady whose obscurity of argument was the forerunner of actual insanity, and Ignatius Donnelly, the Minnesota lawyer with mathematical ciphers in his brain. Among the Oxfordians (and more later of their candidate) are J. Thomas Looney, a schoolmaster, Percy Allen, Mrs. Eva Turner Clark, Miss Carolyn Wells, Colonel B. R. Ward and his son Captain B. M. Ward of the British Army, and Charles W. Barrell, a member (in 1940) of the public relations staff of the Western Electric Company. I do wrong to pass over the British Navy, represented by Rear Admiral H. H. Holland, retired. The latest converts, whose party card is a portentous thirteen-hundred-page volume entitled *This Star of England,* are Charlton Ogburn, a lawyer, and his wife Dorothy.

Their state of mind seems fanatical, their method of reasoning for the most part quite fallacious. Of them all it may be said categorically that not one theory in support of any one candidate has a single shred of positive evidence behind it. All is pure hypothesis. Even opening Spenser's tomb in Westminster Abbey produced no results. That is why the Ashbourne portrait "discovery" by Mr. Barrell, with all the scientific apparatus of infrared light to distract attention from the logical inconsequence of the argument, was made so much of: at last they had something—they hoped.

The Baconian theory by now is rather moth-eaten. It was originally a guess, based on Bacon's being a prominent man, a man of learning and of letters. Fostered for sentimental reasons by Delia Bacon, others, including Donnelly, Mrs. Elizabeth Gallup and William Stone Booth, a well-to-do Bostonian, rallied round the flag. Bacon's claim was chiefly supported by the anagram, acrostic and cipher school of the later nineteenth century, by means of which signals, signatures and messages were unearthed in the First Folio. This pathetically laborious and futile technique was decisively discredited years ago in general terms by F. E. Pierce, and recently by the authoritative analysis of William F. and Elizebeth Friedman, professional cryptologists. Pierce showed that with the options and variations in reading which the Baconians allowed themselves, the results were in general keeping with the mathematical laws of probability and chance. The Friedmans conclude that the bilateral [*sic*] cipher of Mrs. Gallup is the only one which is "a valid system in itself" but "it was not used by her." "As for the others, not only were they not used; they were not usable, nor even credible." Turning their method against them, it has been demonstrated that Shakespeare wrote the Forty-sixth Psalm, that Theodore Roosevelt wrote the Gettysburg Address, and that Bacon was a collaborator in a textbook of freshman English and the Yale catalogue for 1909. It has been pointed out that this theory assumes erroneously that the order of plays in the First Folio and the typographical detail of that volume were controlled by the author. It should be obvious, too, that the form of the plays was determined by literary and dramatic considerations, not by the desire to transmit biographical or other messages to posterity.

Mr. Booth, for example, disregards both these important facts in finding a Baconian acrostic signal in the opening speech of *Troilus and Cressida,* helped by the large initial *C* which gives him two letters from the opening word:

[p. 483]

> CALL here my Varlet, Ile Vnarme againe.
> Why should I warre without the wals of Troy
> That finde such cruell battell here within?
> Each Trojan that is master of his heart,
> Let him to field, Troylus alas has none.

As if we can suppose Bacon arranging this speech as a cautel or warning to the reader to watch for a message below, rather than Shakespeare starting the war and the portrait of his lovesick hero in five terse and pungent lines addressed to the ears of an audience.

Sometimes the supposed message has been proved to be mistaken. Donnelly found (by wishful thinking or manipulation) a cipher account of Christopher Marlowe's death that conformed to the nineteenth-century tradition, instead of anticipating the facts recently unearthed by Leslie Hotson. The Friedmans point out that Mrs. Gallup's "whole case was based on subjective intuitions, on self-persuasion."

A more recent line is that taken by the excavators: the futile opening of Spenser's tomb; the projected excavation in the bed of the river Wye by a Detroit physician; the proposed excavations of Maria Bauer in the burial ground of Bruton Church, Williamsburg, Virginia, thwarted by the "unscientific" and prejudiced church authorities.

A general rejoinder, which should satisfy rational people, is that of Kittredge: that the mind which wrote the plays and the mind which composed the essays and scientific works of Francis Bacon are intellectually incommensurate. If Bacon wrote Shakespeare, then Shakespeare (or someone else) wrote the works of Bacon. This judgment is substantiated by Miss Caroline Spurgeon's analysis of the contrasting character of the imagery employed by Shakespeare and by Bacon.

The most popular candidate at present for the face beneath the mask is not Bacon but Edward de Vere, Seventeenth Earl of Oxford, who was first elaborately supported by Looney in 1920. His *Shakespeare Identified,* like the *Hidden Allusions* of his disciple, Mrs. Clark, is a masterpiece of errors of fact and false logic, as well as amazingly childish naïveté. It is impossible to deal here with either book in detail. I may point out that no connection between Oxford and Shakespeare has been established; that Oxford's extant poems belong mainly to the 1570's and that he died in 1604, while the well-established chronology of Shakespeare's works runs from about 1591 to 1613; that Oxford's temperament was "violent and perverse," while the mood of the plays is in general consonance with the traditional temperament of the "gentle Shakespeare"; that no plays under Oxford's name have survived which might enable us to estimate his quality as dramtist; and that the extant poems by him show hardly a glimmer of the beauty or power which we associate with Shakespeare, and none of the Shakespearian humor.

I will cite only one example—a typical one—of Looney's technique in buttressing the case for Oxford. He quotes Francis Meres as referring to Oxford as "the best in Comedy"—a statement repeated by Mrs. Clark and by Mr. Barrell. This is a clear case of misrepresentation. Meres was the author in 1598 of a trivial and pretentious commonplace book about the literature of the past and the present, *Palladis Tamia: Wit's Treasury.* It has unique importance to Shakespearians because it names most of the plays of Shakespeare then in existence and is therefore of considerable assistance in establishing the chronology of the plays; otherwise, it is mainly a rehash of former treatises. I quote the passage in Meres on which Looney bases his statement. Meres arranges each list in an order dictated not by merit but by social considerations: first nobility, then university scholars, then *hoi polloi.*

> These are our best for Tragedie, the Lorde *Buckhurst,* Doctor *Leg* of Cambridge, Doctor *Edes* of Oxforde, maister *Edward Ferris,* the Author of the *Mirrour for Magistrates, Marlow, Peele, Watson, Kid, Shakespeare, Drayton, Chapman, Decker,* and *Beniamin Johnson.* . . .
>
> The best for Comedy amongst us bee, *Edward* Earle of Oxforde, Doctor *Gager* of Oxforde, Maister *Rowley* once a rare Scholler of learned Pembrooke Hall in Cambridge, Maister *Edwardes* one of her Maiesties Chappell, eloquent and wittie *John Lilly, Lodge, Gascoyne, Greene, Shakespeare, Thomas Nash, Thomas Heywood, Anthony Mundye* our best plotter, *Chapman, Porter, Wilson, Hathway,* and *Henry Chettle.* . . .
>
> These are the most passionate among us to be-[p. 484]waile and bemoane the perplexities of Loue, *Henrie Howard* Earle of Surrey, sir *Thomas Wyat* the elder, sir *Francis Brian,* sir *Philip Sidney,* sir *Walter Rawley,* sir *Edward Dyer, Spencer, Daniel, Drayton, Shakespeare, Whetstone, Gascoyne, Samuell Page* sometimes fellowe of *Corpus Christi* Colledge in Oxford, *Churchyard, Bretton.*

It will be noticed that not only is Looney guilty of *suppressio veri*—seventeen writers "best in comedy" are mentioned and he omits sixteen—but that the passage as a whole demonstrates the separate existence of Oxford and Shakespeare, and gives Oxford no standing whatever in the fields of tragedy or love poetry; yet his (or Shakespeare's) *Richard III, Romeo and Juliet, Venus and Adonis, Lucrece,* and the "sugred" sonnets were already famous, as contemporary allusions reveal.

* * *

Since the Ogburns are the latest champions of Oxford, they require a moment's attention, although they have received the *coup de grâce* from more than one scholar. Like Mrs. Eva Turner Clark before them, though at twice that lady's length, they first revamp the well-established chronology of the plays, 1590-1613, in order to bring them within the lifetime of Oxford, who died, most awkwardly for them, in 1604. They lean heavily, for this, upon identification of the plays with plays of the 1570's and 1580's now known only by title. Thus, to give only one example, they follow Mrs. Clark in assuming that the *Titus and Gisippus* of 1577 was a first edition of *Titus Andronicus,* although from the title it is clear that this lost play was based on a tale in the *Decameron,* with no relation to the pseudo-Roman horrors of Shakespeare's play. Having arranged the plays to their satisfaction, with ascription to revisers of those materials that cannot be dated back, they then proceed to interpret them not as works of dramatic literature but as fragments of the literal or spiritual biography of the arrogant and moody Earl. For this kind of nonsense they have, regretably, some countenance in the work of those "Stratfordians" who hunt the plays for allusions to Shakespeare's friends and [p. 485] enemies, to political events and philosophies, or to his spiritual heights and depths. I allude to Edward Dowden, George Brandes, Frank Harris, Dover Wilson (in *The Essential Shakespeare*), Wilson Knight and the whole school of New Critics. So when Orsino says to Viola, "Let still the woman take An elder than herself," the author was giving a dirty dig to Anne Hathaway, eight years his senior. Alas! Alas!

I must spare a paragraph for a semi-Oxfordian, Percy Allen. A palm should go to him, an active member of that subversive organization, the "Shakespeare Fellowship," for having hit upon a new source of confirmation of these mad theories. In *Talks with Elizabethans* he bridges the gap between this world and the world of spirits with the help of a medium, Mrs. Hester Dowden, daughter of Professor Edward Dowden, who had "mental Shakespearean connections, through her distinguished father." He records his direct conversations with the spirits of Bacon, Shakespeare and others; he puts his crucial authorship questions; he gets some extraordinary replies, and a new Shakespeare sonnet for good measure. Here, if not before, we appear to cross another bridge, leaving our sanity on the farther side.

It would be unfair discrimination not to mention the other competitors, most of them dark horses, in the race for the laurel wreath that the brow of the Stratford boor Shakespeare is too mean to wear. They include: Roger Manners, Fifth Earl of Rutland (proponents Celestin Demblon and Professor Porohovshikof of Oglethorpe University); King Edward VI, who his advocate avers did not die in 1553, but wrote enormously "under many aliases," including the works of Shakespeare and most of Bacon (proponent J. Edward Morgan, a former Nebraska cowboy); Sir Edward Dyer (proponent Alden Brooks, . . .); and Charles Blount, Eighth Lord Mountjoy (proponent Peter Alvor, who believes that Bacon wrote the plays attributed to Ben Jonson). Gilbert Slater in his *Seven Shakespeares* advocates the theory that the plays were composed by a group of writers. This view, which has the advantage of allowing great leeway in conjecture and makes it possible to take up within itself or reconcile various conflicting theories of authorship, is now favored by several theorists. It might be called the appeasement theory or the united front theory. Mr. Slater's seven Shakespeares are as follows:

1. Bacon, author of *Richard III* and *Richard II*.

2. Marlowe, whose death in 1593 was faked and who continued to work for the stage under an alias, helping with his professional technique the work of amateurs, Bacon, Derby, Oxford and other aristocratic patrons. "Note, also," Slater adds, "it was not until December 1594 that the London actor, Will Shakespeare, appears in our records. Was it in that character that Marlowe returned to London life?" (I commend the logical method of this argument to our legal members. As to the facts so deftly manipulated, they are unfortunately not facts, since Shakespeare was famous in London by June of 1592, a year before Marlowe's death; and Marlowe was not an actor. And now Calvin Hoffman, in *The Murder of the Man Who Was Shakespeare,* supports this view with a similar treatment of evidence.)

3. William Stanley, Sixth Earl of Derby—a strong claim to *Love's Labor's Lost, A Midsummer Night's Dream* and *The Tempest.*

4. The Earl of Rutland.

5. Oxford, who is retained with greatly diminished glory.

6. Mary Sidney, Countess of Pembroke and mother of the "incomparable paire of brethren" (the Earls of Pembroke and Montgomery) to whom the First Folio is dedicated. Plays were attributed to Shakespeare by Pembroke and Montgomery to conceal the fact that their mother had something to do with them. "Wilton [her home] is on the banks of the Wiley, a little tributary of the Wiltshire Avon. . . . Does the title 'Sweet Swan' better fit the money-lending maltster of Stratford or the 'peerless Ladie bright' of Wilton? Which of the two would Jonson most naturally think of as 'My Beloved'?"

7. Sir Walter Raleigh, who is said to [p. 486] have had only a slight share; he assisted Mary Sidney.

Slater's argument is a rather charming example of the type—whimsy and fancy triumphing over the pedestrian academic technique of fact-plus-fact-equals-inference. If we had the wings of a bird, like Mr. Slater, how far we could fly in the solution of our scholar's conundrums. But, on second thought, perhaps it is no joking matter. Perhaps we should turn over to the psychiatrists all members of the Shakespeare Fellowship—and their fellow travelers.

The Case for Shakespeare

His voice was propertied
As all the tuned spheres.

It may seem superfluous to argue the case for Shakespeare after refutation of the false conceptions regarding Shakespeare's life and after exposure of the complete lack of an evidential basis for the various other attributions of authorship. But it is evidence of candor to be willing to give his claim a public hearing, even if it seems as superfluous as proving that I am I and you are you. Moreover, we must continue to remember the people who have been deceived by the lunatics and the unmitigated liars of Dr. Tannenbaum's urbane classification. After all, the people deserve to hear the truth as well as to hear folly.

We should realize, first, that no suspicions regarding Shakespeare's authorship (except for a few mainly humorous comments) were expressed until the middle of the nineteenth century (in Hart's *Romance of Yachting,* 1848). For over two hundred years no one had any serious doubts.

Again, we should remember that with minor exceptions at the beginning and the end of his career—easily explained as due to imitation or collaboration—the work of the dramatist is homogeneous, the reflection of a single personality, one side of which is well caught by the contemporary phrases "gentle Shakespeare," "the friendly Author," et cetera. In this work there is an evolution from brilliant but inexpert and unthinking youth through the well-known stages of a maturing art and character, without any obscuring of the fundamental unity of temperament and talent. Thus there is complete confutation of the "group theory"; the theory of multiple hacks, versifying Oxford's prose drafts; and the theories involving the intermittent and casual efforts of noble amateurs.

But what particular facts present to us William Shakespeare of London *and* Stratford-on-Avon, actor, poet and dramatist extraordinary?

The Monument in Trinity Church, Stratford, dating from before 1623, exhibits the half-length bust of Shakespeare.[2] He is holding a pen in one hand and a sheet of paper in the other. The conclusion would seem to be that he had been a writer. The inscription beneath the bust supports that view:

IVDICIO PYLIVM, GENIO SOCRATEM, ARTE MARONEM:
TERRA TEGIT, POPVLVS MAERET, OLYMPVS HABET.

STAY PASSENGER, WHY GOEST THOV BY SO FAST?
READ IF THOV CANST, WHOM ENVIOVS DEATH HATH PLAST,
WITH IN THIS MONVEMENT SHAKSPEARE: WITH WHOME
QVICK NATVRE DIDE: WHOSE NAME DOTH DECK Y^{s} TOMBE,
FAR MORE THEN COST: SITH ALL, Y^{t} HE HATH WRITT,
LEAVES LIVING ART, BVT PAGE, TO SERVE HIS WITT.
OBIIT AÑO DO^{1} 1616
AETATIS. 53 DIE 23 AP^{r}.

Candor requires that I note again that the authority of the monument has been attacked, but on unsubstantial grounds.

The gravestone of Susannah Hall, Shakespeare's daughter, also in Trinity Church, reads:

Heere lyeth y^{e}. body of Svsanna
wife to Iohn Hall, gent: y^{e}. davgh
ter of William Shakespeare, gent:
shee deceased y^{e}. 11th of Ivly. a^{o}.
1649, aged 66.

Witty above her sexe, but that's not all,
Wise to salvation was good Mistris Hall,
Something of Shakespeare was in that, but this
Wholy of him with whom she's now in blisse. . . .

[2] See inside back cover—the editors.

This evidence has apparently been overlooked by the anti-Stratfordians.

Chambers, in tracing the development of the Shakespearian tradition, observes, "Stratford was not unaware of the reputation of its distinguished inhabitant, and became a place of pilgrimage at an early date." In 1634, for instance, one Lieutenant Hammond visited Stratford on a tour of military inspection. [See Documents Section]

* * *

[p. 487] Again, John Ward, vicar of Stratford from 1662 on, made [a significant] entry in his notebook for the years 1661-63. [See Documents Section]

* * *

The inscriptions in the Stratford church and the notes quoted by Chambers alike testify to the early recognition of Shakespeare as a distinguished author, and one associated with Stratford; they assume the identity of the Stratford actor and the great dramatist.

Finally, I shall quote some literary references to Shakespeare by his contemporaries, selecting only those that establish this same identity of persons—denied by the heretics. There are many other striking contemporary allusions, but I pass over them in order to play the game on the enemy's terms and beat him at it.

I will quote first that famous first allusion to Shakespeare, a young man perhaps new to London but already the talk of the town:

> Yes, trust them not [the players]: for there is an vpstart Crow, beautified with our feathers, that with his *Tygers hart wrapt in a Players hyde,* supposes he is as well able to bombast out a blanke verse as the best of you: and beeing an absolute *Iohannes fac totum,* is in his owne conceit the onely Shake-scene in a countrey.

So wrote the dying Robert Greene in September of 1592. Whether he is lampooning Shakespeare the actor or Shakespeare the dramatist is not clear, but he parodies a line from Shakespeare the dramatist, "Tiger's heart wrapt in a woman's hide." And three months later Greene's literary executor, Henry Chettle, apologizing for Greene's pamphlet "in which a letter written to diuers play-makers, is offensiuely by one or two of them taken," blames himself for oversight in publishing the lampoon and declares regarding Shakespeare that he himself has "seene his demeanor no lesse ciuill than he exelent in the qualitie he professes: Besides, diuers of worship haue reported his uprightnes of dealing, which argues his honesty, and his facetious grace in writting, that aprooues his Art."

In the university play, *The Return from Parnassus,* Part III (1601?), in a dialogue between characters representing the comedian and the "heavy" man of Shakespeare's company, Will Kempe and Richard Burbage, Shakespeare, the self-taught (*i.e.,* the "ignorant boor") is said to beat the university-trained dramatist [see p. 31].

* * *

Ben Jonson's famous poetical tribute prefixed to the First Folio is, of course, a prime exhibit. Shakespeare and Jonson were close friends, and had long been associated together in work for the King's men. This is clearly a tribute to Shakespeare of Stratford, with the famous "small Latin and less Greek" and the concluding apostrophe to "Sweet Swan of Avon." Feeble attempts have been made to discredit it, such as Slater's argument that the allusion is to Mary Sidney, and the "ironical" interpretation by Alden Brooks . . .; but they are defeated by their absurdity. Jonson's warm feeling for Shakespeare the man and his reservations concerning his art appear together in the often quoted passage from *Timber* [see pp. 38-39].

* * *

That this [passage from *Timber*] is genuine there can be no doubt. [p. 488] And other tributes, based on personal acquaintance, are extant from the dramatists Heywood and Beaumont. The fellow players of Shakespeare who edited the First Folio, John Heminge and Henry Condell, say they have collected the plays "onely to keepe the memory of so worthy a Friend, & Fellow alive, as was our Shakespeare."

The last witness is Leonard Digges. In verses prefixed to the First Folio, he declares that when "Time dissolues thy Stratford Moniment"[3] men will "view thee still" in this volume of his works—thus once more binding as one the man of Stratford and the writer. Again, in verses prefixed to the edition of Shakespeare's poems in 1640, Digges treats as one man the sonneteer and the dramatist, mentions his limited education, the Globe theater, the tremendous popularity of *Julius Caesar, Othello, Henry IV, Much Ado,* and *Twelfth Night.*

Digges, we now know, is the star witness for Shakespeare. Dr. Hotson has shown that in 1600 Thomas Russell, one of the two "overseers" of Shakespeare's will, married Anne Digges, widow of William Digges and mother of Dudley Digges (Sir Dudley, 1607) and Leonard Digges. The Digges family was well-to-do, the mother of noble ancestry. Leonard with two other boys from the Stratford

[3] See inside back cover—the editors.

neighborhood (one of them William Coombe, brother of the Thomas Coombe to whom Shakespeare bequeathed his sword) entered Oxford at the age of fifteen, in 1603. Leonard made a reputation as a scholar and writer. A translation by him from the Spanish in 1622 he dedicated to the "incomparable paire" of noblemen to whom the Folio was dedicated a year later. Sir Dudley Digges, the older brother, and William Strachey were friends of Ben Jonson and were interested in the Virginia Company; Strachey's account of the ill-omened Somers Expedition to Virginia was used by Shakespeare in writing *The Tempest.* This identification of Leonard Digges and the establishing of a connection between him and Thomas Russell gives us contemporary Stratford recognition of Shakespeare's greatness as a dramatist; and by one who knew Shakespeare the man well.

Let Digges have the honor of the Epilogue:

To the Memorie
of the deceased Authour Maister
W. Shakespeare.

Shake-speare, at length thy pious fellowes giue
The world thy Workes: thy Workes, by which, out-liue
Thy Tombe thy name must: when that stone is rent,
And Time dissolues thy *Stratford Moniment,*
Here we aliue shall view thee still. This Booke,
When Brasse and Marble fade, shall make thee looke
Fresh to all Ages: when Posteritie
Shall loath what's new, thinke all is prodegie
That is not *Shake-speares;* eu'ry Line, each Verse,
Here shall reuiue, redeeme thee from thy Herse.
Nor Fire, nor cankring Age, (As *Naso* said,
Of his,) thy wit-fraught Booke shall once inuade.
Nor shall I e're beleeue or thinke thee dead
(Though mist) untill our bankrout Stage be sped
(Impossible) with some new strain t' out-do
Passions of *Iuliet,* and her *Romeo;*
Or till I heare a Scene more nobly take,
Then when thy half-Sword parlying *Romans* spake,—
Till these, till any of thy Volumes rest
Shall with more fire, more feeling be exprest,
Be sure, our *Shake-speare,* thou canst neuer dye,
But crown'd with Lawrell, liue eternally.

L. Digges.

Appendix A

Further Sources to Consult

Those who wish to consult a more extensive bibliography should refer to the excellent one, to which the editors are heavily indebted, in R. C. Churchill, *Shakespeare and His Betters* (Bloomington, Indiana, 1959).

Allen, Percy. *The Case for Edward de Vere, Seventeenth Earl of Oxford, as 'Shakespeare.'* London, 1930.

Amphlett, H. *Who Was Shakespeare? A new Enquiry*. London, 1955.

Anon. "Another Mystery Solved: The True Identity of Tennessee Williams." *American Bar Association Journal* (Chicago), Jan., 1960.

Appleby, John. *The Stuffed Swan*. London, 1956.

Arensberg, W. C. *The Secret Grave of Francis Bacon at Lichfield*. San Francisco, 1923.

———. *The Shakespearean Mystery*. Pittsburgh, 1928.

———. *Francis Bacon, William Butts and the Pagets of Beaudesert*. Pittsburgh, 1929.

———. *The Magic Ring of Francis Bacon*. Pittsburgh, 1930.

Bacon, Delia. "Shakespeare and His Plays: An Inquiry." *Putnam's Magazine* (New York), Jan., 1856.

———. *The Philosophy of Shakespeare's Plays Unfolded*. Preface by Nathaniel Hawthorne. London, 1857.

Bacon Society, The Francis. *Baconiana: A Journal Devoted to the Study of the Works of Francis Bacon, His Character, Genius and Influence on His Own and Succeeding Times*. (Originally *The Journal of the Bacon Society*.) London, 1886-——.

Baildon, H. Bellyse. Introduction to *Titus Andronicus*. Arden edition. London, 1904.

Bakeless, John. *The Tragicall History of Christopher Marlowe*. 2 vols. Cambridge, Mass., 1942.

Baldwin, T. W. *William Shakespere's 'Small Latine and Lesse Greeke.'* 2 vols. Urbana, Ill., 1944.

Barnard, Finch. *Shakespeare and the Barnard Family*. London, 1914.

———. *More Light on Shakespeare*. London, 1914.

Barrell, Charles Wisner. *Elizabethan Mystery Man.* New York, 1940.

———. "Identifying Shakespeare." *Scientific American* (New York), Jan. 1940.

———. Articles on the *Sonnets* and Oxford's son. *Shakespeare Fellowship News-Letter* (New York), 1942-3; *Tomorrow Magazine* (New York), Feb.-Mar., 1946.

Baxter, J. P. *The Greatest of Literary Problems: The Authorship of Shakespeare's Works.* Boston, 1917.

Baumont, William Comyns. *The Private Life of the Virgin Queen.* London, 1947.

Beeching, H. C., Canon. *William Shakespeare, Player, Playmaker and Poet: A Reply to Mr. George Greenwood.* London, 1908.

Bénézet, Louis P. *Shakspere, Shakespeare and de Vere.* Manchester, New Hampshire, 1937.

———. "A Hoax Three Centuries Old." *American Bar Association Journal* (Chicago), May, 1960.

Bentley, Richard. "Elizabethan Whodunit: Supplementary Notes." *American Bar Association Journal* (Chicago), Nov., 1959.

Biggs, Arthur E. "Did Shaxper Write Shakespeare?" *American Bar Association Journal* (Chicago), April, 1960.

Blumenthal, Walter. "The Phantom Shakespeare." *American Book Collector* (Chicago), Jan., 1960.

———. "Spurious Shakespeare Portraiture: No Authenticated Likeness Known." *American Book Collector* (Chicago), Sept., 1960.

Booth, W. S. *Subtle Shining Secrecies.* Boston, 1925.

Bostelmann, Lewis F. *An Outline of the Life of Roger Manners, Fifth Earl of Rutland.* New York, 1911.

———. *Roger of Rutland: a Drama in 4 Acts.* New York, n.d.

Bowen, Gwynneth. *Shakespeare's Farewell,* Buxton, Derbyshire, 1951.

Brooke, Nicholas. "Marlowe as Provocative Agent in Shakespeare's Early Plays." *Shakespeare Survey,* No. 14. Cambridge, 1961.

Brooks, Alden. *Will Shakspere: Factotum and Agent.* New York, 1937.

———. *Will Shakspere and the Dyer's Hand.* New York, 1943.

Burr, William H. *Bacon and Shaksper.* Washington, New York, Chicago, 1886.

Caldwell, G. S. *Is Sir Walter Ralegh the Author of Shakespeare's Plays?* Melbourne, 1877.

Campbell, John, Lord. *Shakespeare's Legal Acquirements Considered.* London, 1859.

Castle, Edward J. *Shakespeare, Jonson, Bacon and Greene: A Study.* London, 1897.

Chambers, Sir Edmund. *The Elizabethan Stage.* 4 vols. Oxford, 1927.

Chambrun, Clara Longworth, Comtesse de. *Shakespeare: Actor-Poet.* New York, 1927.

———. *Shakespeare: A Portrait Restored.* London, 1957.

Churchill, R. C. "The Baconian Heresy: A Post-Mortem." *Nineteenth Century & After* (London), Nov., 1946.

Chute, Marchette. *Shakespeare of London.* New York, 1950; London, 1951.

Clark, Eva Turner. *Axiophilus; or Oxford alias Shakespeare.* New York, 1926.

———. *Hidden Allusions in Shakespeare's Plays.* New York, 1931. (Published in London as *Shakespeare's Plays in the Order of Their Writing.*)

———. *The Satirical Comedy "Love's Labour's Lost."* New York, 1933.

———. *The Man Who Was Shakespeare.* New York, 1937.

Clarkson, Paul S., and Clyde T. Warren. *The Law of Property in Shakespeare and the Elizabethan Drama.* Baltimore, 1942.

Clements, Rex. "Shakespeare as Mariner." *Shakespeare Fellowship News-Letter* (London), Autumn, 1956.

Collins, John Churton. "Was Shakespeare a Lawyer?" In *Studies in Shakespeare.* London, 1885.

Crewe, E. *Who Wrote Shakespeare?* Cape Town, 1927.

Cuningham, Granville C. *Bacon's Secret Disclosed in Contemporary Books.* London, 1911.

Davis, Latham. *Shakespeare: England's Ulysses.* Seaford, Delaware, 1905.

Dawbarn, C. Y. C. *Uncrowned: The Story of Queen Elizabeth and Bacon.* London, 1913.

Demblon, Célestin. *Lord Rutland est Shakespeare.* Paris, 1912.

———. *L'Auteur d' "Hamlet" et son monde.* Paris, 1914.

Denham-Parsons, John. *Non-Partisan Shakespeare Decipherings.* London, 1927.

Denning, W. H. "Who Wrote the Shakespeare Sonnets?" *English Review* (London), June, 1925.

De Peyster, J. Watts, General. *Was THE Shakespeare after All a Myth?* New York and London, 1888.

Dessart, A. *Lord Rutland est-il Shakespeare?* Liège, 1913.

Devecmon, William C. *In re Shakespeare's "Legal Acquirements."* New York, 1899.

Disraeli, Benjamin. *Venetia.* London, 1837. (*V.* Chapter VI.)

Dodd, Alfred. *Shakespeare: Creator of Freemasonry.* London, 1937.

———. *Who Was Shake-speare?* London, 1947.

Donnelly, Ignatius. *The Great Cryptogram: Francis Bacon's Cipher in the So-called Shakespeare Plays.* 2 vols. New York, 1888.

———. *The Cipher in the Plays and on the Tombstone.* New York, 1899.

———. *Ben Jonson's Cipher.* Minneapolis, 1900.

Douglas, Montagu W., Lt.-Col. *Lord Oxford and the Shakespeare Group.* Oxford, 1952.

Durning-Lawrence, Sir Edwin, Bart. *The Shakespeare Myth.* London, 1912.

Eagle, Roderick L. *Shakespeare: New Views for Old.* London, 1930. (Also an enlarged ed., undated.)

Eggar, Katharine E. *The Unlifted Shadow.* London, 1954.

Ellis, Walter. *The Shakespeare Myth.* London, n.d.

Elze, Karl. "The Supposed Travels of Shakespeare." In *Essays on Shakespeare.* Trans. by Dora Schmitz. London, 1874.

Emerson, Ralph Waldo. "Shakespeare, or, The Poet." In *Representative Men.* Boston, 1850.

Evans, A. J. *Shakespeare's Magic Circle*. London, 1956.

———. "Who Was Shakespeare?" *The Humanist* (London), July, 1957.

Ewen, C. l'Estrange. *Shakespeare, Automatist or Nothing*. Paignton, Devon, 1946.

Forrest, H. T. S. *The Five Authors of Shakespeare's Sonnets*. London, 1923.

Franco, Johan. *Bacon-Shakespeare Identities Revealed by Their Handwritings*. London, 1947.

Frazer, Robert. *The Silent Shakespeare*. Philadelphia, 1915.

Frye, Albert M., and Albert W. Levi. *Rational Belief: An Introduction to Logic*. New York, 1941. (*V*. pp. 363-373.)

Gallup, E. W. (Mrs.). *The Biliteral Cypher of Francis Bacon*. 2 vols. Detroit, 1899.

Granville-Barker, Harley, and G. B. Harrison, eds. *A Companion to Shakespeare Studies*. Cambridge, 1934.

Greenstreet, James. "A Hitherto Unknown Noble Author of Elizabethan Comedies." *The Genealogist* (London), July, 1891.

———. "Further Notices of William Stanley." *The Genealogist* (London), Jan., 1892.

———. "Testimonies Against the Accepted Authorship of Shakespeare's Plays." *The Genealogist* (London), May, 1892.

Greenwood, George. *The Shakespeare Problem Restated*. London, 1908. (Revised ed., 1937.)

———. *In re: Shakespeare: Greenwood vs. Beeching*. London and New York, 1909.

———. *Is There a Shakespeare Problem?* London, 1916.

———. *Shakespeare's Law and Latin*. London, 1916.

———. *Shakespeare's Law*. London, 1920.

———. *Ben Jonson and Shakespeare*. London, 1921.

Greg, Sir Walter. *Facts and Fancies in Baconian Theory*. London, 1903.

Grillo, Ernesto. *Shakespeare and Italy*. Glasgow, 1949.

Halliday, F. E. *The Cult of Shakespeare*. New York, 1960.

Halliwell-Phillipps, J. O. *The Visits of Shakespeare's Company of Actors to the Provincial Cities and Towns of England*. Brighton, 1886.

Harbage, Alfred. *Shakespeare's Audience*. New York, 1941.

Harris, C. Shirley. "Sir Anthony Sherley the Author of Shakespeare's Plays." *Notes and Queries* (London), 13 March 1897.

Harris, Frank. *The Man Shakespeare and His Tragic Life Story*. New York, 1909.

Harrison, G. B. *Shakespeare's Fellows*. London, 1923.

———. *Introducing Shakespeare*. Rev. ed. Harmondsworth, 1954.

Hawthorne, Nathaniel. "Recollections of a Gifted Woman." In *Our Old Home*. Boston, 1863.

Holland, H. H., Rear-Admiral. *Shakespeare Through Oxford Glasses*. London, 1923.

Holmes, Nathaniel, Judge. *The Authorship of Shakespeare*. 2 vols. New York, 1866.

Hookham, George, *Will o' the Wisp, or The Elusive Shakespeare*. London, 1922.

Hotson, Leslie. *The Death of Christopher Marlowe*. London, 1925.

Hutcheson, W. J. Fraser. *Shakespeare's Other Anne*. Glasgow, 1950.

Jamieson, Robert. "Who Wrote Shakespeare?" *Chambers's Journal* (Edinburgh), 7 Aug. 1852.

Johnson, Edward D. *The Shaksper Illusion*. Birmingham, 1944. (Enlarged ed., 1951.)

———. *The Mystery of the First Folio of the Shakespeare Plays*. Birmingham, 1945. (2nd ed., n.d.)

———. *Will Shakspere of Stratford*. London, 1954.

———. *Francis Bacon of St. Albans*. London, 1955.

Johnson, Harold. *Did the Jesuits Write "Shakespeare?"* Chicago, 1916.

Joseph, Bertram. "Who Was Shakespeare?" *The Humanist* (London), May, 1957.

Keeton, George W. *Shakespeare and His Legal Problems*. London, 1930.

Kent, William, and Another. *Edward de Vere, the Real Shakespeare*. London, 1947.

Kittle, William. *Edward de Vere, Seventeenth Earl of Oxford, and William Shakespeare*. Baltimore, 1942.

Lambin, Prof. G. Articles in *Les Langues Modernes* (Paris), 1955.

———. "Shakespeare in Milan." *Shakespeare Fellowship News-Letter* (New York), Autumn, 1957.

Lang, Andrew. *Shakespeare, Bacon and the Great Unknown*. London, 1912.

Lefranc, Abel. *Sous le masque de William Shakespeare: William Stanley, VIe Comte de Derby*. 2 vols. Paris, 1919.

———. *La réalité dans le "Songe d'une Nuit d'été."* Geneva, 1920.

———. *Le Secret de William Stanley: Étude sur la question Shakespearienne*. Brussels, 1923.

———. *A la découverte de Shakespeare*. 2 vols. Paris, 1945, 1950.

Lefranc, Pierre. "Les Études Anti-Stratfordiennes en France." *Études Anglaises* (Paris), April-June, 1960.

Looney, J. Thomas, *"Shakespeare" Identified in Edward de Vere, the Seventeenth Earl of Oxford*. London, 1920. (Reprint, 1949, with introduction by William McFee and notes by Charles Wisner Barrell.)

———, ed. *The Poems of Edward de Vere*. London, 1921.

———. " 'Shakespeare': Lord Oxford or Lord Derby." *National Review* (London), Feb., 1922.

———. "The Earl of Oxford as 'Shakespeare': New Evidence." *Golden Hind* (London), Oct., 1922.

Lucas, R. Macdonald. *Shakespeare's Vital Secret*. London, 1938.

Margrie, William. *Shakespeare Vindicated: An Exposure of Oxford and Bacon Nonsense*. London, 1946.

Maxwell, J. M. *The Man Behind the Mask: Robert Cecil, First Earl of Salisbury, the Only True Author of William Shakespeare's Plays*. Indianapolis, 1916.

Melsome, W. S. *The Bacon-Shakespeare Anatomy*. Ed. by Roderick Eagle. London, 1945.

Millar, J. S. L. *The Man in the Shakespeare Mask*. London, 1946.

Moore, George. *The Making of an Immortal: A Comedy*. London, 1927.

Morgan, Appleton. *The Shakespeare Myth: William Shakespeare and Circumstantial Evidence.* Cincinnati, 1881.

———. *Shakespeare in Fact and in Criticism.* New York, 1888.

Mudie, Alfred. *The Self-Named William Shakespeare.* London, 1925.

"Multum in Parvo" (M. L. Hore). *Who Wrote Shakespeare?* Denver, 1885.

Nicol, J. C. *The Real Shakespeare.* London, 1905.

Norris, J. Parker. *The Portraits of Shakespeare.* Philadelphia, 1885.

O'Connor, Frank. *Shakespeare's Progress.* Cleveland, 1960.

Ogburn, Dorothy and Charlton. *This Star of England.* New York, 1952.

———. *The Renaissance Man of England.* New York, 1955.

———. "Shakespeare or Shaksper?" *American Scholar* (Washington, D.C.), Spring, 1960.

O'Neill, Rev. George. *Could Bacon Have Written the Plays?* Dublin, 1909.

Palk, Robert. Letter on Raleigh and Shakespeare. *Times Literary Supplement* (London), 20 April 1916.

Pares, Martin. "Francis Bacon and the Knights of the Helmet." *American Bar Association Journal* (Chicago), April, 1960.

Pearson, Hesketh. *A Life of Shakespeare.* New York, 1961.

Pemberton, Henry, Jr. *Shakspere and Sir Walter Ralegh.* Ed. by S. L. Pemberton and C. Smyth. Philadelphia and London, 1914.

Penzance, Lord. *A Judicial Summing-Up on the Bacon-Shakespeare Controversy.* London, 1902.

Porohovshikov, Pierre S. *Shakespeare Unmasked.* New York, 1940; London, 1955.

Pott, Mrs. Henry. *Did Francis Bacon Write "Shakespeare"? Part One: 32 Reasons for Believing That He Did.* New York, 1884. *Part Two: The Lives of Bacon and Shakspere Compared.* New York, 1885.

———. *Francis Bacon and His Secret Society.* New York, 1891.

———, ed. *Bacon's Promus of Forms and Elegancies.* New York, 1883.

Robertson, J. M. *The Baconian Heresy: A Confutation.* London and New York, 1913.

———. *The Problem of the Shakespeare Sonnets.* London and New York, 1926.

———. *The Genuine in Shakespeare: A Conspectus.* London and New York, 1930.

Roe, Frank Gilbert. "The Marlowe Fiasco: Shakespeare Is As Shakespeare Does." *Queens Quarterly* (Kingston, Canada), Spring, 1957.

Roe, J. E. *The Mortal Moon: Bacon and His Masks.* New York, 1891.

———. *Sir Francis Bacon's Own Story.* New York, 1918.

Rushton, W. L. *Shakespeare a Lawyer.* Liverpool, 1858.

———. *Shakespeare's Testamentary Language.* London, 1869.

———. *Shakespeare Illustrated by the Lex Scripta.* London, 1870.

———. *Shakespeare's Legal Maxims.* London, 1907.

"Shakespeare Arena." Letters about the authorship controversy. *American Bar Association Journal* (Chicago), June, 1959.

Shakespeare's England. 2 vols. Oxford, 1916.

Shatford, Sarah, ed. *My Proof of Immortality.* By *Sir* William Shakespeare. New York, 1924.

Sheppard, Thomas. *Bacon Is Alive!* Hull, Yorkshire, 1911.

Slater, Gilbert. *Seven Shakespeares.* London, 1931.

Smart, John. *Shakespeare: Truth and Tradition.* London, 1928.

Smith, Logan Pearsall. *On Reading Shakespeare.* London, 1933.

Smithson, E. W. "Ben Jonson's Pious Fraud." *Nineteenth Century & After* (London), Nov., 1913.

———. *Baconian Essays.* Introduction and two essays by Sir George Greenwood. London, 1922.

Spedding, James. *Letters and Life of Francis Bacon.* 7 vols. London, 1861-1874.

Spielmann, M. H. "Shakespeare's Portraiture." In *Studies in the First Folio.* Oxford, 1924.

Standen, Gilbert. *Shakespeare Authorship: A Summary of Evidence.* London, 1930.

Stopes, Mrs. Charlotte Carmichael. *The Bacon-Shakspere Question Answered.* 2nd enlarged ed. London, 1889.

———. *Shakespeare's Warwickshire Contemporaries.* Stratford-on-Avon, 1907.

———. *The Life of Henry, Third Earl of Southampton.* Cambridge, 1922.

Stotsenburg, John H., Judge. *An Impartial Study of the Shakespeare Title.* Louisville, Kentucky, 1904.

Sullivan, Sir Edward. "Shakespeare and the Waterways of North Italy." *Nineteenth Century & After* (London), Aug., 1908.

———. "Shakespeare and Italy." *Nineteenth Century & After* (London), Jan.-Feb., 1918.

Surtees, Scott F. *William Shakespere of Stratford-on-Avon.* Dinsdale-on-Tees, 1888.

Sweet, George Elliott. *Shake-speare the Mystery.* Stanford, 1956.

Sydenham of Combe, Lord. *The First Baconian.* London, n.d.

Sykes, Claud W. *Alias William Shakespeare?* Preface by Sir Arthur Bryant. London, 1947.

Theobald, Bertram G. *Shake-speare's Sonnets Unmasked.* London, 1929.

Theobald, R. M., ed. *Dethroning Shakspere: A Selection of Letters to the "Daily Telegraph."* London, 1888.

———. *Shakespeare Studies in Baconian Light.* London, 1904.

Thompson, Godfrey. "Who Didn't Write Shakespeare?" *Humberside* (Hull, England), Autumn, 1956.

Thompson, William. *William Shakespeare in Romance and Reality.* Melbourne, 1881.

———. *Bacon and Shakespeare.* Melbourne, 1881.

———. *The Political Allegories in the Renascence Drama of Francis Bacon.* Melbourne, 1882.

Thomson, J. A. K. *Shakespeare and the Classics.* London, 1952.

Titherley, A. W. *Shakespeare's Identity: William Stanley, Sixth Earl of Derby.* Winchester, 1952.

———, ed. *Shakespeare's Sonnets, as from the Pen of William Sixth Earl of Derby.* Liverpool, 1939.

Townsend, G. H. *William Shakespeare Not an Impostor; by an English Critic*. London, 1857.

Ward, Capt. B. M., ed. *A Hundreth Sundrie Flowres*. London, 1926.

———. *The Seventeenth Earl of Oxford*. London, 1928.

Ward, B. R., Col. *The Mystery of Mr. W. H.* London, 1923.

Webb, T. E., Judge. *The Shakespeare Mystery*. New York, 1902.

Wham, Benjamin. "'Marlowe's Mighty Line': Was Marlowe Murdered at Twenty-nine?" *American Bar Association Journal* (Chicago), May, 1960.

White, Richard Grant. *Studies in Shakespeare*. London and New York, 1885.

Wigston, W. F. C. *Bacon and the Rosicrucians*. London, 1899.

Willis, William, Judge. *The Baconian Mint: Its Claims Examined*. London, 1903.

Wilson, J. D. *The Essential Shakespeare*. Paperback ed. Cambridge, 1960.

Windle, Mrs. C. F. A. *On the Discovery of the Cipher of Francis Bacon*. San Francisco, 1881-1882.

Wright, Louis B. *Middle-Class Culture in Elizabethan England*. Chapel Hill, 1935.

———. "The Anti-Shakespeare Industry and the Growth of Cults." *Virginia Quarterly Review* (Charlottesville), Spring, 1959.

Wright, Louis B., and Virginia LaMar. "The Author." Pp. xi-xxii in *The Tragedy of King Lear,* by William Shakespeare. *The Folger Library General Reader's Shakespeare*. New York, 1960.

Yeatman, J. P. *The Gentle Shakspere*. London, 1896.

Zeigler, Wilbur Gleason. *It Was Marlowe: A Story of the Secret of Three Centuries*. Chicago, 1895.

Appendix B

Suggested Research Topics and Questions

I. For brief research papers based on this text:

A. Choose two or three sources in the text and evaluate their reliability. In order to begin such evaluation, one might ask questions like the following:

1. How far can one depend on the public and official documents in "Records Relating to William Shakespeare" to give an insight into the personality and character of Shakespeare?
2. What kinds of information and inference can one legitimately abstract from Lieutenant Hammond's remarks?
3. How useful is Fuller's brief biography of Shakespeare?
4. Is Richard Davies a good authority for the statements that Shakespeare died a Catholic and was a poacher?
5. Are Davies' statements more trustworthy than those of Aubrey?
6. Are Heminges and Condell reliable witnesses to the authorship of the plays?
7. Can one trust the statement of authorship printed on the title page of a book?
8. What sort of information does Robert Greene give about Shakespeare?
9. How reliable is Manningham's anecdote about Shakespeare and Burbage?
10. Is it likely that Shakespeare wrote the verses about John Combe?

Other questions of this sort are easy to frame. The answers to them depend, of course, on one's ability to exercise his common sense.

B. Discuss the logic or arguments of two or more controversialists.

1. Whose arguments are better, Heilbroner's (to the effect that Marlowe wrote the Shakespearean plays) or Harage's (to the effect that Shakespeare did)?
2. Evaluate the basic procedures used by Spurgeon and Mendenhall. Do they have weaknesses? Include consideration of Bergen Evans' comment about revealing imagery.
3. Who presents the better case in the authorship controversy, Spurgeon (Stratfordian) or Mendenhall plus Hoffman (both pro-Marlowe)?
4. In what ways does Kocher support the Stratfordian position generally and Spurgeon's position in particular?
5. Whose argument is the more effective, Mark Twain's or Dorothy and Charlton Ogburn's? Why?
6. Review the two basic arguments presented by both Hoffman and Heilbroner; next consider G. B. Harrison's objections; finally discuss which of the viewpoints is correct.
7. Which method of using internal evidence is best suited to proving the authorship of the works of Shakespeare? Mendenhall's, Hoffman's, Spurgeon's, or William Ross'?
8. Describe and evaluate the basic techniques for determining authorship used by Kocher, Hoffman, Allen, and Ross.
9. Whose logic is the better, William Clary's or John Hauser's?
10. Compare the cut version of the passage from *Every Man out of His Humour* given by Durning-Lawrence with the complete text of the passage in question (the editors present the omitted portion in a footnote). Then compare his selection from the *Parnassus* plays with the selection given in "Contemporary References to Shakespeare." Decide how valid Durning-Lawrence's conclusion is that these plays ridicule Shakespeare. Does Durning-Lawrence's editing tend to mislead the reader?
11. In what various ways is the Francis Meres' material used by the controversialists? Which of these ways are invalid and why?
12. Analyze the validity of reasoning used in the letters

written to the editor of the *Saturday Review of Literature* by William A. Klutts, Marcia M. Roof, the Countess de Chambrun, Alden Brooks, and F. Y. St. Clair.

13. Discuss the value of the opinions of authority. Use the opinions of Henry James, the Cook County judge (cited in Wadsworth), and Ralph Waldo Emerson (cited in Durning-Lawrence).
14. Using appropriate material from Durning-Lawrence, the Friedmans, and the Ogburns, discuss the logical validity of ciphers in establishing the authorship of the plays and poems.

C. Check the accuracy of selected facts presented by three or more of the controversialists. The following are merely examples of the sort of things that may be verified.

1. Were crosses and other signs used as signatures by literate men of the period?
2. Were books expensive and difficult to obtain in Elizabethan England?
3. Were there the remnants of nunneries, as Ross maintains, in Elizabethan England?
4. Has the Shakespeare monument been changed since it was first set up?
5. Would a wound over the eye like the one inflicted on Marlowe have been immediately fatal?
6. Do we have, as some scholars claim, "more reliably documented information about Shakespeare than about Aeschylus, Sophocles, Euripides, Aristophanes, Plautus, Terence," any medieval English playwright, and most of Shakespeare's contemporaries? Pick two or three dramatists and check the number and nature of the documentary materials available for their lives.
7. Was the authorship of *Tamburlaine* ever doubted?
8. Did Elizabethan noblemen and clergy use stooges who fronted for the works they wrote?
9. Was the Earl of Oxford called "Will" by his intimates?
10. Is Bergen Evans correct in his listing of errors in Shakespeare's plays?
11. Can evidence be found to substantiate Gelett Burgess's statement: "The anonymity of several important Elizabethan works has never been pierced"?
12. Is Jonson quoted accurately by Heilbroner (*see* p. 132)?

Does Jonson's statement agree with one made by Heminges and Condell on the same point?

13. Was Marlowe Walsingham's "illustratious protégé"?
14. Was the Earl of Oxford, as Harbage maintains, "humorless, bigoted, and morally confused"?
15. Check any biographical sketch of Shakespeare given by one of the controversialists against the documentary evidence given in this text and determine how accurate the sketch is.

D. Consider the interpretations that a number of controversialists give to various facts. Are these the only interpretations possible? If alternative interpretations are possible, how valid is the process of selecting only one interpretation and using it? The following questions challenge some of the interpretations given by controversialists.

1. Was Stratford a dirty town because some of its inhabitants were fined for having muck heaps?
2. Does the presence of an epitaph on Shakespeare's tomb mean that Shakespeare wrote the epitaph?
3. Is it necessarily improbable that the person who wrote Shakespeare's will also wrote the plays?
4. Does the fact that Shakespeare's plays were not published as soon as they might have been necessarily mean that Shakespeare was fronting for Marlowe?
5. Does knowledge of courtly behavior mean that one must be a courtier?

E. Using the materials in this text, construct a sketch of John Shakespeare's life in order to show the sort of background in which William Shakespeare grew up. Support or refute some of the controversialists' stands, for example, that John was illiterate or ignorant or that William had no basis for knowing anything about Latin or law.

F. Using the entries from the church register, write a genealogical essay on the Shakespeare family and draw some conclusions about its social position and culture. Relate your findings to the controversy.

G. What do the documents in this text reveal about Stratford-on-Avon? How is this information relevant to the authorship controversy?

H. What do the contemporary records and allusions indicate about Shakespeare's popularity and success?

I. Choose two or three of the selections by controversialists and discuss the amount of conjecture in their recapitulations of Shakespeare's life.

J. How effectively has humor been used in the various writings on the controversy?

K. Discuss the Shakespeare controversy conducted in the pages of *The Saturday Review of Literature.*

L. How much name-calling and vilification is resorted to by various authors? Is this device effective? Which side uses it more?

M. How important is it that the true authorship of the works be established?

N. Discuss the rhetorical devices and slanting in Bergen Evans' "Good Frend for Iesvs Sake Forbeare" and in Fruedenberg's letter.

O. What do the portraits of Shakespeare and the church memorial prove about the authorship of the works of Shakespeare?

II. For longer research papers based on this text:

A. In the *American Bar Association Journal* for March, 1959, Ogburn says, "The Dramatist was obviously a trained lawyer." Muster the data and opinion for and against this position and then evaluate it.

B. Identify and describe the points that the anti-Stratfordians consider most telling. Evaluate them, indicating which are strongest, which are weak, and which are fallacious.

C. What evidence of emotional bias do you find in your survey of this text?

D. Discuss the psychological aspect of the controversy. Look at Twain and Clary to begin with.

E. Evaluate the rival claims put forth by the supporters of Bacon and those of Oxford. If you had to choose between the two, which would it be? Why?

F. Was Bacon (or Marlowe or Oxford—choose one) the author of the works commonly attributed to Shakespeare?

G. What are the major Stratfordian arguments used to support Shakespeare's claims to the plays and poems, and how valid are they?

H. Write a biography of William Shakespeare in order to prove that Shakespeare was or was not the author of the works attributed to him.

I. After reading the text, decide what information (now lacking) is needed to bring the authorship controversy to an end.

J. Write a history of the Shakespeare controversy.

K. Is there any evidence that the editors have taken sides in the controversy? Evaluate this text on the matter of bias.

L. Expand any of the topics in Section I that will lend themselves to the process. For example, instead of discussing the amount of conjecture in the arguments of two or three controversialists, consider the use of conjecture by ten or more of the writers.

M. Which of the Stratfordians makes the strongest case? Explain why.

N. Which of the anti-Shakespeareans makes the best case? Explain why.

O. Compare the quality of the controversy in the *American Bar Association Journal* with that in *The Saturday Review of Literature*.

P. In the *American Bar Association Journal,* Mr. Bentley asserts that the proper province of scholars is limited to clarifying language, aiding the appreciation of content and structure, and identifying sources used by authors. He claims, however, that establishing identity is a matter dependent upon evidence and, therefore, a matter for lawyers. Oppose scholars (Hastings, Evans, Campbell, Harbage, Harrison, etc.) and lawyers (Clary, Hauser, Ogburn, Bentley, etc.). Which group does the better job of establishing the identity of the author?

Q. Discuss the ways in which the minds of the controversialists go astray in the course of their arguments, and explain the causes of error.

R. Discuss the problems that beset a biographer or historian.

III. For long research papers using materials in the text and those obtained from the library.

A. As the following relate to the Shakespeare controversy, discuss patronage in Elizabethan times, the propriety of a nobleman's acknowledging authorship of poetry and plays, and conventions concerning women as authors.

B. Expand any suitable portion of this text. Examples follow.
   1. In addition to data presented in this text, what can you discover about Stratford between 1550 and 1600? Was it a dirty, backward community filled with illiterates? Relate your answer to the controversy.
   2. Study the Elizabethan and Jacobean actors and companies of actors. Try to determine their social status, their literacy, their ability as actors and businessmen, their *modus operandi,* and anything else that might provide evidence that Shakespeare could or could not have written the plays.
   3. Write a paper on Alden Brooks' position in the Shakespeare controversy.
   4. Supplement the documents section of this text by collecting documentary material that might have been included in the text. Explain the relevance of this material to the controversy in order to demonstrate that the information should have been included.

C. Investigate the 1601 performance of *Richard II* as it relates to the Essex Rebellion and the authorship problem. Consult *This Star of England* and *Shakespeare and His Betters,* to begin with.

D. Write an essay on logical fallacies. Define the various kinds of fallacy and illustrate each, as far as possible, by using examples from this text or other writings related to the controversy.

E. Survey some of Bacon's works (include his essays and poetry) and note their nature and extent, as well as the author's characteristic mode of expression. Read a biographical sketch of Bacon's life. On the basis of Bacon's known activities, his style, his interests, and the extent of his known writings, decide whether Bacon wrote Shakespeare. Use material in this text in order to provide an introduction to your subject.

F. Using sources outside this text, evaluate the reliability of all the items included in "The Shakespeare Documents" and "Contemporary References to Shakespeare."

G. Read the sections of the text dealing with Shakespeare's sonnets and their relationship to his life and the authorship question. Then collect other opinions on the matter. Finally decide what you think the relationship is.

H. Read Marchette Chute's *Shakespeare of London.* From the viewpoint of a controversialist, evaluate it as biography.

I. Look up book reviews of the writings of controversialists and give a survey of opinion about the value of those works. Some review material is included in the text.

J. Assemble the documetary evidence relating to the life of another Elizabethan writer (e.g., Jonson, Spenser, Kyd, Nash, Lyly, Peele, Marlowe) and compare it with that given here for Shakespeare. Use your findings to evaluate the statement of Stratfordians that we know more about Shakespeare than we know about any of his fellow dramatists. Also decide whether the data for the other author give you valuable insight into the trustworthiness of the Shakespeare documents.

K. Expand Professor Evans' list of Shakespeare's errors in various fields of knowledge and reach some conclusion about the assertion that the author of the works must have been a man of universal learning.

L. Investigate the idea, held by some controversialists, that Shakespeare was a man of great learning by ascertaining how learned he was in a particular field such as the classics, law, astrology, astronomy, religion, medicine, war, geography, history, nautical matters, or the like.

M. Check the controversialists on Shakespeare's personality by reading one of the plays and using it, plus information from this text, to reconstruct Shakespeare's personality. Then compare your image with that given by a controversialist. Decide why the two differ.

N. From the anti-Stratfordians, draw up a list of the qualifications that they feel the author of the plays must have had. Then apply the list to Sir Walter Raleigh. Could he have written the plays? Investigate Raleigh further as a claimant to the title of author.

O. Note the suggestions in this text that topical allusions in the Shakespeare plays refer to the author's life and, hence, reveal the true author. Mr. Hoffman, Mr. and Mrs. Ogburn, and Mrs. Clark, among others, use this line of reasoning in their books. Consult pertinent passages and determine the soundness of this technique.